JUST WAR AND TERRORISM

THE END OF THE JUST
WAR CONCEPT?

<small>EDITED BY</small>

W. SMIT

PEETERS
LEUVEN - DUDLEY, MA
2005

Library of Congress Cataloging-in-Publication Data

Just war and terrorism: the end of the just war concept? / edited by Wim Smit.
    p. cm.
    Includes bibliographical references and index.
    ISBN 90-429-1697-4 (alk. paper)
    1. War--Moral and ethical aspects. 2. Terrorism--Moral and ethical aspects.
3. Just war doctrine. I. Smit, Wim.

B105.W3J84 2005
172'.42--dc22   2005054740

© 2005 – Peeters – Bondgenotenlaan 153 – 3000 Leuven

D 2005/0602/130
ISBN 90-429-1697-4

Contents

Acknowledgments

In 1998, under the inspiration of Chaplain Claude Selis, the *Belgian Catholic Army Chaplaincy* founded the *Center for Theology and Military Ethics* (CTME). The necessary reorientation of the chaplaincy after the far-reaching reforms of the Belgian army led to the initiative to found this Center. The transition toward a professional army, and participation in new (humanitarian) missions ('peacekeeping' and 'peaceforcing'), has also called for a renewal of consciousness on ethical issues. One of the main purposes of the Center, is to publish articles on topics in military ethics, religion and war, violence, war and peace in Church history and the Bible, and much more.

The undeniable presence of religious factors in today's conflicts calls for a thorough rethinking of the relationship between religion and violence. This is all the more apparent as international political and military attention is being focused on terrorism in the wake of the September 11th attacks. Hence the CTME decided to organise a seminar on the topic of terrorism. Preparations began in 2003 with the seminar taking place on 21 and 22 October 2004. This was the second seminar of the Center, but the first where the decision was made to print the contributions of the speakers.

With this initiative, the CTME intends to offer a contribution to the philosophy of just war in light of global terrorism, arguably one of the most serious challenges facing the world today, and one that demands a critical and balanced reappraisal on many levels. The publication of this book can also be seen as a new impulse in the activities of the Center, and an opportunity to reach a broader public.

It is clear that this book is not the result of one man's work. Many people need to be thanked for their contributions. First of all I want to thank Nick Fotion, not only for his much appreciated effort to be present in Belgium for the seminar and for his valuable contribution, but also for his willingness to do the first and most important corrections of the English texts. How could we have done it without him? Together with the second native speaker, David Pratt, he did an exceptional job. Many thanks to both of you.

There would never have been a seminar without the help of my colleagues Claude Selis and Johan Van Den Eeckhout. They are to be thanked for their penetrating criticism of the texts of the contributors, and their constant moral support which helped me to prepare and lead the seminar. Together with them I want to thank Cyriel Desmet, former professor in military history at the Royal Military Academy in Brussels. I see him as a wise owl from whom I am certain to learn quite a lot more. His viewpoints are challenging and not seldom provocative, so one always departs his company with much to think about.

Of course I also want to thank our former Chief of Chaplains Roger Van den Berge who supported our ideas for the seminar from the beginning, and who, in the name of the Chaplaincy, agreed to finance this project.

Wim Smit
(Editor)
www.army-chaplaincy.be

Introduction

Part of the task of an introduction to a collection of essays is to give some information on how they came into being and how they cohere in their present form. The material in this book first began to take shape in 2003 when the *Center for Theology and Military Ethics* set about organizing an expert seminar devoted to exploring the question of terrorism and the concept of the just war, or more precisely, the fate of any future just war theorizing in the face of terrorism and pre-emptive military action. The seminar was given the title *Just War and Terrorism: The End of the Just War Concept?* The question mark was not simply an eye-grabbing device. The question was genuine and not rhetorical because the seminar's steering committee believed the present situation of world terrorism has put traditional just war thinking to such a test as to cast doubt over its future as such, though the concept is far from finished. So a number of scholars from Belgium, the Netherlands, Germany and the United States were invited to this seminar. Fortunately, several respected authors responded favorably. So the project was off to a strong start with the likes of Carl Ceulemans, Nick Fotion, Fred Van Iersel, Johan Verstraeten and Alphart von Horn attending.

These key participants were tasked with preparing a position paper on the question, something not too lengthy (about 15 pages), wherein the fundamental problems of the just war theory might be confronted. They were asked to give a brief description of the development of the just war tradition while pointing up difficulties and nuances in the concept, and attending to these four fundamental questions:

1) What is specific about battling terrorism? And what is the difference between a classical war and one fought against terrorism?

With that distinction in mind, what is the feasibility of conducting a classical just war (*ius ad bellum*) in this new situation?
2) Is a pre-emptive attack against terrorism justifiable when it is
used to protect a state's civilians? If so, what does that mean for
the concept of just war? If not justifiable, then in what ways can
terrorism be fought? Include your personal view and opinion
in your answer.
3) When the United Nations remains uninvolved, can we say that
states have '*carte blanche*' to protect themselves? Does UN non-
involvement legitimate pre-emptive war as a way to protect
one's own civilians? Furthermore, why is the UN powerless?
Is it uninterested or unable to answer this threat? Or is it only
capable of making political and military decisions in classical
war situations?
4) In your own view, how do you see the peace of tomorrow?

By Spring 2004, the first drafts of these papers were ready, and
as one might expect, they were divergent, so much so as to cast
doubt on whether they could be effectively debated. It was obvious
that the original questions were insufficient and some additional
guidelines would be needed in order to make the seminar produc-
tive. So the following topical questions were imposed on the participants:

1) How should 'terrorism' be defined?
2) What are the origins of the just war concept? How did it develop
historically?
3) Is the just war tradition now outdated due to terrorism?
4) Is pre-emptive war a just means in the fight against terrorism?
5) How should we deal with terrorists?
6) What are the roles of NATO, the UN and the EU in fighting terror?
7) What hope is there for a just peace?

With these new questions in place, the seminar occurred on 21
and 22 September 2004 in the Royal Military Academy in Brussels. The traditional academic format where contributors read their

papers and then reply to questions was abandoned in favor of having each speaker take an ample amount of time to formulate a position on a certain question and then respond to the reactions of the other participants. What resulted was a sustained discussion of several different points of view. This format led to some sharp debate, which in turn grew more nuanced as the proceedings moved along, and in a few instances caused some changes of opinion. After two days of thrashing one another's positions, the participants were asked to re-write their papers. In early 2005 these finished papers were collected and edited once more, and now appear here for the first time under the original title of the seminar. Hopefully, some of the energy of the original debates in Brussels can still be detected in these essays.

Three new essays round out the discussion. The first by Claude Selis, addresses the conditions of the just war in relation to the new conflicts. The second by Wim Smit, presents new thoughts on the violation of human rights occurring in counter-terrorist actions. A third new essay is by David Pratt; who discusses "how and why just war thinking has become conflicted and less influential in the public forum." He concludes with some suggestions on how it might be renovated, by virtues beyond justice.

This book offers the interested reader a wide spectrum of views on one of the most challenging issues in politics today – war and its justification. It is being offered as a call to stir up and reconsider our settled opinions on the matter. If it succeeds in that, then it will have paid the best of compliments to its authors and editors, and to the lively interactions that brought it about in the first place.

CARL CEULEMANS

War Against Terrorism
Some Ethical Considerations from the Just War Perspective[1]

1. INTRODUCTION

Just a few days after the suicide attacks of September 11, 2001, US President George W. Bush declared war on terrorism. At the same time, it was also made clear that this war would not be like any other war. There would not be one single military battle, but a wide ranging effort going from coalition building and intelligence gathering to fighting actual wars. Victory, the warning went, would not come easy – if at all. International terrorism, although not a new phenomenon in itself, was definitely here to stay, and the international effort to fight it practically monopolized the entire debate on international peace and security. Like in any other war, the major concern in this one was that of effectiveness and efficiency. How should we proceed in order to obtain the greatest probability of success and the fewest number of casualties on our side? One answer to this question is the pre-emptive action doctrine. The American National Security Strategy of September 2002, said that in the post 9/11 era, the notion of self-defense needs to be re-defined.[2] In order to protect oneself and others against possible terrorist attacks, it is necessary to address these kinds of threats well before they are fully formed.

---

[1] In this contribution the author made use of some of the arguments he developed in a previous published article (C. CEULEMANS, *Ethische grenzen aan de oorlog tegen het terrorisme*, in *Militaire Spectator*, 172 (4) (2003), pp. 165-176.) and a presentation he made on the US preventive war doctrine at the Renmin University (Beijing) in October of 2003.

[2] http://www.whitehouse.gov/nsc/nssall.html

However, despite the general concern about the international terrorist threats, there is no general consensus on the need of a pre-emptive action doctrine. In an address to the UN General Assembly on September 23, 2003, the UN Secretary general Kofi Annan expressed his concern that this new doctrine might well lead to a proliferation of unilateral and lawless use of force. He furthermore made it clear that this new logic represents "a fundamental challenge to the principles on which, however imperfectly, world peace and stability have rested for the last 58 years."[3]

It is no doubt true that the introduction of the pre-emptive action doctrine puts a good deal of pressure on the post World War II paradigm that considers defensive military action as the primary legitimate form of military action. The objective of this essay is to look at this "new" kind of warfare from a moral point of view, and to ask – Do the changes in the international reality justify a more offensive military approach? Or, on the contrary, has a very dangerous evolution occurred which risks re-establishing war as a normal instrument of international statecraft? In order to get a somewhat clearer insight in this matter, we will try to discover what the just war theory has to say about the war against terrorism.

From a methodological point of view, this essay will be divided into two parts. In the first part, just war theory will be discussed, followed by an examination of the non-paradigmatic nature of the war against terrorism. The second part will explore the specific moral issues associated with the challenge of fighting terrorism based on the principles of the just war theory.

2. THE PRINCIPLES OF THE JUST WAR THEORY

One way to describe just war theory (or *bellum justum* theory) is to say that it is a *normative ethical tradition* that determines *when* and *how* military force should be used. For the adherents of just war

---

[3] http://www.un.org/apps/news/printnews.asp?nid=8330

theory, war is essentially an evil that must be avoided as much as possible. There are times, however, when the use of military force can be justified. Basically this position reflects the idea that just war theory perceives the use of force as an occasion in which two basic moral precepts come into conflict. On the one hand, there is the duty not to harm – which implies the avoidance of the use of military force; and, on the other, there is the duty to defend oneself or others, which can necessitate the use of force. According to James Childress the former obligation is generally considered in our society as a prima facie principle.[4] Only in very specific circumstances can this duty not to harm others be overridden. Now this is where the first basic component of the just war theory comes in: viz., that of the *jus ad bellum*. This principle sums up all the criteria one has to respect before starting a war. It offers to the decision-maker a deliberation instrument that allows him to determine whether he is justified in putting aside his duty not to harm others. Although the principles of the *jus ad bellum* differ somewhat from one author to another, generally the following are listed:

— 1. A war can only be waged for a just cause;
— 2. A war has to be waged with good intentions;
— 3. A war has to be the last resort;
— 4. A war must only be waged if there is a reasonable chance of success;
— 5. A war must only be waged if the good one hopes to obtain outweighs the evil that will be caused by the war;
   6. The decision to go to war has to be taken by the legitimate authority.

Even if the *ad bellum* criteria are satisfied, and as a consequence one is justified in starting a war, just war theory also requires restraint during the actual hostilities. Just because one is justified in putting aside the duty not to harm others, doesn't mean that

---

[4] J. CHILDRESS, *Moral Responsibility in Conflicts. Essays on Nonviolence, War, and Conscience*, Baton Rouge/London, Louisiana State University Press, 1982, pp. 63-94.

"anything goes" once hostilities commence. Overriding a basic moral precept, like not harming others, leaves what Childress calls "moral traces" or "residual effects."[5] This is where the second just war component comes in: viz., that of the *jus in bello*. Whereas the *jus ad bellum* is concerned with the initiation of war, the *jus in bello* (the right in the war) focuses on the way a war should be fought. In particular, *jus in bello* consists of the principles that need to be respected during the hostilities. Traditionally there are two *jus in bello* principles:

1. One must never intentionally target non-combatants (the discrimination principle);
2. The military advantage obtained with a particular act of war has to outweigh the damages this act will cause (the proportionality principle).

Both these basic components of the just war theory are considered to be logically independent.[6] One can start a war in a just manner, but fight it unjustly. Or, a war that doesn't respect the *jus ad bellum*, can be conducted according to the *jus in bello*. This logical independence of the *ad bellum* and the *in bello* principles is also reflected in the fact that the decisions regarding both components reside essentially in different realms. Indeed, the *jus ad bellum* decisions reside in the realm of politics, whereas the *jus in bello* decisions basically take place within the military realm. An important corollary of this moral divide is that of the moral equality of the combatants on both sides. Although soldiers may fight in an unjust war, they are ordered into battle by their government, just as are the enemy soldiers who fight against them are ordered by theirs. Whatever the justness of the war, the military has the duty to fight – and if necessary they are forced to do so – for the causes of their country. They are the human instruments of state policy, who, as Walzer expresses it, recognize those on the other side as "poor sods, just like me," trapped in a war that they didn't make.[7]

---

[5] *Ibid.*, p. 69.

[6] M. WALZER, *Just and Unjust Wars. A Moral Argument with Historical Illustrations*, New York, Basic Books, 1992, p. 21.

[7] *Ibid.*, p. 36.

The just war principles are not a-historical moral precepts. Indeed, no one person developed the *bellum justum* doctrine. Rather, it is the synthesis of an ancient way of thinking about war and peace. In this respect James Turner Johnson very appropriately talks about the just war as a tradition rather than a theory.[8] Although St. Augustine is generally considered as the father of the just war, he was not the first to think about the issue of war and peace from a normative point of view. Before him, in the early Greek civilization with Plato and Aristotle and in Ancient Rome with Cicero, we find traces of moral reflection on war and peace. After him, there were theologians, like St. Thomas Aquinas, and the canon lawyers, like Gratian, who mainly contributed to the development of the *jus ad bellum*. The development of the *jus in bello*, on the other hand, was essentially based on the code and customs of chivalry. From the sixteenth century on, it was especially the Spanish neo-scholastic school with Francisco de Vitoria and Francisco Suarez which based just war thinking on the natural law perspective. With the Dutch jurist Hugo Grotius the secularization of the just war doctrine continued within the framework of international law theory.

During its more than two thousand-year history, just war thinking has not always been popular. After having reached its peak in the Middle Ages, the notion of a *bellum justum* began to lose its attractiveness and authority during and after the seventeenth century. With the Peace of Westphalia (1648) state sovereignty became a dominant feature of the international community. In order to avoid the destructive wars of religion, it was agreed that states should not interfere with the internal affairs of other states. This meant that the moral universalism of the *Republica Christiana* had to make way for the moral particularism of the individual state. An important corollary of the loss of this common morality was the undermining of the *jus ad bellum* component. In an environment where the political entities were thought

---

[8] J.T. JOHNSON, *Just War Tradition and the Restraint of War. A Moral and Historical Inquiry*, Princeton, Princeton University Press, 1984, p. XXI.

to be the only ones that could legitimately decide on the appropriate use of force, it does not make much sense to talk about just and unjust wars. Each war started by a sovereign state was *per definition* considered as legitimate.

This situation would change somewhat in the first half of the twentieth century. In a relatively short period of time, the international community of sovereign states was confronted with two devastating world wars. The idea that states have the absolute right to decide autonomously on the appropriateness of the use of military force was no longer acceptable. The result was that the *jus ad bellum* component reappeared as an item in international law. After the First and more so after the Second World War, the state's authority to wage war became severely restricted. With the Briand-Kellogg Pact (1928) the contracting parties outlawed war as an appropriate instrument in their relations with other states, and committed themselves to resolve their differences in a peaceful way. In the UN Charter we find a similar ban on wars of aggression.[9] Except for the inherent right of individual and collective self-defence (Article 51 of the UN Charter) all Member States committed themselves to "refrain in their international relations from the threat or use of force against the territorial integrity or political independence of any state" (Article 2 paragraph 4 of the UN Charter).

But the twentieth century presented the just war theory with still other challenges. One of these was the introduction of weapons of mass destruction (and in particular nuclear devices) on the international scene. The existence of this kind of armament led to a serious questioning of the moral validity of the *bellum justum*. Was a theory claiming that war could still be just not a moral outrage in an era where any war could lead to the

---

[9] The General Assembly of the UN accepted in 1974 the following definition of the concept of aggression: "Aggression is the use of armed force by a State against the sovereignty, territorial integrity or political independence of another State, or in any other manner inconsistent with the Charter of the United Nations, as set out in this definition." See: Y. MELZER, *Concepts of Just War*, Leyden, A.W. Sijthoff, 1975, p. 29.

annihilation of mankind? However, with the end of the Cold War it seems that the questioning of the moral validity of the just war doctrine has abated somewhat. What is more, with the introduction of all kinds of "new" forms of use of military force – peacekeeping, peace-enforcing and humanitarian interventions – the principles of the just war seem to provide an attractive framework of moral analysis.

3. FIGHTING TERRORISM – A NON PARADIGMATIC TYPE CASE

As we already indicated earlier, just war principles are not a-historical criteria, but are in fact the synthesis of the moral wisdom contained in a long tradition of practical and theoretical reasoning. So in the following pages we will bring this moral wisdom to bear on the war against terrorism. Using the principles of the just war as a starting point in the process of "moral mapping" of a new form of contemporary warfare, is in itself, a contribution "to the ongoing development of that tradition by entering into a critical dialogue with the wisdom it contains."[10] But, of course, such a further moral development requires first of all a better insight into the particular character of the war against terrorism. How does it differ from a conventional war?

Terrorism in all its forms and appearances is not something new.[11] Probably the phenomenon of using terror as a weapon is as old as human society itself. Indeed, in human history there have always been governments and groups within society that have taken recourse to violence or the threat of violence against civilians to instill fear in the hearts of the people in order to acquire or keep political power. Although terrorism was already very much part of our contemporary society – just think about the IRA in

[10] J.T. JOHNSON, *Morality and Contemporary Warfare*, New Haven/London, Yale University Press, 1999, p. 39.
[11] For a historical overview of international terrorism, see: C. CARR, *The Lessons of Terror. A History of Warfare Against Civilians – Why it Has Always Failed, and Why it Will Fail Again*, London, Little Brown, 2002, p. 271.

Northern Ireland and the ETA in Spain – it has practically monopolized the attention of the international community since the suicide attacks of September 11th in the US. Shortly after the 9/11 attacks, President Bush declared war on terrorism. Though counter-terrorism is probably as old as terrorism itself, the warlike rhetoric in use today to talk about terrorism was unknown to the past.

No doubt this explicit reference to war conveys the relentlessness and the thoroughness with which terrorism in general, and those who were responsible for the attacks in particular, need to be dealt with. It should be obvious, however, that the war against terrorism is nothing like an "ordinary" war. When we talk about war, we usually think about an armed confrontation between two states, and more in particular about a confrontation between the armed forces belonging to those states. Fighting terrorism is no doubt also about a confrontation and it also no doubt involves the use of force. But it is not in *the first place* an *interstate* confrontation. The most distinctive difference is perhaps the nature of the enemy. Unlike a particular enemy-state and its national armed forces, terrorist groups like al-Qaida are internationally organized and make use of very elusive independent functioning cells. Closely linked to this dissimilarity is the fact that in most cases the enemy does not limit itself to attacking military objectives, but intentionally targets the civilian population.

In the next part we will analyze a number of specific moral issues entailed by the war against terrorism within the framework of the just war theory. The main issue in that discussion is pre-emptive military action. Can pre-empting a terrorist threat ever be considered as a just cause? And besides these concerns about justice, there is also the concern of prudence. Can we still consider the use of force as a last resort in the context of fighting terrorism, or can the war against terrorism ever have a reasonable chance of success, let alone be proportional? Another basic issue here is that of proper authority. Who gets to decide on issues of military force when it comes to fighting terrorism? Finally, we will tackle the *in bello* issue, by asking ourselves whether those who fight terrorism

should respect the *in bello* principles, or whether they should fight
terror with terror?

4. PRE-EMPTING TERRORIST THREATS – A JUST CAUSE?

The first and no doubt one of the most important just war principles is *just cause*. This principle, in effect, says that you can only
start a war when you have a good reason to do so. A reason might
be defending oneself or another state. It also says that you can
intervene to stop another state from participating in ongoing
humanitarian crisis. What is essential for just cause is the presence
of an injustice that needs to be corrected or punished, or, when the
injustice is about to occur, pre-empted. Indeed, within the tradition of the *bellum justum*, the possibility of a pre-emptive action
isn't excluded. Just war theorists such as Grotius (1583-1645) and
Vattel (1714-1767) clearly state that, under certain conditions, an
action to pre-empt an injustice might very well be considered a
just cause. But also more recent adherents of the just war doctrine
admit the possibility of a legitimate pre-emptive action. The most
influential is no doubt Michael Walzer. It is his insight on this
matter that will shape our analysis of the US pre-emptive action
strategie defined in the National Security Stategy (2002).[12]
    The fundamental characteristic of a pre-emptive military action
is trying to avert a danger or an injustice that is about to occur. As
a first use of military force, such an operation is indeed very sus-
pect in an international context where the only authorized use of
force is that of self-defense. Walzer is very aware of the sensitivity
of the issue. In order to explore what can be morally accepted and
what not, Walzer presents us with what he calls a spectrum of
anticipation. On the one side of the spectrum there is what he
calls a form of anticipated reflex. This kind of action is initiated at
the point where the aggression hasn't occurred yet, but is about to

---

[12] M. WALZER, *o.c.*, p. 361.

happen. According to Walzer, it is like throwing up one's arms at the very last minute to avert an incoming blow.[13] The extreme at the other side of the spectrum is all but the result of a reflex. Here the action taken is deliberately and very well thought through. This kind of anticipative action – here Walzer talks about **_preventive_ action** – is based on the idea that international peace is best served by maintaining a certain balance of power. If a neighboring country threatens to overrun us, it is absolutely necessary to take action. Not doing so would not avoid war, but would simply mean fighting it later on a larger scale and at worse odds, precisely because of the increased strength of the adversary. Both these extreme forms of anticipated action pose no real problem from a moral point of view. An anticipated reflex is without any doubt a clear form of self-defense. Anticipated action in order to maintain the balance of power is, on the other hand, clearly unacceptable because such an action tends to reduce war to an all too common instrument of the state. So a real anticipative action that is more than pure self-defense, but less than pure power management, – here Walzer talks about *pre-emptive* action – needs to be situated somewhere between these two extreme forms.

A justified pre-emptive action is characterized by what Walzer calls a "sufficient threat." For a threat to be sufficient, it needs to satisfy three conditions. First, the potential enemy needs to manifest a clear intent to injure. Second, there has to be a degree of active participation that makes that intent a positive danger. Finally, one has to be confronted with a general situation in which waiting, or doing anything other than fighting, greatly magnifies the risk. With this last condition Walzer indicates that a legitimate pre-emptive action can go further than merely a reflex action. Waiting at the last moment to react does indeed jeopardize one's own chances to defend oneself successfully. The first two conditions on the other hand, exclude anticipative action inspired by power games. A change in the balance of power alone is not enough.

[13] *Ibid.*, p. 75.

Walzer illustrates this notion of justified pre-emptive strike by referring to the Six Day War (1967).[14] This war began on June 5 with a first strike by Israel against Egypt and its allies (Syria, Jordan and Iraq). Walzer analyses the narrow time frame (three weeks) that preceded the actual attack and concludes that there were abundant reasons for believing that Israel was faced with what he calls a sufficient threat. First, there was a manifest intent to injure. In a speech on May 29, the Egyptian president Nasser made it clear "that if war came, the Egyptian goal would be nothing less than the destruction of Israel."[15] Second, there were clear signs that Egypt and its allies were making active preparations in order to accomplish their hostile intentions toward Israel. From May 14 on, the Egyptian government began to move its troops into The Sinaï. Egypt also ordered the United Nations Emergency Force to leave, and announced that the Straits of Tiran would no longer be accessible to Israeli shipping. At the end of May, Syria, Jordan and Iraq had formed a military alliance with Egypt. Finally, there was what Walzer calls "a basic asymmetry of forces."[16] Egypt had the military capacity to deploy a large army over a long period of time on the Israeli border. In contrast, Israel had to mobilize its reserve troops each time a crisis occurred. These reserves could only be used for a short period of time, which meant that Israel could not 'sit out' the crisis, as Egypt could. In other words, Israel did not have the luxury of postponing its military actions indefinitely without jeopardizing its chances of defense.

But how should we evaluate the US pre-emptive war doctrine based on Walzer's view? Is such a strategy justified by the presence of a "sufficient threat"? As was obvious from the above, Walzer's approach of a legitimate pre-emptive action has to be understood in a framework of interstate relations. As war against terrorism falls somewhat outside this framework, one might ask whether Walzer's criteria of a sufficient threat is actually helpful

---

[14] *Ibid.*, pp. 82-85.
[15] *Ibid.*, p. 83.
[16] *Ibid.*, p. 83.

here. Indeed, as long as we talk about interstate relations, it makes sense to distinguish a war of self-defense against an ongoing aggression, and a pre-emptive strike. This is no longer obvious when we focus on the war against terrorism. The preparation and the execution of terrorist attacks are nothing like the preparation and the execution of a traditional military offensive. The preparation of a large-scale military operation is always to some degree detectable, which leaves room for those who feel threatened and who want to take pre-emptive actions to act. This is usually not the case with terrorist attacks. Here a limited number of people prepare their attacks in the utmost secrecy, so that in effect it is hard to predict *where* and *when* they will strike. All this makes it virtually impossible to resist an actual ongoing terrorist attack. The only sensible form of self-defense is simply to prevent such actions from happening in the first place by attacking, as mentioned in the US National Security Strategy, the terrorist leadership, its command, control, and communication centers, its training facilities, etc.

But there is still a more fundamental argument in favor of rethinking the notion of sufficient threat within the framework of the war against terrorism. The main purpose of the concept of sufficient threat is precisely to indicate under what conditions another country may be attacked first. Such a pre-emptive attack against another country is, however, an exceptional situation. Most of the time other states do not present threats that justify such actions. This is not so when we are dealing with international terrorist organizations. Because they have already killed and/or have threatened to kill innocent people, these organizations have already opened "the hostilities." This means that the idea of striking before they do no longer makes any sense, because they have already struck first. So when we do talk about conducting pre-emptive actions against terrorist organizations, it is because these organizations are *per definition* a sufficient threat. Their very existence implies that they are actively preparing other attacks. That is what they do; that is their very nature. The al-Qaida network is no exception. Bin Laden's organization was not only involved in previous attacks against American targets (the bombing of the American Embassies in Kenya and Tanzania in October 2000), it also declared in 1998 that it was the duty of all Muslims to kill US citizens and their allies everywhere.[17] ✓

But, one might ask, does the obvious nature of a pre-emptive action as described above, extend to attacking states who are suspected of supporting these terrorist organizations? Again, it is not clear if Walzer's notion of "sufficient threat" can be applied here. The threat such a state presents does not reside in the fact that it is about to attack the potential victim state. It "only" contributes to the creation of a terrorist threat. In that sense we might say that such supporting states are part of what we could call "the terrorist chain of agency." This means that the supporting activities of these states constitute a logical part of the enterprise of intentionally harming innocent people. Now, because they are part of this terrorist chain of agency, the victim state has a just cause in stopping their supporting activities. One might still speak in this respect about pre-empting a sufficient threat, be it in a more indirect manner. As will be made clear in the next section, prudential just war considerations – like last resort – will require a somewhat different approach to terrorist organizations and their supporting ← states. Indeed, to put it in terms of a domestic analogy, stopping someone who has vowed to kill you whenever he has the chance to do so, and stopping someone who "only" provides this person with a gun, are, from a moral point of view, two different cases.

And what should the scope of such an intervention be? Should we topple the government and replace it with a "terrorist-free" regime, or should we limit our scope and strike in such a way as to make it very difficult for that government to continue its supporting activities? Obviously, the former option is the more thorough one, but it requires a long-term commitment in order to stabilize the country (cf. Afghanistan and Iraq). The latter option demands less commitment, but it can never really eliminate the possibility that some form of support for terrorism will continue to exist.

---

[17] L. BEYER, *Roots of Rage*, in *Time* (October 1, 2001), pp. 52-54.

5. PRUDENTIAL CONSIDERATIONS

Until now the argument has focused on the question whether pre-empting terrorist attacks could be considered as a just cause. Having a just cause, though, is not enough. There are also a number of prudential conditions that need to be satisfied. Military force not only needs to be a last resort, it also has to offer a likelihood of success and its use must be proportionate. Now because the struggle against terrorism is often thought of as a battle against an ultimate evil, one might seriously question the need for burdening oneself with such prudential considerations. In what follows we will have a closer look at these prudential just war criteria, and try to determine whether they are still relevant within the framework of fighting terrorism.

Before taking recourse to any military option, the reasonable non-military alternatives should be exhausted first. The range of options here in applying the principle of last resort are from negotiations to economic and political sanctions. But the relevance of this principle in the context of fighting terrorism is not so self-evident. Because of their very nature, terrorist organizations aren't very prone to engage in negotiations. Additionally, most governments have a strict policy of not negotiating with terrorists. It is also difficult to see how economic or political sanctions could deter future terrorist attacks. The conventional alternative means are simply not reasonable within this context. Given the constant threat terrorist organizations present to a society, immediate forceful actions to reduce the terrorist danger seem to constitute a first and last resort. But a distinction has to be made here between a struggle against terrorist organizations and a war against a state supporting terrorism. Because we know *who* they are and *where* they are, there is some room to give the government of such states the possibility to stop supporting terrorist organizations, for instance, by presenting them with an ultimatum.

The *likelihood of success* principle says that one should only consider the military option to obtain justice if there is a reasonable chance that such a course of action will yield the desired result. This implies that sometimes we should decline the military option, even it appears that we have a clear just cause and no real alternative course of action to obtain satisfaction. The underlying philosophy is of course closely linked to the very nature of war. It would indeed not be very wise or prudent to risk the lives of so many people in such a deadly endeavor as war when in fact there are good reasons to believe that all these lives will be wasted for nothing.

Now in what measure can we extrapolate this principle in the realm of fighting terrorism? Can we, for instance, say that we should drop our fight against terrorism once it becomes clear that it will be nearly impossible to eradicate this phenomenon? Here the dissimilarity between an interstate war and fighting terrorism becomes relevant. Fighting terrorism is not just about the use of force. It is in fact a multifaceted effort. It involves internationally coordinated intelligence gathering and analysis. It involves international investigations into the structures, funding and affiliations of the terrorist networks. It involves the building up of airtight security systems to protect potential targets. But it also involves training special forces for counter-terrorism activities. Now when we talk about the likelihood of success in the context of fighting terrorism we need to distinguish two levels. The first level is that of the overall effort. At this level we cannot afford to give in to the "defeatist" logic of the success principle. Even when there is no immediate perspective of defeating terrorism, we cannot just drop counter-terrorism in all its aspects all together. Fighting terrorism is a long-term effort that seldom yields total and absolute victories. The second level is that of the specific use of force. Here the likelihood of success principle can be used in much the same way as in the war context. Only when it is reasonable to believe that military and/or police actions will be successful, can such actions take place.

Not only must the war effort offer a reasonable chance of success, it also needs to be *proportional*. This means that the good one hopes to obtain with the war has to outweigh the unavoidable bad consequences that that war will entail. The basic philosophy is the same as that for the success principle: don't waste lives for a futile cause. When we apply the proportionality criterion in the context of fighting terrorism we again need to distinguish the two levels we talked about in the likelihood of success discussion. On the overall effort level, the fight against terrorism cannot be assessed other than proportionally. Indeed, what is at stake here is not just the prevention of material damage and the loss of life but the protection of our society values and the functioning of our society as a whole. This does not mean, however, that in the overall enterprise of fighting terrorism anything should go. In the effort of defending oneself, the danger exists that society would start limiting certain liberties and begin invading the domain of personal privacy. From a proportionality point of view this is, of course, detrimental since it begins to undermine the very values we seek to protect. On the level of military action, the proportionality assessment is not so straightforward. Here one needs to weigh carefully the pros and cons before initiating a military operation. It is also at this level that the inherent difficulties of applying the proportionality principle become painfully apparent. How many lives is our way of life worth? (This is the incommensurability problem itself.) Or, what kind of damage will ensue from the military action? Or, what are the chances that we will attain our objective?

6. WHO SHOULD DECIDE?

In order for a war to be just, the decision to go to war needs to be made by a *legitimate authority*. The main purpose of this principle is to limit the number of authorities who can declare war. This principle was especially relevant in the feudal system of the Middle Ages when political authority was indeed very dispersed. Could lower nobility for instance start wars, or was that privilege reserved for kings and emperors, or even clerical authorities? Nowadays the UN Charter distinguishes two legitimate authorities. The first recognized legitimate authority is the state. According to Article 51 of the UN Charter each state has the right to use force to defend itself or others against an occurring attack. The second legitimate authority is the Security Council. In case of a threat against or a breach of the international peace and security, the Security Council has the authority to decide on the use of force (Article 42). Now can a state that decides to use force in order to fight terrorism be considered as a legitimate authority? In response to the 9/11 attacks, the US commenced military attacks in Afghanistan. But as the military response took place almost a month after the attacks, it could no longer be considered as a case of self-defense against an ongoing attack. It might be argued, however, that given the specific nature of fighting terrorism the interpretation of Article 51 should be broadened to include pre-emptive actions. Indeed, as argued in a previous section, resisting an ongoing terrorist attack is, although not impossible, very difficult as it can take place at any given time and place. So the only effective form of self-defense in this context is to prevent terrorists from executing their attacks in the first place.

But what about the UN Security Council? What role – if any – can it play in the war against terrorism? Since the end of the Cold War the UN has been confronted with an increasing demand to respond more actively to threats to international peace and security emanating from intrastate ethnic struggles and humanitarian crises. There were those who claimed that the UN was the only organization that could guarantee an impartial intervention. Others argued that in some cases – when for instance the Security Council is paralyzed by the use of the right of veto – individual states, or a coalition of states, should have the right to intervene. Still others believe that only states can be considered as a legitimate authority, because only they have the real power to intervene.

In the period following the 9/11 attacks, the role of the UN in the war against terrorism seemed to be much less an issue of dispute. Contrary to stopping a humanitarian crisis in some far-off land, fighting terrorist organizations that attack one's own population is definitely a cause where the legitimate authority problem seems to be more straightforward. If one's own citizens are under attack, then one has the right and even the duty to protect them. The need to call upon the Security Council to authorize a possible military intervention is in such a case much less sharply felt. This doesn't mean, however, that the exercise of the right to defend one's citizens is always beyond suspicion. Just as interventions for humanitarian reasons, military interventions in the framework of the war against terrorism are susceptible of being abused. Any country suspected of sponsoring terrorists indeed risks being attacked in the name of self-defense. Or worse, the war on terrorism might be used as a pretext to intervene militarily in the internal affairs of other states. In order to avoid these kinds of abuses as much as possible, the Security Council should continue to play its role when it comes to authorizing the use of military force. Whether exceptions should be allowed to this rule need to be the subject of a case-by-case analysis. Unilateral intervention without UN authorization might be justified in cases where, for instance, a government has reliable information about the whereabouts of key terrorist leaders, but has not the time to obtain due UN authorization.[18] Overthrowing a government, on the other hand, suspected of supporting terrorist organizations, without there being hard evidence to corroborate this suspicion, is certainly not a good candidate for unauthorized intervention.

But the involvement of the UN in the war against terrorism needs to be considered for yet another reason. The threat of international terrorism is a global threat and should be addressed accordingly. If the war against terrorism is to be successful, the members of the international community should cooperate as much as possible in such areas as intelligence gathering, police

---

[18] Obviously the UN wants to avoid such non-authorized interventions as much as possible. In his address to the General Assembly on 23 September 2003 the UN Secretary-General suggested for instance that there should be a discussion on the early authorization of coercive measures to address certain types of threats, like for instance, terrorist groups armed with weapons of mass destruction. (http://www.un.org/webcast/ga/58/statements/sg2eng030923.htm)

investigations, extradition and prosecution of suspects, and suppression of money laundering. The UN can provide such a forum. In the direct aftermath of the 9/11 attacks the Security Council voted Resolution 1373 (28 September 2001), in which it reaffirmed that the terrorist acts had to be considered as threats to the international peace and security. In this resolution, voted under Chapter VII of the UN Charter, the Council urged all states to cooperate and to prevent and suppress all terrorist activities, including the support of these activities, on their territories.

The question is, however, whether the UN has the structural capacity to tackle these new kinds of threats. Indeed, the UN was created in the aftermath of the Second World War, and its main objective was precisely to prevent such conventional interstate wars. Now, as indicated earlier, the war against terrorism isn't exactly a conventional war. UN Secretary-General Kofi Annan recognizes this challenge and urges the member states to question the adequacy, effectiveness, and instruments at its disposal. In this respect, Kofi Annan proposes to rethink the UN on two fundamental levels. The first is that of the international peace and security. According to him, the Security Council needs to regain the confidence of the states and world public opinion "both by demonstrating its ability to deal effectively with the most difficult issues, and by becoming more broadly representative of the international community as a whole, as well as the geopolitical realities of today."[19] The trouble with this proposition is, however, that generally the need for more legitimacy and the need for more effectiveness do not go well together. Increasing the number of Security Council members – and thereby increasing the legitimacy of the Council – may very well decrease its effectiveness still further.[20] The second fundamental level is the social-economic.

[19] http://www.un.org/webcast/ga/58/statements/sg2eng030923.htm

[20] Frederic Bozo puts it as follows: "The legitimacy of a collective security action … grows proportionally to the number and the representativeness of the states involved. Contrariwise, its effectiveness depends upon a coalition which is as organised, workable and therefore as restricted as possible, controlled by those states which are both willing and able to act." Frederic Bozo cited in

Here Kofi Annan pleads for the strengthening of the Economic and Social Council of the UN. This strategy seems to move into the direction of taking on the social-economic grievances that are among the root causes of terrorism. Although doing something about social-economic injustices is no doubt a good thing to do, there is no consensus as to whether these are a root cause of terrorism. The history of terrorist movements seems to show that those involved in terrorist activities belong in fact to the relatively privileged class.[21] Bin Laden and those who were responsible for the 9/11 attacks were no exception to this rule.

7. FIGHTING WELL: MORAL NECESSITY OR TACTICAL WEAKNESS?

The principle of *non-combatant immunity*, also known as the *discrimination* principle, says that only military targets may intentionally be attacked. Does this principle still apply in the fight against terrorism? One might argue that it is not a good idea to fight morally against an immoral adversary. If they don't respect the rules, why should we?

There are a number of reasons why we should. A first obvious reason is that copying the indiscriminate methods of the adversary would turn those who fight terrorism into terrorists themselves. Secondly, it is very doubtful whether acting indiscriminately would yield any tactical advantage. It is highly unlikely that such conduct would deter the terrorists. On the contrary, chances are that one might get caught up in a brutally escalating cycle of violence and terror. The third reason for respecting the discrimination

C. GUICHERD, *Regional Collective Security*, in B. WICKER & F. VAN IERSEL (eds.), *Humanitarian Intervention and the Pursuit of Justice. A Pax Christi Contribution to a Contemporary Debate*. Kampen, Kok Pharos Publishing House, 1995, p. 97.

[21] M. RADU, *The Futile Search for the 'Root Causes' of Terrorism*, E-Note on Foreign Policy Research Institute website, April 2002. (http://www.fpri.org/enotes/americawar.20020423.radu.futilesearchforrootcauses.html)

principle is the need to be truthful to the values of one's own society. Giving in to the highly emotional cries to repay the adversary
in kind – cries often heard in the direct aftermath of a terrorist
attack – might in the long run cause severe moral traumas in a
society. Is this the kind of society we want? Are these the values we
stand for? Finally, there is the consideration that acting indiscriminately in the fight against terrorism can very well lead to international isolation, whereas building and maintaining an international coalition is generally recognized as a necessary condition for
success.

Although the discrimination principle remains very relevant
in the context of fighting terrorism, its application is not without difficulties. One of the central problems is that of the exact
status of the terrorists. It cannot be said that they are regular
combatants. Contrary to the armed forces of an enemy-state,
the members of a terrorist organization are not recognizable as
legitimate targets in so far as they avoid open confrontation at
all times. Indeed, the success of their operations depends to a
large degree on the secrecy in which they can be prepared and
conducted. This is exactly why an important part of the effort
of fighting terrorism is about the identification and the local-
ization of those involved in the terrorist activities. Terrorists
cannot be considered as regular combatants in another sense.
They are simply not the moral equals of the military and police
forces that fight them. Soldiers and policemen get ordered to
fight the enemy by a public authority. In that sense they constitute an instrument to protect the integrity of society. The
members of a terrorist organization are not in a comparable
fashion the instrument of a community. Those who execute the
terrorist attacks also participate to some degree in the planning
and the participation of those attacks. Or, to put it in the terms
of just war theory, those who decide whether to use force (*ad
bellum*) and those who use it (*in bello*) are to some degree the
same. One could of course argue that those who do the actual
bombing are just the "poor sods" who are indoctrinated by the
leaders of the terrorist group. In that sense they would be as

much an instrument as soldiers are. Now, independent of whether this claim of instrumentality is true or not – here we would have to venture into some serious empirical discussions – it is hard to contend that someone who deliberately kills innocent people is the moral equal of those who try to respect the *in bello* principles as much as possible.

Nonetheless, terrorists are not common criminals either, like the members of the Mafia for instance. International terrorism acts for ideological or religious reasons. They are in addition highly trained and destructive paramilitary units that conduct well-orchestrated campaigns against the social and political systems of a state.[22] The US, for instance, considers the members of al-Qaida and the Taliban as *illegitimate* combatants. As a consequence the captured members or suspected members are denied the treatment of a regular combatant – cf. the Geneva Conventions – and the treatment of a suspected criminal. In reality they are intentionally kept in a legal *no-man's-land*, where there are no clear rules and procedures. The arbitrary treatment of al-Qaida and Taliban prisoners kept at Guantanamo Bay in Cuba illustrates this clearly. According to Ronald Dworkin such a legal vacuum should be avoided. He suggests that besides the existing war model and crime model a third scheme should be introduced.[23] The main purpose of this third model is to establish basic constraints in the domain of fighting terrorism that would aim to exclude arbitrary treatment of prisoners. In a first phase a decision would have to be made – on a case by case basis – whether a prisoner will be treated as a prisoner of war (POW) or as a criminal. Once this decision has been taken (Dworkin suggests that this should be done within a three-month period) the prisoner would be subject to the rules and procedures of the crime or the war model. In order to take into account the specificity of the war against terrorism, both models would have to be

[22] C. CARR, *o.c.*, p. 9.
[23] R. DWORKIN, *Terror & the Attack of Civil Liberties*, in *The New York Review of Books* 50 (17) (2003). (http://www.nybooks.com/articles/16738).

slightly modified. For instance, in the case where a prisoner is considered as a POW, the rule that he or she can be released when the war is over is no longer realistic. The war against terrorism, Dworkin remarks, is not a conventional war with a formal beginning and end, but could go on for generations to come. Dworkin's suggestion is therefore that the legislative authority should stipulate the maximum period during which a prisoner may be detained. In the crime model, Dworkin gives the example of courts being created to address problems specific to the fight against terrorism. Regardless of their special nature, however, these courts should respect some basic requirements like the separation of judicial and executive power, and the possibility to appeal decisions taken.

The second *in bello* principle is that of ***proportionality***. Contrary to the *ad bellum* proportionality, the *in bello* proportionality requirement tries to weigh the costs and benefits associated with an *individual* war action, and not with the war effort in its entirety. Basically this principle says that the damage and destruction caused by a military action should not outweigh the military value of the target. Sometimes this principle is also referred to as that of avoiding unnecessary damage and suffering. Only a necessary amount of force may be used to take out the target. If you can eliminate a tank with a conventional weapon, you shouldn't take recourse to a nuclear device. Like the discrimination principle, the *in bello* proportionality requirement remains relevant within the context of fighting terrorists. Potential targets need to be assessed and selected carefully based on (among other things) their counter-terrorist value and the probable damage its destruction will entail. Because of the threat terrorism presents to the well-functioning of society, chances are indeed high that all potential terrorist linked targets will be attributed a military priority. Some anti-terrorist actions require difficult ethical decisions from the perspective of proportionality and discrimination. Is it legitimate, for instance, to shoot down civilian airplanes that have been hijacked by terrorists in order to be used as weapons against civilian targets?

30 CARL CEULEMANS

8. CONCLUSION

So what should we conclude from all this? It should be clear by now that the war against terrorism is not a classic war in which two countries try to resolve their differences through military means. Since the attacks of September 11, 2001, the international community seems to have entered into a new era in which it must rethink its overall strategic, moral and legal approach in the domain of international peace and security. For instance, should we try to integrate offensive military action into the international legal and moral reality, or should we just hold to our defensive post-World War II paradigm? Another issue is that of proper authority. As the war against terrorism can easily be interpreted as a war of self-defense, the urge to act as one sees fit in order to protect one's own citizens is indeed overwhelming.

Given the global and complex nature of the terrorist threat, one should realize that the unilateral approach cannot offer a way out. As both the interventions in Afghanistan and Iraq have shown, the US as sole superpower is capable of winning a war, though it is not capable of restoring and keeping the peace by itself. Fighting terrorism necessarily requires a shared responsibility on different levels. In that perspective international organizations and structures need to be adapted and empowered to meet this new reality. But, of course, legal and institutional adaptations alone can never provide an answer to every problem. In many instances moral deliberation on a case-by-case basis will remain necessary. Here, then, the tradition of the just war will once again show its usefulness.

NICK FOTION

Applying Just War Theories to Wars Involving Terrorism

1. GENERAL BACKGROUND

Just war theory is a secondary ethical theory. It is developed or generated from a primary theory which typically ranges over the entire ethical landscape. Utilitarianism is an example of a primary theory[1] in that it claims to tell us what rules and principles we should follow in all aspects of our lives. It also claims to tell us what we should do when our rules and principles come into conflict with one another. Deontology is another example of a primary theory.[2] It similarly tells us what rules and principles we should follow. Contractualism is yet another primary theory,[3] as is virtue theory[4] which places less emphasis on rules and principles and purports to guide us by focusing on character development. Rather than asking the rule-oriented question "What should I do?" it asks "What kind of life should I lead?" One other primary theory should be mentioned: viz., religious-based theory. With this sort of theory ethical rules, principles and/or virtue claims are generated from religious commitments (e.g., via commandments from the Deity).

Surprisingly, as a secondary theory, just war theory can be generated from any of these primary theories. It is as if travelers

---

[1] R. M. HARE, *Moral Thinking*, Oxford, Clarendon Press, 1981.

[2] C. KORSGAARD, *The Sources of Normativity*, in *Moral Discourse and Practice*, S. DARWALL, A. GIBBARD & P. RAILTON (ed.), New York and Oxford, Oxford University Press, 1997, pp. 389-406.

[3] T.M. SCANLON, *What We Owe to Each Other*, Cambridge, The Belknap Press of Harvard University Press, 1998.

[4] R. HURSTHOUSE, *On Virtue Ethics*, Oxford, Oxford University Press, 1999; M. SLOTE, *Morals From Motives*, Oxford, Oxford University Press, 2001.

coming from different directions all converge on Brussels, and even converge on the same street of that city at the same time. Thus a utilitarian is likely to tell us that one of the principles of just war theory is last resort, to which a deontologist, a contractarian, and the others would likely agree though each of them offers radically different pictures of the nature of ethics.[5]

Let us be clear about what it is that these various theorists agree on. Just war theory is not only a secondary theory in the way explained already. It is also a secondary theory in being topical. It is concerned with the domain of ethics having to do with military activity and so differs from primary theories that range over all the ethical domains. But there are other (topical) domains. These include law enforcement, law, medicine, business, education and the family. Of course these domains overlap some, as when we are concerned with the ethical problems a family business might encounter. Nonetheless, each domain has a unique set of ethical problems to deal with. As a result, it is possible to imagine each domain developing one or more theory to help it deal with its own special problems. These cross-domain theories may in fact, overlap to some extent, but they most likely will exhibit differences that will help make each theory unique. These domains can be divided into sub-domains. For example, within medicine we can develop thinking and theories having to do with nursing, access to health care and experimenting on humans and sub-human animals. Within business there are the sub-domains having to do with computers, information technology, journalism, personnel matters (e.g., sexism) and international affairs.

With these distinctions in mind, we can begin to appreciate how just war theory deals with *some* of the problems found in the

[5] See R.B. BRANDT, *Utilitarianism and the Rules of War*, in M.M. Wakin, (ed.), *War, Morality and the Military Profession*, Boulder, CO, Westview Press, 1979, pp. 393-413; J.F. CHILDRESS, *Just War Theories: The Bases, Interrelations, Priorities, and Functions of Their Criteria*, in M.M. WAKIN (ed.), *War, Morality, and the Military* Profession, Boulder, CO, Westview Press, 1986, pp. 256-276; J. RAWLS, *The Law of Peoples*, Cambridge, MA, Harvard University Press, 1999; M. WALZER, *Just and Unjust Wars*, New York, Basic Books, Inc., 1977.

military domain. It is a sub-domain theory falling within the larger domain of military ethics. As such, it is not designed to deal with all of the military's problems. For example, just war theory tells us very little about what virtues need to be developed in the armed forces. We get guidance from another theory, probably a primary one, on what the military virtues are and which ones are the most important. Nor does just war theory tell us about the ethics of personnel issues such as whether women should be allowed to fight in trenches alongside men. Nor does it tell us about the ethics of military spending. Rather, it is expressly designed to handle only two questions, albeit two very important questions:

1. When can a nation, or any other political entity, rightly (justly) go to war? This is the *jus ad bellum* question.
2. Once the war starts, how can it be fought rightly (justly)? This is the *jus in bello* question.

2. THE JUS AD BELLUM QUESTION

As it developed historically, the theory answered the *jus ad bellum* question primarily in terms of wars fought between nations. This is certainly true since the Treaty of Westphalia in the seventeenth century after which nations became the centers of political power, and the standards identified by the *jus ad bellum* portion of just war theory became national in nature. Thus, before a nation could rightly go to war, the war had to be started legitimately. That meant that only certain authorities in the nation (e.g., the king, parliament, the dictator, or the president) could rightly involve a nation in a war. If a maverick general or a radical political group actually started a war by invading a neighbor, the war would be said to be unjust (i.e., not rightly started). Notice that with wars fought between nations, the standard of legitimate authority was (and is) applied symmetrically. Both (or all) nations had (have) to meet the standard.

Similarly, the other standards found in just war theory have symmetrical status. One of these standards is the good reasons (or just cause) principle.[6] To be involved rightly in war a nation must have a good reason, such as, at this very moment it is being invaded, or has suffered that fate recently. Other good reasons are that one of the nation's allies is being invaded or has recently been invaded. Still another reason is that the nation is acting to stop a humanitarian catastrophe. Finally, and more controversially, a nation can rightly go to war preemptively if it is faced with an attack that is clearly present, and is both serious and *imminent*. If the threat were clear and serious, but not imminent (i.e., if the threat were in the future), then the theory would not permit an attack (i.e., a preventive one). More on this point below.

Traditionally, four other standards need to be met before a nation could be said to be rightly at war according to just war theory. These include good intentions, likelihood of success, proportionality and last resort.[7] As most often interpreted, *all* of these standards have to be met before a nation can be said to be rightly involved in a war. Failure to meet any one of them marks that nation's involvement in war as unjust.

Unfortunately, the nation vs. nation version of just war theory suffers from a variety of problems. Uppermost among them is the vagueness of its principles. Take last resort as an example. The theory never makes clear what last resort means. The principle sounds more like hyperbole than a straightforward honest principle. How does a nation identify its latest effort to avoid war (e.g., negotiations) as its last resort? Isn't it possible to try some different negotiations before resorting to war? And if that fails, isn't it possible to try imposing sanctions? And, if that effort fails again, what about starting another round of negotiations? In short, none of the options that a nation can take identifies itself as the last resort. Realizing this, some theorists talk about not going to war

[6] C. CEULEMANS, *Just Cause*, in B. COPPIETERS & N. FOTION (eds.), *Moral Constraints on War*, Lanham, Boulder, New York and Oxford, Lexington Books, 2002, pp. 25-39.

[7] N. FOTION, B. COPPIETERS & R. APRESSYAN, *Introduction*, in B. COPPIETERS & N. FOTION (eds.), *o.c.*, pp. 1-22.

without first reaching the last *reasonable* resort.[8] That makes more sense, but then there is no agreed upon test to know which policy is the last reasonable one. Without a doubt, there is an inherent vagueness in the last resort principle. Vagueness plagues other principles in the theory as well. The likelihood of success principle tells nations that they should not allow themselves to go to war without having a (reasonable) likelihood of success of reaching whatever goal triggered the war in the first place. But the principle does not tell us what counts as likelihood of success.[9] What odds are considered successful? One in two, four, ten or more? The proportionality principle is similarly vague. It tells us that a nation should not involve itself in a war if the benefits are not proportional to the costs. But does that mean that the benefits should be equal to the costs, or slightly greater or much greater? The vagueness of the principle leaves followers of just war theory wallowing in disagreement. As a result, the theory cannot be applied uniformly. One official involved in deciding whether to go to war may suppose that his nation has appealed to and failed to get a response to his last reasonable resort, while another official in the decision process may suppose that her nation has not yet reached the point of last reasonable resort. These same two officials might also disagree about likelihood of success. The one may feel that having one chance in four of succeeding is good enough while the other may feel that her nation should not become involved unless the likelihood of success is three in four.

There are other problems with the theory. Take the good (right) intentions principle. What does it mean for a nation to have the right intentions? It is difficult enough identifying the intentions of individuals, given that intentions are subjective in nature. But identifying the intentions of nations is far more difficult. Is it done by obtaining the average of the intentions of key

---

[8] J.F. CHILDRESS, *o.c.*
[9] N. FOTION, & B. COPPIETERS, *Likelihood of Success*, in B. COPPIETERS & N. FOTION (eds.), *o.c.* pp. 79-90.

governmental officials? Or, is it done more behaviorally by seeing what a nation does once the war starts and, later, what it does when the war is over? If the latter is the right way to go, what specific kinds of behavior need to be monitored? Economic? Political? Military?

These and other problems, then, plague the application of just war theory. Specifically, they plague the theory when the war being contemplated is between two nations. But when the contemplated war is between a nation and some non-nation group (e.g., rebels, guerilla fighters, terrorists) even more problems emerge. I will list and briefly describe some of them.

    1. Legitimate Authority. It is impossible to apply this principle to many non-nation groups since they literally have no legitimate leaders. A rebel group may have a leader (e.g., as in the Castro-led Cuban revolution) but that leader is not necessarily recognized by anyone as a *legitimate* leader. Thus, applying the just war principles symmetrically seems impossible in nation vs. non-nation conflicts. The nation involved in the conflict needs to satisfy this principle, but the rebel group apparently does not. This is a problem for the theory since it appears now that the two sides are not fighting by the same rules.

    2. Likelihood of Success. A nation involved in war must assess its involvement in terms of its likelihood for succeeding, but a rebel group would probably not. It would be unreasonable to expect most non-nation groups to satisfy this principle. At the start of hostilities, most rebel groups have such a low chance of success that if the principle were applied strictly, all or almost all rebel efforts would automatically be condemned as unjust (not morally right). So again we have asymmetry in applying the theory, and again two sides apparently not fighting by the same rules.

    3. Good Reasons (Just Cause) and Last Resort. Classically, as noted already, a nation is allowed to strike another nation preemptively, that is, if the threat is clear, serious and imminent (e.g., there is overwhelming evidence that the enemy

will strike at dawn). But, as we have seen, the theory does not allow for a preventive strike. Such a strike is meant to deal with a clear and serious threat that, as a matter of fact, is in the distant future. The reason preventive strikes are not allowed, while preemptive ones are, is that future threats can be dealt with under the last resort principle. A nation can resort to all kinds of policies if a threat is in the distant future while it has no such option if the threat is from an attack planned at dawn. But the distinction between pre-emption and prevention seems to disappear, or at least to be less crucial, when dealing with wars between nations and non-nation groups. Generally, non-nation groups plan for war non-contingently. That is, their plans represent the first step of an actual attack. All nations plan for war contingently. Their plans say, in effect, that *if* a war starts, we will do such and such. In contrast, non-contingent planning (of most rebel groups) treats planning as the first step in the war against the enemy. In effect, rebel groups are in the process of starting their attack even if the physical attack has not yet literally started. For this, and other reasons (e.g., rebel groups have a tendency to use mass destruction weapons and a tendency to attack 'soft' civilian targets), it seems that a nation can claim that it has a good reason (just cause) to attack a rebel group preventively and to claim, as well, that it need not employ the last resort principle. One problem with modifying the classic version of just war theory (designed for nation vs. nation conflicts) in this way is that the theory seems to allow nations to go to war too quickly. If nations can go to war against non-nation groups for preventive reasons, the theory fails since it no longer constrains wars as it was supposed to do. Nations, it appears, can resort to war just about anytime they imagine that some rebel group is in the making. Any threat, real or imagined, is enough to get a war started.

In summary, it appears that two versions of just war theory are needed – one for wars between states (nations) and or

between nations and non-nation groups. The classical theory on
when a war can start (*jus ad bellum*), faces many problems. But, I
am arguing, it is still viable. This is because it is often able to do
its job of constraining the start of war even if it does not constrain
war as much as many would like. The modified theory for 'irregular' war (i.e., nation vs. non-nation) also faces problems, but it
too seems to be viable. Considering all their weaknesses, neither
theory is as powerful as many would like. But in defense of both
versions of just war theory, they seem to be the best of a bad lot.
Or, putting it another way, those who reject such theories take
the burden upon themselves of showing us another theory, or a
different way of thinking about war, that is better. So far no one
has.

3. THE JUS IN BELLO QUESTION

The second part of just war theory deals with the conduct of a war
once it starts. Like the first part which attempts to limit war by
doing whatever is possible to prevent it from starting, the second
tries to limit what political and military leaders, as well as their followers, do during war. Traditionally two principles are invoked to
bring off this limiting policy. The first is proportionality and the
second is discrimination. The latter is thought to be the more
important.

The principle of discrimination urges the war participants to
distinguish between those who should not be targeted in war and
those who can be. It is easy enough to start making a list of those
who should not be targeted. The list includes children, their
mothers, retired people, those who are wounded or sick (in hospi-
tals), health-care workers, religious officials, farmers, and those
who work in offices, factories and shopping centers that serve the
civilian sector of society. On the other side, those who can be targeted are uniformed members of the military establishment – but
excluding those in uniform working in the health-care field and in
the religious sphere. Depending on their degree of involvement in

war, others as well can be targeted. Civilians who labor to repair damaged military equipment, those who work to bring military supplies to the front, etc. usually can be targeted. Less clear is what should be done to workers in facilities that serve both the military and the civilian community. Certainly munitions workers are legitimate targets, as are the plants where they work; but workers (and their plants) who serve both those in war and those not in war show us once again how the vagueness problem in applying just war theory refuses to go away. If seventy percent of what the factory produces is sent to the military, is that enough to make that factory a legitimate target? What about fifty-five percent? Forty-five percent? Twenty-five percent? Ten percent?

Actually these questions cannot be answered in the abstract. Various factors, such as the seriousness of the situation at the front, need to be taken into account. If the war is nearly over, an attack on the clothing factory that produces military uniforms is hardly justified. However, if the factory makes sophisticated camouflage equipment, and victory is still in doubt, then that factory may be 'attackable'. Another factor that comes into play in applying the discrimination principle is the type of military equipment available. If a nation produces and can deploy a wide variety of smart weapons, it acquires a duty to employ them to prevent harming those who should not be harmed. Notice at this point that the asymmetry issue enters into the picture again. Third-world nations and rebel groups possess few or none of these smart weapons. So quite naturally the requirement to discriminate will be less stringent for those less technologically sophisticated war participants.

Realizing, then, that no blanket policy of discrimination makes much sense, those participating in war have gradually come to adopt the concept of rules of engagement.[10] Rules of engagement are specific verbal guides that tell military personnel how to behave when they are under attack or when in a threatening situation. The rules of engagement will be different for a submarine

---

[10] A. HARTLE, *Discrimination*, in B. COPPIETERS & N. FOTION (eds.), *o.c.*, pp. 141-158.

commander, a bomber pilot, and an officer or soldier patrolling a village that has just been occupied after a difficult battle. Focusing on the latter for a moment, these rules would tell soldiers to <u>defend themselves if attacked.</u> They might also tell the soldiers that if they feel threatened, but are not under attack, they should first issue a verbal command such as "Halt!" Failing to get the proper response, the rules might then tell the soldiers to show their weapons in a threatening manner. Failing again to get a proper response, they should next fire a warning shot. They would shoot to kill only after they have applied all the above rules first.

The rules of engagement would no doubt be different when searching for terrorist leaders. A possible set of rules for one kind of terrorist scenario might include the following:

1. <u>Positively identify</u> those individuals who are known to be terrorist leaders.

2. Determine who is with the leaders. If they are family (including children) do not attack but, instead, continue to monitor the terrorists' movement.

3. When the terrorist leaders are alone (or when there are many leaders and followers together with only a few family members) then commence an attack. [Note that Rule #2 might be different if the terrorist leader is someone like Osama bin Laden. He might be so important to the war against his group, and so hard to find, that once found, the rules might say that he should be attacked even if his whole family is put under serious threat as a result.]

The rules of engagement for searching a hostile village where terrorists are suspected to be hiding might be as follows:

1. Enter the village with loaded weapons held in a ready-to-fire mode.

2. Search each home by first commanding the occupants to vacate the home.

3. Search each person who has vacated.

4. Enter each home as if it contains terrorists who are ready to attack.

5. Open fire only when fired upon or when the remaining occupants of the home have weapons in hand.

Understandably, we think of such rules as applying to those nations who are defending themselves against terrorist attacks. Understandably, as well, we don't expect the terrorists themselves to formulate and follow rules of engagement that discriminate in any meaningful way. Our expectations here are very low. But these facts of life should not deter us from judging terrorist behavior on ethical grounds. It is in their power to attack military targets primarily and, by doing so, terrorize a nation. Their rules of engagement (for acting properly) might sound something like the following with respect, say, to using suicide bombers. The bombers would not detonate their bomb on a civilian bus, in a crowded café, in a religious institution, etc. The bomber would also not detonate his/her bomb at a checkpoint where many civilians are mixed in with military personnel. Only if the checkpoint is manned mainly by military personnel would the bomber sacrifice him/her self by detonating the bomb. In other words, there is no reason to excuse 'terrorists' from following a set of rules that, in one way or another, honors the principle of discrimination. In this regard, even terrorists can act morally.

Certain things need to be said about the other principle of justice-in-war (*jus in bello*). As noted earlier, it is called proportionality. Like the principle of proportionality having to do with starting war (*jus ad bellum*), the in-the-war version tells us that the good of some battle or campaign should be proportional (greater than?) the bad (harm) it entails. Vagueness plagues this principle as it does its sister *jus ad bellum* principles. But there is an additional problem facing both *jus in bello* principles which does not impact the *jus ad bellum* principles since they are applied serially. The problem has to do with a possible conflict between the two *jus in bello* principles themselves. The question is: if one principle tells us to do one thing and the other principle to do something else, which one should we follow? This classic conflict was what Harry Truman faced in 1945 when he had to decide whether the United States should use the atomic bomb on Japan. Had he treated discrimination as the dominant principle, he would have had no other choice but *not* to deploy the bomb. There were no 'rich' military targets the bomb could be used on and, for several reasons, he could not authorize dropping the bomb at sea to demonstrate its power. It could only be used on a city where civilian casualties would be very high. So the use of the bomb unavoidably involved intentionally attacking a large number of civilians. So, putting priority on the *jus in bello* principle of discrimination would have meant not dropping the bomb.

But a different story emerges if the focus shifts to the principle of proportionality. Yes, civilian casualties would be high if the bomb were used. But civilian casualties, along with military casualties on both sides, would be predictably very much higher if the bombs were not dropped and an invasion of the main islands of Japan were carried out instead. In other words, much less harm would have been done if the bomb were used than if it were not. The story in effect says in certain special circumstances the principle of proportionality trumps the principle of discrimination.

Now the problem with the *jus in bello* portion of just war theory is that it does not make clear which of the two *jus in bello* principles has trumping status. Those who incorporate the principle of double effect (PDE) into the debate argue that the discrimination principle does the trumping.[11] They cite the PDE to the effect that it is simply (and absolutely) wrong to intentionally attack civilians. Under PDE there are no exceptions. But those who argue that the discrimination principle is not absolute (i.e., has some exceptions) give (limited) trumping powers to the proportionality principle. They argue that if the loss of life in

---

[11] There are many versions of the principle of double effect. One that will do for our purposes goes like this: Many intended actions that we perform in order to bring about some good effects have unintended and negative effects. To be morally permitted, the good effects must be predicted to be greater than the bad ones (e.g., more military targets will be destroyed – intentionally – than civilian targets – unintentionally). It must also be clear that there is no other way of bringing about the good intended effects and so no way to avoid bringing about the bad ones.

dropping the bomb would turn out to be very significantly less than the loss of life resulting from an invasion, then the bomb should have been dropped.

This problem of trumping is truly a serious one for just war theory since it divides this theory's advocates irrevocably. There does not seem to be any way of resolving the disagreement. But for the sake of argument, let us assume that some rebel group is leaning in the direction of allowing the proportionality principle to have some trumping power over the principle of discrimination. Such a group might be tempted by such a trumping policy because its leaders suppose that it gives them more tactical and strategic flexibility. Somewhat like the situation in which Truman found himself, they could suppose that they have an excuse to attack a civilian population for the overall good of the cause they favor.

However, notice a key difference between the situation of President Truman and that of the rebels. In effect, Truman made an exception to the discrimination rule because the United States found itself in extraordinary circumstances. In a sense, Truman made a once-in-a-lifetime decision. His was not a decision of principle whereby discrimination could be overridden frequently and in a variety of situations from then on. Instead, his decision was based on realistic proportionality measurements concerned with a specific situation. It is true that the measurements were crude. But no matter how crude they were, they told him that the loss of life (on both sides) if an invasion were to take place would be larger many times over when compared with the loss of life resulting from dropping the atomic bombs on Japan.

In contrast, when rebels make an exception to the discrimination rule by favoring the principle of proportionality they are not typically dealing with extraordinary circumstances. Rather, in using terror tactics on 'soft targets', they are making a decision on principle that allows them to do what they are doing over and over again. There is no restraint on their actions. For them, the principle of discrimination is not overridden just this one time (or very infrequently) and remains intact thereafter. Rather, in making so many exceptions, they are burying the principle.

Further, they are not making a realistic proportionality measurement the way Truman did (or is said to have done historically). They of course can make realistic assessments of the casualties they create as the result of their rebellion. But they can't realistically tell a story about the casualties (suffering, etc.) that would be caused should their rebellion not take place. So unlike the situation in Japan in 1945, rebel behavior that leans heavily on terrorist activities cannot appeal to the principle of proportionality to trump the principle of discrimination. They cannot appeal to the trumping powers of that principle and also claim that they are behaving morally. Of course they can make the claim. They can claim anything that they want. But their claim is a hollow one since they cannot justify their terrorist actions by appealing to either of the forms of just war theory discussed above.

4. TWO MORE APPLICATIONS

I would like now to move to a different setting where one can and often does apply just war theories. I am using the plural here because, remember, I am arguing for (at least) two forms of just war theory. I will apply these theories to the 2002 war in Afghanistan and the war in Iraq begun in 2003. I begin with the former.

The Afghanistan war requires that both the state vs. state and the state vs. non-state versions of the theory be applied since that war was really two wars. Dealing with the al-Qaida forces based in Afghanistan, the state vs. non-state model of just war theory fully justifies an attack on these forces. The aim of the attack was to prevent further attacks by al-Qaida; and the state vs. non-state version of just war theory allows for such preventive attacks. But of course, the al-Qaida forces that were attacked were based in a sovereign state. That meant the United States and its allies had to appeal to the other version of just war theory as well. In fact they did in so far as they applied, for example, the last resort principle (and the other principles). They said to the Taliban rulers of

Afghanistan that they had to hand over the (supposed) guilty al-Qaida leaders they were protecting. Only if the Taliban refused to do that would the US coalition initiate hostilities in Afghanistan as an act of last resort.

But now contrast the Afghanistan war with the war in Iraq. The latter was a war exclusively between states and so required an appeal only to the state vs. state version of just war theory. This being so, the last resort principle needed to be honored as it was not in dealing with al-Qaida. Nor will it do to claim that initiating a preventive war is justifiable because the state vs. state version of just war theory does not allow preventive wars. This, as we have already noted, is because preventive wars violate the principle of last resort. Wars that prevent future wars are ones that can be avoided. But, it also would not do to claim that this was a pre-emptive war. Such claims tell us that a nation is facing an imminent and serious threat to its existence, and that simply was not the case since Iraq was clearly in no position to threaten the United States in 2003.

5. CONCLUSIONS

The purpose of this paper is to suggest that it makes sense to have and to employ two separate theories of just war for two separate kinds of war. I have not tried to prove that a dual theory approach is the best way to go. Indeed, it may also make sense in dealing with state vs. state *and* state vs. non-state wars to employ one overarching theory only. However, what I am suggesting is that the dual theory approach begins to make sense if one thinks of theory formation in ethics (and for that matter in any other field) instrumentally. If theories are thought of as useful instruments for helping us to think through our problems, then there can be no objection, in principle, to employing more than one instrument to get the job done. If the job is, in fact, two separate jobs, it would not be surprising if two instruments, each tailored to a task, get the job done best.

In this paper I have not actually shown in detail how classical just war theory works best with state vs. state wars and then how a modified version of that theory works best with state vs. non-state wars. To show in detail how this all works out would require writing a document of book length proportions. Examples of many wars, and many different kinds of wars, would have to be cited. And each war would need to be analyzed in terms of each of the principles found in the version of the theory appropriate to it. Further, it would also have to be shown that the dual theory approach does not seriously run afoul of the problem of dealing with wars that fall between state vs. state and state vs. non-state wars. Short of presenting such a comprehensive portrait of the two-theory approach, what I have done is point our thinking in the direction of that approach. But beyond that, I have also suggested by the examples of the wars I cited that the application is not that difficult. Working with two theories is not going to over-burden our minds. I am suggesting that it may be more convenient to have two tools in hand, a hammer and a wrench as it were, when there are two different jobs to be done.

DAVID PRATT

Realism and Just War Fictions
Theory Failings and Cosmopolitan Virtues

Sometimes art tells us exactly what we need to know about difficult moral problems. Concerning the justification of violence, the opera *Khovanshchina* teaches us some hard lessons. In its final scene, Russian Old Believers choose self-immolation in a chapel as their only valid response to a political and military situation gone out of control against them. As the closing bars are heard, troops rush in, too late to stop the flames or save the dying. Mussorgsky's music heightens the sense of moral tragedy as the curtain falls and audiences are left hushed and disturbed. The opera makes a blunt commentary on what happens when civil and ecclesial authorities lose their ethical balance and align on a course of war. *Khovanshchina* is fiction based on history. Its themes are corruption, paranoia, and inevitability.

The American war on terrorism has many similar moral notes and scripting, all non-fictional, and set to play for years to come. As of this writing, the conflict in Afghanistan and Iraq continues with few signs of peace on the horizon. The terrorist leaders of al-Qaida remain at large and their operatives form new cells abroad. The U.S. defensive posture is locked on course, inevitably, unimaginatively, while losses mount. One of the less obvious casualties in this global battle is the just war theory itself. The appearance of internationally organized terrorists and the American 'forward defense' policy has for all intents and purposes vacated the middle position that is just war thinking. What remains is either pacifism or a new realism, 'just war fictions,' or better yet, '*Khovanshchina* realities'. In the following essay, I will be tracing some philosophical points involved in this decline in just war thinking. Specifically, I will be taking up what is regarded as the 'epistemic problem' of justification. This will lead us to several types and examples of justification, and to a closer look at the notion of direct and indirect intentions in warfare. This analysis will reveal how and why just war thinking has become conflicted and less influential in the public forum. It is more or less dead-locked and going nowhere at present. I will conclude with some suggestions on how it might be renovated. Here, I will turn to Martha Nussbaum's cosmopolitanism, to the problem of knowing our duties to others, in order to argue for at least one virtue that can be a corrective element for any future just war theory.

1. AN OLD REALISM IS NEW AGAIN

Much will be written about the failure of classical just war theory to restrain the rush to arms in Afghanistan and outright preventive war in Iraq. The terrorist crisis has brought about a new defense approach which weighs potential harm against preventive action, a 'direct action rationale'. The analogy of burning a small forest in order to keep the larger adjacent one from catching fire comes to mind here. The paradigm example was made famous by Thucydides in his account of Athens conquering the island of Melos. The story bears repeating as we try to parse the just war thinking that has occurred since September 2001.

The Athenian generals arrived with a simple demand – give up neutrality and align with Athens at once. Athens was on hard times in its war with Sparta. Melos was Spartan in origin and conspicuously outside Athenian hegemony, and as the story goes, an inspiration to those who might one day rebel. In modern parlance, the island was a security threat. Melos refused the 'offer'. Athens attacked. No help from Sparta arrived. The Melians were either killed or enslaved and their island annexed. Melos' leaders took a bold principled stand but failed to save their people[1].

---

[1] M. WALZER, *Just and Unjust Wars: A Moral Argument with Historical Illustrations*, New York, Basic Books Inc., 1977, pp. 5-7.

This situation is echoed in Belgium's neutrality in World War I, and any nation found to be supporting or harboring al-Qaida personnel in 2002. Michael Walzer reminds us that the Athenians made no pretext to justify or make proportionate their actions. They could argue amongst themselves that the invasion was a necessity, and present that to the Melians as inevitable. Walzer notes how this sort of realism negates the freedom that makes moral arguments meaningful and possible in the first place.[2] Power, advantage, and fear overtake reason in these situations.

It is disturbing, therefore, to find lines in the *U.S. National Security Strategy*[3] which the Athenians might have been comfortable using. Consider these excerpts:

- "The United States possess unprecedented – and unequaled – strength and influence in the world. Sustained by faith in the principles of liberty, and the value of a free society, this position comes with unparalleled responsibilities, obligations and opportunity. The great strength of this nation must be used to promote a balance of power that favors freedom." (p. 1)

- "The U.S. national security strategy will be based on a distinctly American internationalism that reflects the union of our values and national interests. Our goals on the path to progress are clear: political and economic freedom, peaceful relations with other states, and respect for human dignity." (p. 1)

- "We will disrupt and destroy terrorist organizations by... identifying and destroying the threat before it reaches our borders. While the United States will constantly strive to enlist the support of the international community, **we will not hesitate to act alone,**

---

[2] *Ibid.*, pp. 8;10. Walzer's three propositions for Athenian amoral realism are (1) there is no freedom to choose morally in the international arena; (2) moral arguments are meaningless to international affairs; and (3) 'moral' warfare is more destructive than an amoral version. Moral discourse is likely a veiled discourse for more power. See: B. OREND, *Michael Walzer on War and Justice*, Montreal, McGill-Queen's University Press, 2000, pp. 62-65.

[3] Text on line at http://www.whitehouse.gov/nsc/nss.html For criticism see the Cato Institute's analysis at http://www.cato.org/pubs/pas/pa-496es.html

if necessary, to exercise our right of self-defense by acting preemptively against such terrorists, to prevent them from doing harm against our people and country; and by denying further sponsorship, support, and sanctuary to terrorist by convincing or **compelling states to accept their sovereign responsibility."** (p. 6, emphasis added)

The Strategy's rationale for pre-emption/prevention is in fact a blend of assessments about terrorists and their sponsors, the threat table, and passing references to just war norms. Its logic goes roughly in these four steps:

• "The gravest danger to freedom lies at the crossroads of radicalism and technology. When the spread of chemical and biological and nuclear weapons, along with ballistic missile technology – when that occurs, even weak states and small groups could attain a catastrophic power to strike great nations. Our enemies have declared this very intention, and have been caught seeking these terrible weapons. They want the capability to blackmail us, or to harm us, or to harm our friends – and we will oppose them with all our power." (p. 13)

• "We must be prepared to stop rogue states and their terrorist clients before they are able to threaten or use weapons of mass destruction against the United States and our allies and friends." (p. 14)

• "In the Cold War, weapons of mass destruction were considered weapons of last resort whose use risked the destruction of those who used them. Today, our enemies see weapons of mass destruction as weapons of choice. For rogue states these weapons are tools of intimidation and military aggression... **We must adapt the concept of imminent threat to the capabilities and objectives of today's adversaries...** Rogue states and terrorists do not seek to attack us using conventional means. They know such attacks would fail. Instead, they rely on acts of terror and, potentially, the use of weapons of mass destruction... The targets of these attacks are our military forces and our civilian population, in direct violation of one of the principal norms of the law of warfare. As was demonstrated by the losses on September 11, 2001, mass civilian casualties is the specific objective of terrorists and these losses would be exponentially

more severe if terrorists acquired and used weapons of mass destruction."[4] (p. 15, emphasis added)

- "We will always proceed deliberately, weighing the consequences
of our actions. To support preemptive options … to eliminate a
specific threat to the United States or our allies and friends.[5] The
reasons for our actions will be clear, the force measured, and the
cause just." (p. 16)

What is uneasy about the *National Security Strategy* are the vestiges
of the just war tradition that it does retain. A patina of justification? A vocabulary for delusion? These questions suggest that just
war reasoning is suffering from internal difficulties and is unable
to revise itself for the terrorist situation, hence its shrinking political significance. We can see this in a debate between two leading
just war proponents on the Afghanistan invasion.

2. Priorities of Justice and Presumptions for Restraint

In April 2002 the journal *First Things* ran a piece featuring profes-
sors Paul J. Griffiths and George Weigel, two American Catholic
experts on war ethics, debating the invasion of Afghanistan. Their
points are as fresh as ever. Griffiths noticed that the Catholic
debate on either side, while full of appeals to just war theory and
magisterial documents, was more guided by political convictions.
American Catholics failed to ask the telling questions of their
government in the build up to war. The burden of proof falls on
the advocates of war, and that burden was not met. The war
was illegitimate, he says, and war proponents (like Weigel) were

---

[4] See www.lastbestchance.org for a sobering look at the prospects of terrorist nuclear strikes. Also on this site is the May 29, 2005 *Meet the Press* (www.
msnbc.com) transcript of the 9/11 commission members and their report, equally
chilling that nuclear attack is seen as inevitable to al-Qaida's goal of breaking the
will of the United States in the Middle East.

[5] The military implementation of this policy is summed up as "Full Spectrum
Dominance." See the text *Joint Vision 2020* at http://www.dtic.mil/jointvision/
jvpub2.htm

"bewitched by their political convictions into abandoning the grammar of the faith and thereby misrepresenting Catholic teaching to others."[6] The required *jus ad bellum* criteria were unmet when hostilities commenced. He calls this disregard of criteria "epistemic immodesty" – the position of knowing more than what can be known in fact, and then rushing to combat on that basis. At issue here is the conduct of information from the government, the media, and foreign media sources. His point is that "we have no good reason to think that any of these sources is sufficiently reliable to provide what we need." Griffiths goes on to note the painful episodes in World War II where the U.S. and British governments lied and distorted information. The modern post-Westphalia state is adept at deceit and omission, he contends. So there is no effective way for citizens to rebut government convictions at the critical decision moments, and certainly not when national interests are teamed with revenge and fear motives. So a 'mendacity principle' has to be overcome before the *jus ad bellum* criteria can be honestly determined.[7] This means the Catholic position against killing (the default position as it is called) should be made all the stronger. And since we do have governmental deceits, that position must still hold. 'Epistemic immodesty', blasts of rhetoric, and American exceptionalism (the notion that the U.S. is good and does good to others and stands above the world because of that) all undermine the restraining principles of just war thinking. Griffiths argues that Catholic teaching overrides this exceptionalism. The sketchy information given prior to the Afghanistan operations should have given Catholics pause.

These remarks are amazingly prescient given the reasons that would soon be advanced in favor of attacking Iraq. Griffiths does not specify what his objections mean for the just war theory itself. I would posit that his 'mendacity principle' makes the *jus ad bellum* criteria more unreliable than he admits. Actually, governmental

---

[6] P.J. GRIFFITHS & G. WEIGEL, *Just War: An Exchange*, in *First Things* 122 (April 2002), p. 31.

[7] *Ibid.*, p. 32.

REALISM AND JUST WAR FICTIONS

deceit voids the criteria since a legitimate government declaring a war is presumed to be honest even if not forthcoming about every detail. We will return to this when we look at justification in more detail. Meanwhile, the response to Griffiths turns out to be equally corrosive on just war theory.

George Weigel is well known for his criticism of Catholic anti-war approaches after Vatican II. The 'default position' of Griffiths and others, he regards as a departure from classic thinking about peace. The 1983 pastoral letter *The Challenge of Peace* is an example of the activist antiwar strain of thought from the Vietnam era that has entered the mainstream of Catholic thinking. This he contends, has led to skepticism about any legitimate use of military force and amounts to a 'functional passivism' that attempts to pass itself as the Catholic tradition on war.[8] Central to this mistaken approach is the idea that just war thinking must begin with a presumption against violence. Precisely the opposite is true, he argues, since the pursuit of the public good sometimes requires violence. In the medieval view, rulers were expected to defend the public good even at the expense of their own life, and by extension, the common folk as well. Any sort of just war thinking starts with a judgment about rightly constituted public authority and a 'presumption for justice.' "In suggesting the reverse," he says, "the new Catholic 'default position' confuses ends and means and makes a tremendous hash out of moral reasoning – and out of the history of theology." With a rhetorical flourish he adds that those who would argue for the presumption against violence on the basis of Aquinas' *Summa Theologiae* question "Whether It is Always Wrong to Wage War?" which begins the article on war would be forced into a presumption against the existence of God on the basis of his question "Whether God exists?" which opens the article on God's existence. (He avoids discussing whether the war question has a different function since the two questions do not share the same logical form and are dealing with different realities. How much stronger his argument here would have been had he

---

[8] *Ibid.*, p. 34.

demonstrated such a similarity in the questions.) His real point is that rightly ordered public authority is obliged to hold a 'presumption for justice.' This is what sets the horizon for a moral analysis of just war thinking.[9] Governments are supposed to use the legal and political instruments at their disposal to achieve a peaceful order of things (*tranquillitas ordinis*). This sometimes requires using armed force. And the world's leading nations bear this obligation above others.

For Weigel, the crucial distinction here is that war is public force (*bellum*) not private conflict (*duellum*). This makes the *ad bellum* issues – just cause, right intention, legitimate authority – the most important. Those who hold the 'default position' overweight the *in bello* considerations and thereby bog down normal political reasoning. For instance, undue attention on the noncombatant immunity prior to the war on the Taliban would have interfered with the obligation of U.S. leaders to open hostilities against al-Qaida in Afghanistan, a moral necessity under justice. Priority must also go to the *ad bellum* questions because we can know them; we can determine just cause, etc., even with the 'epistemic modesty' Griffiths mentions. To privilege *in bello* details beforehand would lead to uncertainty, and that would paralyze politicians. Weigel seems to hold that *post bellum* concerns would be secondary also, even though they factor into the viability of *ad bellum* considerations as such. In a telling remark, Weigel criticizes *The Challenge of Peace* for overemphasizing proportionality and discrimination and pressing for arms control at the height of the Soviet-American cold war. This was bad political advice, he says, because the problem was not nuclear weapons but Soviet communism. Once that went, the threat of nuclear war did too, and real disarmament began. The 'default position' gives similarly bad advice on global terrorism. Eradicating this threat is a duty to world security. Its existence automatically puts America in a state of last resort because any fainthearted response would only encourage more attacks. The celebrations in Kabul after the fall of

[9] *Ibid.*

the Taliban suggest that the intention and execution of the war had been right. Weigel concludes with a prediction that Baghdad will rejoice in much the same way. Had he been writing this in 2005 his optimism would have been more tempered. The Abu-Graib trials, the on-going suicide bombings and the shaky Iraqi government seem to prove Griffiths right.

These differences between Griffiths and Weigel illustrate exactly what has happened to just war thinking. It is locked in an impasse between the presumption against violence and the presumption for justice, a restraint versus security deadlock.[10] In other words, the conception of the public good has been narrowed down to such a point that the Athenians could have worked their seizure of Melos under these terms. And if that is so, then we are left with simulacra rather than theory and rationality. We have vestiges and vocabulary of a tradition but no tradition. Hence the question of delusion is all the more relevant today. This brings us to the problem of justification.

3. THE EPISTEMIC PROBLEM: THREE EXAMPLES OF MORAL JUSTIFICATION

As wars drag on, the rhetoric of their justification drifts too.[11] The present conflict is no exception. The movement from 'lesser evil' to 'necessary evil' to 'necessary good' has occurred in military parlance. The 'necessary good' of regime-change is now being accepted as a sufficient rationale for the war. This is what Griffiths noted about mendacity and media blindness. This is also what Weigel's priority of justice and proper authority eschews. 'Rhetorical

---

[10] G.M. REICHBERG, *Is There a 'Presumption Against War' in Aquinas's Ethics?*, in *The Thomist* 66 (3) (2002), pp. 354-359 casts the problem as permissible versus meritorious uses of violence. His detailed analysis throws the question back on Aquinas' theory of *prudentia* in statecraft (p. 363) weighted on the side of the moral demands of natural and positive right (*ST* II-II 60.5).

[11] See: S. SMILANSKY, *Terrorism, Justification, and Illusion*, in *Ethics* 114 (4) (2004), p. 799.

drift' also points to something else in the debate on terrorism, namely, that there are varying degrees of belief and certitude in the justifications we form about it. The sin of war rhetoric is that it enables us to turn beliefs into facts. I will now illustrate how this happens with examples from three different church leaders who attempted to justify defensive war.

In 1813, the head of the Russian Orthodox Church exhorted the faithful: "If you avoid dying for the honor and freedom of the Fatherland, you will die a criminal or a slave; die for the faith and the Fatherland and you will be granted life and a crown in heaven."[12] With Napoleon still in Russia, Moscow burned, and the country in upheaval, Metropolitan Philaret of Moscow was clearly issuing a statement about national defense. We attempt the same thing in secular language with phrases like 'preserving our way of life' and 'defending freedom in the world,' and we consider them binding on secular citizens in much the same way. Religious language aside (in so far as we can set it aside given that American Evangelicals and Islamists are perfectly at home with Philaret's language), the moral justification in 1813 was based on a belief in positive information. There was no possible way to doubt Napoleon's invasion or the malice behind it. Compare this with a later war. As World War I went from bad to worse for Russia, church leaders called people to arms with similar exhortations. But in 1918, Patriarch Tikhon of Moscow condemned the Bolshevik government for quitting the war on Imperial Germany, though it was already lost for Russia by then. His argument was based on a strong belief that continuing the war was mandatory for justice, on two counts – so as not to dishonor the many who had died thus far for the cause, and to honor the alliances that brought them into war in the first place, a duty to the allies who were still fighting. His statement said: "You have taken from our soldiers everything for which they

---

[12] See this and the following example in: A.F.C. WEBSTER, *Justifiable War as a 'Lesser Good' in Eastern Orthodox Moral Tradition*, in *St. Vladimir's Theological Quarterly* 47 (1) (2003), pp. 5-6;47. See my response to this article, *Dual Trajectories and Divided Rationales, o.c.*, pp. 83-95 for an earlier version of the argument advanced here.

fought splendidly in the past. You have taught those, who not long ago were brave and invincible, to abandon the defense of the motherland, to run from the battlefields. You have extinguished in their hearts the conscience that 'greater love has no man than this, that a man lay down his life for his friends' (Jn 15:13)." This is a different kind of moral justification, one that we hear in secular discourse in phrases like 'staying the course' and 'finishing the job.' (American leaders have been issuing such appeals as unrest in Iraq goes unchecked.) What these two examples tell us is that conceiving a justification is more complex than we admit, with or without mendacity in our public authorities or media. Here is the technical reason why this is so.

Moral justification has two kinds of certainty. For want of better terms I will call the first sense foundational or ontic.[13] It concerns the acts and conditions that make it possible for reason to apply the terms 'justified' and 'justification' to a situation. A foundational moral justification (FMJ) is one that gives unequivocal reasons for permitting an act that would otherwise be impermissible, such as resorting to violence when lethally attacked, or declaring war in response to an ongoing invasion, or shooting an armed robber who draws his gun. The facts that compose our beliefs are unimpeachable in these cases. Now, the call to arms in 1813 appears to be FMJ, though its unequivocal reasons get cloudy the more Napoleon retreated and the more his forces were systematically destroyed, thus weakening him for the counter-offensive envisioned by the Russians. So even in this solid example of FMJ, there is a downward tendency in the reasoning, in the deliberation itself, as the circumstances of defense changed. The threat in 1813 was much different than 1812. So as time went on, the fine line between a licit defense and an excuse for vengeance got thinner by the day. The justification was growing invalid from the moment it was issued, which means even the FMJ is more fluid than its name suggests, at least in some situations.

---

[13] See: E. REITAN, *The Moral Justification of Violence: Epistemic Considerations*, in *Social Theory and Practice* 28 (3) (2002), pp. 445-464.

The other kind of certainty is called epistemic. This concerns the beliefs and perceptions that make up a justification per se. An epistemic moral justification (EMJ) gives permission for an act that might be questionable, though justifiable, such as resorting to violence in the face of impending attack, or calling for war because of threats of attack, or perhaps a hostile gesture from a would-be robber. In these instances there is a presumed certitude, a nearly unequivocal reason for action, or at least one that is approaching that level. What is occurring here is a weighting of beliefs in expectation of certainty. The appeal in 1918 was weighted in notions of justice (retribution) and loyalty, and in the presumption that a greater harm would come for not attending to these virtues even though continuing the war had no chance for success. These were seen as reasons enough for EMJ. The possibility the whole war might have ended earlier had Russia not capitulated is an outside consideration when assessing the Patriarch's mind. He may not have thought that, but he did understand the need to have the Bolsheviks stay in the alliance and be in the peace process in order to restrain their revolution at home, which was positively known to him. So the EMJ here is clouded with considerations which obscure its presumed certainty. Thus there is even more risk of downward reasoning in this sort of deliberation.

From these distinctions it should be clear why the U.S. invasion of Iraq or the Israeli bombing of the Osiraq reactor are barely able to qualify as EMJ and cannot make the grade to FMJ. Yet just war theory calls for FMJ. This is true even if we are following Weigel's presumption for justice. The real problem here is that we tend to suffice with EMJ. Griffiths' worries about information and deceit are only half of the problem because we are inclined to set aside just war reasoning for realism from the very start. We suspend the theory with the theory's own terms as it were. What results is a kind of fictional justification, a masking of utilitarian or realist motives. This will become clearer in the next example, but first a bit more clarification on the epistemic distinction itself.

People are content to justify violence epistemically because it presents a kind of straight-up certainty from the point of view of the defender. Its simplest form looks like this: believing that X is an unjust aggressor licenses me to use force against X whether or not the aggression in question is a matter of fact. A fundamental justification puts much steeper demands on the defending party, and as proponents of EMJ point out, this is too much for the defender when physical harm or destruction of the common good is at stake, or when it is happening too suddenly. This strengthens what would otherwise be a lesser warrant for violence. James Sterba argued effectively for this several years ago, and his approach turns out to be ideally suited for the kind of deliberation that occurs in pre-emptive decisions since it widens the opportunity for resorting to violence. He says:

"In order for defensible action to be morally justified, it is not necessary that one's defense be directed only at persons who are *actually* engaged in or are *actually* preparing to engage in unjust aggression; rather, it suffices if one's defense is directed at persons whom one reasonably believes are engaged in or preparing to engage in unjust aggression."[14]

His argument depends on a prior distinction, namely, if we say something is right for us to do, then it must make sense to us, which means that knowledge must be accessible to us, and in such a way that any discrepancy between our thinking and doing what is right can be traced to a failure in deliberation.[15] In other words, the perception of threat is sufficient. As beauty is in the eyes of the

[14] J. STERBA, *Justice for Here and Now*, Cambridge, Cambridge University Press, 1998, p. 170. He goes on to remark: "Accordingly, once we recognize that aggressors should be defined *epistemologically* as persons of whom it is reasonable for defenders to believe that they are engaged in or are preparing to engage in unjust aggression, rather than *metaphysically* as persons who are actually engaged in or are actually preparing to engage in unjust aggression, we can see why it is reasonable to deny nonaggressor immunity, not only to soldiers generally, but also to those who work in munitions factories or who are in other ways inextricably tied to aggressive military actions." See: E. REITAN, *a.c.*, pp. 447.

[15] J. STERBA, *o.c.*, pp. 15-16.

beholder, so is threat in the perception of the defender, and that warrants action. We are now a full step removed from questioning our perception since reasonable beliefs about a threat are now able to qualify as reasons for violence.[16] Everything here turns on whether this justification can be said to be necessary and sufficient for that. There are good grounds to say it is not. For one, to say that violence is epistemically justifiable is to say that it is permissible on the basis of what the agent believes about the actions of an unjustified aggressor. This means my fallible but epistemically justified beliefs about violence generate an infallible conclusion about its moral permissibility. For another, this line of thought collapses the Thomistic distinction between the material and formal rightness of an act, the objective rightness of the act itself and the subjective rightness of the agent's motives and intentions.[17]

There are number of negative outcomes when an epistemic justification is taken to be necessary and sufficient. First, this tends to erode any incentive to avoid errors in judgment, and it reduces the need for regret when error does occur.[18] The decision to attack Iraq lacked the incentive to have the critical intelligence be strictly error-free since EMJ was presumed in the decision from the start. And no regrets for that have been issued. The second problem with embracing EMJ is that it inevitably lets beliefs stand as certainties, the epistemic becomes foundational, and excuses pass for justifications. A proper justification allows one to reasonably believe that an act is morally permissible even though it is prima facie forbidden. To say that an act is excused, however, says nothing about its moral permissibility, only that the agent is more or less blameworthy for having done it. This is why Francisco de

[16] E. REITAN, *a.c.*, p. 450.

[17] *Ibid.*, p. 456. See also C. MCGINN, *Ethics, Evil and Fiction*, Oxford, Clarendon Press, 1997, p. 14 for his criticism of requiring moral properties to have causal-explanatory power when in fact they do not. The delusion here is to assign a causal character to goodness when it is merely evaluative. This is another aspect of the EMJ.

[18] E. REITAN, *a.c.*, p. 459.

Vitoria rejected the possibility that both sides in a war could be called just. Only one side is just, properly speaking, the other is either wrong or merely excused due to ignorance (invincible ignorance) or sin.[19] This distinction between justified and excused is also vitiated when EMJ is taken to be necessary and sufficient.

It is hard to imagine a better mechanism for justifying preventive warfare than EMJ. Nor will it do to say that the church has lost its voice in the debate since there is much religious-based input in it. The just war line of advice can no longer assert itself on politicians because it cannot counter their urge to have a simple notion of justified war as Weigel's presumption for justice gives, and different forms of EMJ give more, and realism gives the most.[20]

With these distinctions in mind, we can study another church leader who tried to cope with an immoral activity in an otherwise justified conflict. This is the well known case of William Temple, Archbishop of Canterbury, and the policy of area bombing.

It is generally agreed today that the practice of city bombing in World War II was unjustified. Though at the time, it was widely supported on the basis that it would hasten the end of the war and halt the evils going on inside Germany. This question was debated in the Anglican Church until late 1944. Temple stands out for several reasons. First, he shared the view of many that modern citizens were so intertwined in the efforts of their country as to implicate them in its actions, thus making them liable to (all) the effects of war. Strategic reasons could override their noncombatant immunity. Secondly, he condemned hate and revenge

[19] *Ibid.*, p. 457. C. MCGINN, *o.c.*, p. 15.

[20] In other words, just war theory is unable to claim its own rationality in the debate. The debate has gone tone-deaf to its meanings. See: J. MILBANK, *The Gift of Governing: Secularization and Political Authority*, in *New Blackfriars* 85 (996) (2004), pp. 217;223-35 for his analysis of a neo-Gothic entrenchment in the West which despite commitments to liberalism is not truly liberal at all (because it does not grant free choice but limited conditional choices) and is therefore less able to respond to militant Islam and is prone to violence itself. Islamic fundamentalism is a parallel to the Western liberal (religious) market state.

as motives in the air war and did not condemn the Nazis bombing of Britain. He was consistent in that. He also wanted retribution on Germany to be short-lived in order to allow the country
to return to normal as soon as possible. He understood that the
war had its roots in a lack of *post bellum* justice at the Treaty of
Versailles, not an easy argument to make in Britain then. Thirdly,
his view that the state exists to serve the individual not the individual the state was a position completely opposite from the Nazis
theory of the individual, and this disposed him to see the allies in
too good a light. Fourthly, as the practice of area bombing
expanded and the debates dragged on, the Archbishop's endorsement of the policy became increasingly important to the Air
Ministry, while Temple's need to know that there were restraints
on the policy likewise increased. One can sense that the ecclesiastical party is the one to get hoodwinked in this bargain.

Assurances were given by the Air Ministry to Temple's prede-
cessor in 1939 that only identifiable legitimate military targets
would be bombed. This was to ensure that operational negligence
would not target civilians.[21] By 1942, with the bombing program
well underway, the Air Ministry assured Temple that only factories
were being targeted. Of course that was not the case, and that fact
soon came to light, forcing a decision from Temple. He chose to
justify the policy by arguing that the circumstances of modern
warfare now made bombing a necessity for avoiding defeat. That
opinion had weight during the height of the German air war on
Britain, but by late 1943 and after, with the allies controlling the
skies, area bombing was being conducted to achieve victory.
Temple's support of it was couched in utilitarian terms – the practice was gaining in effectiveness so it had to continue. But this was
not a utilitarian reading of the just war tradition.[22] His view that
state and citizens are indistinguishable in time of war pushed him

---

[21] S.E. LAMMERS, *William Temple and the Bombing of Germany. An Exploration in the Just War Tradition*, in *Journal of Religious Ethics* 19 (1) (1991), p. 76. B. PASKINS & M. DOCKRILL, *The Ethics of War*, Minneapolis, MN, University of Minnesota Press, 1979, p. 246.

[22] S.E. LAMMERS, *a.c.*, pp. 80-82.

to conclude that effectiveness trumps non-combatant immunity. Or in classical terms, the remote end of the bombing (the faster ending to the war) was allowed to condition the morality of its proximate ends (the targeting of factories and then cities as such). This is a perfect example of just war thinking deteriorating under the pressure of government deceit. But Temple's descent into utility is not all the fault of lies. There is an epistemic justification (EMJ) here too. He was arguing for justice, namely, that it was more just to speed the end of the war than to achieve it more slowly by heeding *in bello* norms. This is a stark instance of how the presumption for justice can unravel the just war theory, at least the *in bello* portion of it.[23]

The Temple case shows how an illicit bombing strategy was able to become central to the war and then derive its own validation from that. In the war on terrorism, a pre-emptive/preventive strategy has been allowed a similar validation. Area bombing for the sake ending a war is a breakdown of *in bello* principles, while regime-change for the sake of security is a breakdown *ad bellum*. Both moves are theory failures. The pitfalls of epistemic justification (EMJ) are proof enough that just war theory can be compromised from within itself. To see this more clearly, we must turn to a subtler philosophical problem at the core of just war thinking.

4. Privileging the Intention: Strong and Weak Versions of Double Effect

So far, I've been raising doubts about the viability of just war theory in terms of its functioning. In this section, I turn to some fine points internal to the theory, especially a neglected distinction in the principle of double effect.[24]

---

[23] The fact of the holocaust, and what the allies knew of it, is another (epistemic) complication in this case.

[24] See: F.M. KAMM, *Failures of Just War Theory: Terror, Harm and Justice*, in *Ethics* 114 (4) (2004), p. 653 for double effect as detrimental to the theory.

To the catalogue of cases in the double effect literature, al-Qaida has bequeathed the example of the hijacked airliner headed for a building and the fighter jet about to shoot it down. That act eliminates the terrorists and saves the people in the building, but it kills the passengers on board. Thus the phrase "the good we intend and the evil we do" summarizes what the principle of double effect attempts to solve. Centuries of commentary have made this principle into a boutique field of ethics. What concerns us here is a recent trend to put more emphasis on the intention of the agent in these situations. We need to attend to this because the necessary and sufficient justification we saw earlier depends on a heightened sense of intentionality, and could not occur without it, and because the language of double effect is everywhere in war. So it is no accident that its *locus classicus* is to be found in Aquinas' treatment of self-defense (*ST* II-II 64.7).[25] Here he tells us why self-defense is licit, saying:

> "Nothing stops one act from having two effects, since only one effect is intended, while the other is beside the intention (*praeter intentionem*). Now moral acts receive their species according to what is intended, not from that which is beside the intention, since that is accidental… Therefore from the act of self-defense itself, two effects can occur – the saving of life and the death of the assailant. Thus in as much as the act is intended to preserve life it is not unlawful, as it is quite natural to save oneself as much as possible. But even if it proceeds from a good intention, an act may be rendered unlawful if it is out of proportion to the end. Wherefore if a man in self-defense uses more violence than necessary, the act will be unlawful. But if he repels the attack with moderate force his defense will be lawful."

This text has been decisive in the history of moral theology for the idea that an action gets its moral specification (or species) from the intention that brings it about and not from anything beside the intention. This framework of intention and specification gives an

---

[25] J. FINNIS, *Aquinas: Moral, Political and Legal Theory*, New York, Oxford University Press, 1998, p. 277.

abstract (analogical) clarity to the moral act. This schema comes at a price though. Not everyone has been convinced that violence can be so cleanly delineated. It also carries religious assumptions about virtues that most secular discussions would omit out of hand. We will look at these two points further on. The tradition, meanwhile, has struggled to sort out the question of agency in double effect (DE) situations by speaking of direct and indirect intending and willing. This has given rise to a set of conditions and cases for spelling out the principle of double effect (PDE). The classic DE cases are: 1) surgical intervention – where the evil of removing a limb is accidental to the intention to save the patient's life; 2) indirect abortion – where the decision to remove a cancerous uterus entails the death of the fetus; 3) city bombing – where the evil of killing non-combatants is not part of the mission to destroy enemy war production; and of course, 4) killing in self-defense. Agents are said to be moral in so far as they do not will these evil effects and act proportionately toward a good end. Hence the four conditions for DE are: 1) The act must be good in itself; 2) The evil effect cannot be intended, only permitted or tolerated; 3) The good intended must not be ordained by means of the evil effect; 4) There must be appropriate serious (proportionate) reasons to permit the evil effect.[26]

These cases and conditions were formulated to limit the PDE. Modern criticism has focused on the fourth condition. 'Revisionist' moral theologians in particular have questioned whether the PDE is even necessary since everything can be explained by proportionate reasoning.[27] But more recent criticism has turned to

---

[26] See: D.S. ODERBERG, *Moral Theory: A Non-Consequentialist Approach*, Oxford, Blackwell, 2000, pp. 90-91 for a recent defense of the four conditions, with emphasis on the fourth condition.

[27] See: K.L. FLANNERY, *Acts Amid Precepts: The Aristotelian Logical Structure of Thomas Aquinas's Moral Theory*, Washington, DC, Catholic University of America, 2001, p. 187. Rather than focusing on the intention, he relocates PDE back to law, the licit, and to what he calls "fixed paths" of action that exist in us due to natural and positive law, and how we conceive of goods and go about protecting them. He reminds us that the self-defense question asks if such an act is lawful. The legal paradigm sets the horizon for PDE.

the third condition and to the meaning of the direct/indirect distinction. Proponents of it maintain that there is a crucial difference between choosing something good and allowing some evil to result from that choice, and choosing to do something evil as a means to achieving something good.[28] The problem is: when does the evil effect of a good action become a directly intended element in that action? This question is paramount because, first, it points to a fine-line distinction in deliberation similar to what we saw earlier in the two kinds of justification – and there is a type of DE reasoning at work in epistemic justification (EMJ). Secondly, the question points to what the third condition is really all about – it forces us to distance intending from foreseeing in the moral act so as to realize the PDE. In other words, in each of the paradigm cases, we are able to render foreseen evil outcomes as *unforeseen,* intellectually speaking, at those moments throughout the act as we try to attain our moral view of the situation.[29] The language of 'beside the intention' accomplishes this function. The framework of intention and specification delivers this kind of distinction-making to the argument. Now such an analysis is plausible in the medical cases because the DE situation is unexpected and accidental. But in war situations, where planning leaves nothing to chance and sets up the DE conditions in the first place, it is nearly impossible to speak of foreseen evil effects as anything but

[28] E. KRASEVAC, *The Good that We Intend, and the Evil that We Do. A New Look at* Praeter Intentionem *in Aquinas,* in *Angelicum* 79 (4) (2002), p. 841.

[29] 'Unforeseen' is a term that needs to be defended. When good and evil effects are simultaneous in an act it is not possible to speak of setting aside the evil in view of the good because the two are equally in view. So throughout the DE event, reason must remove the evil effect from view or bracket it away in order for the action to be judged licit, and therefore do-able. And this bracketing happens at the action or motivational level, and when a moral appraisal is given after the act. Similarly, I have introduced the term 'subsumed' as an alternative to 'beside the intention' to better sum up how a duly proportionate reason accommodates an evil effect within a licit action. 'Unforeseen' and 'subsumed' are fulfilling intentional and justificatory roles. See: D.S. ODERBERG, *o.c.*, pp. 106-110 for distinguishing intention from motive and foresight. Such distinctions support the idea that evil effects are being subsumed under a general intention.

intended. In a fashion, *praeter intentionem* seems like fiction when applied to war. The PDE is hardly realized in these situations. Asking about the psychology of the agent – trying to know what the bombardier 'really' intends when releasing his ordinance – does not vindicate the PDE either.

The tradition has responded with more distinctions. It tries to say what is a due proportionality between means and intention by speaking about the means that is *essentially* determined by the intention.[30] In the case of self-defense, when deadly force is the only means to ward off attack, this is proportionate to the good intention and is thus subsumed in it, and therefore realizes the aim of the defender. Its lethality is outside the intention. But when such force is not the only recourse it is disproportionate with self-defense, and falls under a different intention, namely homicide.[31] Everything comes down to reason's role in saying what is duly proportioned. Hence, the tradition has emphasized the structure of the act itself. The physical happening (*genus naturae*) is as important as the moral meaning (*genus moris*).[32] What

---

[30] There are two important distinctions here: First, Aquinas' distinction between choosing and intending. While they are materially the same they are formally distinct: election signifies the means, the variables elements of the act, taken in light of the end, while the intention is the end, the specifying element of the act as such. (*ST* 1-II 1.3; 8.3) For an exhaustive account see: T.A. SALZMAN, *Deontology and Teleology*, Leuven, Peeters, 1995, pp. 311-324. Second, there is the per se and per accidens distinction of means to an end. Aquinas says: "An object of an external act can be related to the end of the will as per se ordained to it (as fighting well is per se ordained to victory) and as accidentally ordained to it (as when taking what belongs to another is accidental to almsgiving). Therefore, when the object is not per se ordained to the end, the specific difference which is derived from the object is not an essential determination of the species derived from the end, nor the reverse either. So one of these species is not under the other; thus the moral action is under two disperate species. This is why we say someone who steals in order to commit adultery commits two evils in one act. But if the object is per se ordained to the end, then one difference essentially determines the other. Hence one of these species is contained under the other." (*ST* I-II 18.7)

[31] E. KRASEVAC, *a.c.*, p. 843.

[32] *Ibid.*, pp. 844-845.

followed was a tendency to interpret the third condition to mean that an evil effect had to come after the good effect, at least causally if not temporally, to prevent intending an evil means. But this places a hardship on cases where good and evil actions are inseparable. So the fighter pilot ordered to down the hijacked airliner, and the bombardier aiming at factories in cities, barely qualify under the third condition because their commanded actions are simultaneous with evil effects. This has caused some moralists to go looking for a way to include these borderline cases under the third condition, by focusing exclusively on what it is we are choosing to do, and thereby widening the notion of *praeter intentionem*.[33] This has given rise to 'strong' and 'weak' versions of the PDE.

In the 'strong' version, as long as the commanded acts are pro-portionate to the end any sort of evil outcome in the act is *praeter intentionem*, even if that outcome is inevitable and known from the start. This does not render the act immoral, at least not direct-ly. The direct/indirect distinction allows us to speak of subsuming evil under the good we intend.[34] The intention to shoot down the hijacked airliner is so weighted in the third and fourth conditions of DE as to overwrite the evils in that act. The 'weak' version, says when an evil effect is inevitable and always an outcome of the commanded acts it cannot be merely accidental to the action and important to the agent in the same way. The evil effects are still being intended. When self-defense is necessarily lethal, then the assailant's death is a means to one's defense. Likewise, if the evil effect is instrumental to realizing the good effect it is not *praeter*

---

[33] *Ibid.*, p. 852. Putting attention on what we are choosing and wanting in a DE situation is another way to re-assert that evil effects can be subsumed under the good we intend. This is the framework of intention and specification in Aquinas. Jean Porter (in *Moral Action and Christian Ethics*, Cambridge, Cambridge University Press, 1995, p. 72) speaks of "more and less exigent responsi-bilities" to those we help and harm when deciding to act in a DE instances.

[34] E. KRASEVAC, *Can Effects that are Inevitable and Instrumental be* Praeter Intentionem? *Another Look at Aquinas' Understanding of* "Sit Proportionatus Fini," in *Angelicum* 82 (1) (2005), pp. 77-78.

intentionem but willed as such. Downing the airliner necessarily causes the terrorists and passengers to die in order to protect the Pentagon and its people. It is difficult not to see their deaths as instrumental to this outcome. This is why the 'weak' version is critical of intentionality and lays stress on what it is we are doing rather than what we want to do.[35]

Proponents of the 'strong' version admit that shooting down the airliner has a direct causal relation to stopping the terrorist hijackers and killing everyone aboard, but the connection is on the physical level (*genus naturae*), not the moral level which is to stop the attack (and protect the Pentagon's people). This is what the agent really wants to do, and that explains the commanded acts. Killing all the passengers aboard is outside of that, though unavoidable.[36] So we are faced with having to explain how an unavoidable evil can be abstracted from the commanded acts at the moment they are forming in the agent and when the reasoning (*ratio*) for the whole event takes hold and moves the agent to his or her task.[37] The 'strong' version eschews the psychological debate here with a philosophical account concentrating exclusively on the moral dimension (*genus moris*) of our reasoning. This amounts to a claim for unimpeded rationality in crisis cases. And if that is the claim (and I believe it is among strict just war theorists) then we have now uncovered the mainspring for all just war reasoning.

'Strong' version PDE is the sort of reasoning that politicians want to claim in their decisions for war, and church leaders would

---

[35] *Ibid.*, p. 79.

[36] *Ibid.*, p. 85. The problem centers on the status of the effects that are 'foreseen' in this process, the contrast between intention and foresight. See: A. MCIN-TYRE, *Doing Away with Double Effect*, in *Ethics* 111(2) (2001), pp. 221;224-226. The distinction (pp. 237-240) between "screened-off consequences" and merely foreseeing as opposed to intending instrumental consequences fails to show that evil effects are in fact *praeter intentionem*. In other words, only when the evil is genuinely an accident (unforeseen) can it be outside the moral purview.

[37] S.L. BROCK, *Action and Conduct*, Edinburgh, T&T Clark, 1998, pp. 127-132;221 discusses DE situations in terms of agent causality by distinguishing intentional from mechanical causality.

rely upon for their endorsement of it. This expanded emphasis on the intention and moral dimension of an act makes a perfect theoretical backdrop for the presumption for justice over the presumption against violence. The *ratio* of the 'strong' version underwrites the epistemic justification (EMJ) we criticized earlier. Therefore, the recent trend to downplay the more conservative 'weak' version and its emphasis on the physical act in favor of an ultra-intentionality, at a time when physical circumstances and details are supremely important in deciding on warfare against terrorism, stands as a dark coincidence in just war theory.[38]

'Strong' version PDE also makes Aquinas' framework of intention and specification appear quite rationally solid. But that is a bit of fiction too since the framework is rather delicate for the fact that it is secured by a set of virtues which the secular debate on war does not accommodate very well, if at all, namely charity and mercy. The larger outline of the *Summa Theologiae* presupposes these virtues. This means charity sets the horizon for moral action more than justice. Charity's action on all the virtues, especially justice, cannot be minimized when taking up the question of licit forms of violence. This is simply another way of stating that the Thomistic framework favors restraint as a matter of course. The problem we face is how to get charity and the deliberation that it entails into secular discourse under another name, without losing any of its original meaning. This forces us to own up to the fact that Aquinas' justification of violence is inherently fragile and not as clean and neat as the advocates of pre-emption/prevention warfare tend to suggest. Our urge to affirm our own perceptions and overrate our intentions always threatens the truth of the framework. Its fragility comes from the fact that it is able to become untruthful while seeming completely otherwise.[39]

[38] A.R. JONSEN & STEPHEN TOULMIN, *The Abuse of Casuistry*, Berkeley, University of California Press, 1988, p. 312.

[39] C. McGINN, *o.c.*, p. 19 explains this as the error of putting moral judgments ahead of the goodness they are suppose to be tracking, making it a property that consists in being judged rather than a concept prior to judging. This underlies what he calls "epistemological queerness" (see pp. 57-60).

Once again, we are confronted with the ineluctable conclusion that just war thinking is at risk of veering into error on its own terms. This must be corrected. We need to rebuild its rationality from within.

5. THEORY RENOVATION AND GLOBAL VIRTUES

My critics will note that this essay has produced no knockdown arguments against the just war theory. The theory is too resilient for that. My argument says the theory can no longer hold its ground because it is unable to give compelling reasons for adopting it over realism in the present conflict with terrorism. This inability stems from difficulties internal to the theory, specifically an overblown view of intentionality and justification. So we are faced with having to decide to repair or retire just war thinking as such. This is where ethicists are put to the test to deliver something constructive, either a whole new theory or some kind of renovation of what we already have. Given the problems of justification and intentionality we have just studied, it should be clear that either solution has to meet a steep theoretical challenge in order to keep the notion of justifiable war from becoming little more than a slogan in the political arena. The task is to make it post-9/11 meaningful. By way of conclusion, I want to pursue this task in a modest way by describing precisely what is needed for a more coherent just war theory. As it turns out, only one thing is needful.

What we are looking for is something that can tie together *ad bellum* and *post bellum* concerns in such a way that our pre- and post-war responsibilities are clear from the start, so that our deliberations are as seamless as possible. We need something that can assert itself in the justification process and restrain our urge to regard our beliefs as facts and prematurely warrant violence, as happens in epistemic justifications (EMJ). We need to temper the rationality of the 'strong' version of the PDE without overturning the Thomistic framework of intention and specification. We need to recover the 'weak' version of the PDE and not get mired in the

various conditions of double effect or reduce that principle to
proportionate reasoning alone. The direct/indirect distinction
must be preserved. In order to renovate the just war theory, we
will have to translate the religious sensibility of the framework to
a secular context without loosing its basic content. What we need
is some way to go between the demands of justice and security on
the one hand, and the requirement for mercy and restraint on the
other. We need a corrective that can address jingoism, mendacity,
paranoia, greed and all the other illicit motives for war, and yet
still face the political realities of West versus Middle East. This
means sorting out crusade and 'crescade' mentalities.[40] This tall
job description obviously calls for a virtue that can accomplish all
of these theoretical and procedural demands evenly while functioning as a mediating principle in the theory. We need a virtue
that can make the values behind the just war criteria more explicit in the criteria itself, and do this in such a way as to be organic
to the theory.[41] That one virtue is benevolence.

What I am actually proposing is benevolence and beneficence
together under one word. This is to emphasize the aspect of willing and deliberating which is present in both of them. I am calling on Aquinas' description of benevolence as an act of charity
and beneficence as an action included under charity.[42] The source
behind his thinking is Aristotle's discussion of friendship as a

[40] See: A.L. SILVERMAN, *Just War, Jihad, and Terrorism: A Comparison of Western and Islamic Norms for the Use of Political Violence*, in *Journal of Church and
States* 44 (1) (2002), pp. 89-91 for Wahhabi sectarianism and its violent interpretation of jihad, including recruiting the wealthy and educated. This is not a
spiritual struggle but a 'crescade' by design, with little prospect for dialogue and
accommodation.

[41] Mark Douglass attempts this in *Changing the Rules of War: Just War Theory
in the Twenty-First Century*, in *Theology Today* 59 (4) (2003), pp. 536-538. But
the practical criteria he demands (like shared authority for all and full access of
information – pp. 541-543) are external to the theory and unworkable. Tinker-
ing with the criteria like this does not repair the theory.

[42] See: *ST* II-II 27.2 for benevolence as an act of the will to love (defined in
Q. 27.1 as "fitting of charity in so far as it is charity."). See: *ST* II-II 31.4 for
beneficence as an act indistinguishable from charity.

regard for one's neighbors stemming from the regard we hold for ourselves, a kind of seeing and considering which applies especially to our rational side.[43] It is this 'rational side' that is most important because of the role benevolence ought to play in deciding about war. Too often we forget that the just war theory is a structure about decision-making more than a set of checks and tests. I am also looking to the work of a contemporary Aristotelian who has written widely about compassion and our duties to others. This is Martha Nussbaum on virtue and cosmopolitanism. Her many insights on deliberation and the rationality of emotions tend to support the kind of enlarged concept of benevolence I am discussing here. Unfortunately, to fully defend this proposal means spelling out a theory of the common good and showing how this virtue would function in a variety of situations. That would require another essay in itself. What is needed here instead is some discussion on how benevolence can be a guiding principle in just war thinking and thereby fix the theory. What is necessary is that we restructure the existing form of just war deliberation. And that means we must bring on a change of language, a slight change only. It is not necessary to upend the theory in order to repair it. What follows is three short points for insisting that benevolence be part of the standard just war vocabulary:

1. **Benevolence is a comprehensive concept**. It straddles Christian charity and justice, and appeals to religious and secular interests alike. It brings the benefits of a theological principle without the demands of faith. Its appeal is rational and universal since reasonable people are generally open to it. When formulated as a principle of action, it adds back to the Thomistic framework of intention and specification an appeal to charity which goes missing otherwise. When proposed as a principle of justice, it adds a consideration for charity under a different name. As a general principle, it does not require an elaborate explanation since it only

---

[43] See: *Nichomachean Ethics* IX 4.1 and 3, and especially IX 5.1 for goodwill toward strangers which is characterized by its ability to arise suddenly without intimacy or familiarity.

needs to be posed as a question at any given point during deliberation. The "where is benevolence?" and "what is benevolent here?" types of questions are sufficient to put it on the horizon or at the center of decision-making, as the case may be. Even when it is dismissed, having simply asked such questions can be crucial when humanitarian interventions are being decided or when the full scope of a war plan is in question. If benevolence were at the center of just war language, it would have been much harder to ignore genocides as in Rwanda and Cambodia, or to have rushed to pre-emption/prevention after 9/11. Benevolence also comes without most of the hair-splitting distinctions that litter just war thinking and make it so frustrating and difficult for politicians and military leaders to correctly use. It is much more straightforward to ask what sort of good we are willing for ourselves and others than to ask if our intention is right and our cause just. Case in point, the *National Security Strategy* would have had to have been written differently if a benevolence principle had accompanied the presumption for justice and security. The outcome might have been the same, but at least the rationale behind it would have been challenged. Furthermore, benevolence is perhaps the only concept that can gather up the so called *post bellum* norms (which are presently a jumble of considerations for peace-building without clear consensus) and link them to *ad bellum* considerations. Without it, there is no way to intrinsically connect both sets of norms.[44] *Post bellum* norms remain extrinsic to the theory and are easily set aside, which suggests that their claim to be items of justice is vague. Benevolence as a kind of charity – rationally understood – makes direct claims for peace-building when the question of resorting to war first appears.

---

[44] A good example of this lack of connection is in B. OREND, *Jus Post Bellum*, in *Journal of Social Philosophy* 31 (1) (2000), pp. 123-124;128-129 where peacemaking norms are mainly a replication of restraint norms. He shows how they work but presents no inner reason why they should. A practical consideration, like cost or timeliness, could override them. Benevolence too, though it is a harder principle to trump.

2. **Benevolence perfects justice.** It does this without precluding warfare. It is equally a motive for humanitarian intervention and a restraint on going to war too hastily. It can stand alongside just cause and right intention as an *ad bellum* condition; and it fits into the just cause for terminating war in the *post bellum* conditions. It acts as another guarantee that the good we intend in war is aimed beyond ourselves.[45] But this gives the impression that benevolence is simply another patch on a quilt of rules, another item on a list, in other words, more theory bog-downs. It would be wrong to characterize it as a rule though it should be on such lists. What is needed is a motive or purpose that is synonymous with the justice we are seeking to achieve when we decide to apply violence or withhold it. What commends it is its ability to function as a bi-valent principle in those deliberations, a kind of motive-clarifying principle. By definition it is just and merciful at once, a kind of thin principle of conscience in practical affairs. Put differently, it is what we want (*ad quem*) and that by which (*a quo*) we want the good to occur. It is also fluid enough to be counted in all the criteria; we can ask benevolence questions of any of the criteria and expect an answer. It would seem that this is what has to be asked in order to settle them. And this is what is not being asked when they are abused. So there is no need to tinker with the existing list of rules once this principle is in place. This kind of bi-valence is what the truth and reconciliation process in South Africa, for example, has tried to achieve. Northern Ireland is another situation where it could have positive effects.[46] Its effect on the just war theory is even more clear. Benevolence stands as a

---

[45] See: B. OREND, *a.c.*, p. 128 for his description of a *jus post bellum* just cause for termination based solely on vindicating the just cause criteria that launched the war in the first place. What is missing is a principle that looks beyond that kind of justice.

[46] D.B. FORRESTER, *Violence and Non-Violence in Conflict Resolution: Some Theological Reflections*, in *Studies in Christian Ethics* 16 (2) (2003), pp. 70-74. He cites Desmond Tutu's "difficult but ultimately rewarding path of destroying enemies by turning them into friends" (*No Future Without Forgiveness*, p. 138) but gives no rules for bringing this about.

'third presumption' between justice and security on one hand, and the presumption against violence on the other. It tempers the one without going over to the other. It is neither warism nor pacifism and does not tie up the political-military decision process with extra prejudices. The 'third presumption' does not favor excessive caution or faintheartedness. Nor does it support flimsy excuses for armed conflict. So it is ideal for breaking the security versus restraint deadlock we illustrated earlier. But its most important feature is its ability to assume a normative and a procedural form.

Of course I am glossing over the problem of how this virtue generates the duties that bring it to life. What is important to note here is its ability to be non-relative and flexible. I am invoking Nussbaum's interpretation of Aristotle which says virtues have a fixed primary reference in our basic experience of them; we have a common understanding of what they are about and what happens when they are lacking. We constantly draw upon that stable sense of what they are. Virtues have a more buoyant second reference in the concrete choices we have to make. In this arena there are shades of meaning; virtues appear more variable though reliable. With benevolence, we recognize it from our basic experience of injustice, and that shapes its meaning. What changes is how we apply it in different situations. Going from a nominal definition of 'willing good for others' to concrete instances of causing good to happen means constantly having to re-specify that virtue.[47] Its normative meaning is always being re-aligned against our spheres of experience. What this does for just war thinking is to open the possibility of an additional layer of evaluation about justice from the perspective of charity. I am recalling Aquinas on the various effects of charity, namely, peace, mercy, beneficence and those sentiments that oppose it,[48] and his contention that there are only imperfect virtues without charity

[47] M. NUSSBAUM, *Non-Relative Virtues: An Aristotelian Approach*, in J.P. STERBA (ed.), *Ethics. The Big Questions*, Oxford, Blackwell, 1998, p. 263-265.
[48] G.M. REICHBERG, *a.c.*, p. 348. *ST* II-II 29.1-3.

(*ST* II-II 23.7). My contention is that an evaluation according to benevolence re-specifies the justice of the just war toward charity and moderation, and that this is enough to refresh the tradition. But to press that claim involves showing how a benevolence principle concretely alters our deliberations about war. This brings us back to the problem of duties to others.

3. **Benevolence is cosmopolitan.** To better understand this point, and answer the problem we just stated, we should look at a classical failed example. There is a flaw in the Western justice tradition dating back to Cicero. The greatness of his *De Officiis* is that it names material aid for our neighbors and warding off aggression against them as duties of justice. To do nothing while others are harmed is to commit passive injustice, a shame on any civilized person or nation. The smallness of *De Officiis* is that its justice and beneficence do not include relieving the poor of their poverty. That omission is not a passive injustice even though poverty is as sure an assault on a fellow human being as any. Nussbaum's criticism here is important: It is not possible to require money and effort for one kind of relief and not the other. What she uncovers is a high view of humanity alloyed with the dubious notion that external goods are not truly necessary for happiness. It is simply wrong to say material aid is non-necessary for flourishing when speaking of the poor, as if poverty were merely something external and not striking the core of our humanity.[49] What results is a compromised benevolence. It slips into being an imperfect duty behind property rights, and other things. There is a similar compromise in the classic just war theory in as much as it does not take up the problem of owing certain duties to the enemy in the process of declaring him fit to be defeated according to justice (just cause, right intention). The analogous error is to think the unjust aggressor does not merit *post bellum* goods, and that the just defender can remain virtuous for withholding them. That last misstep is all too important here. So the classic just war

---

[49] M. NUSSBAUM, *Duties of Justice, Duties of Material Aid: Cicero's Problematic Legacy*, in *The Journal of Political Philosophy* 8 (2) (2000), pp. 196,189,191.

theory suffers its own kind of Ciceronian error on transitional obligations. This is what plagues attempts to layout a program of *post bellum* norms. The solution for poverty is to increase public spending and create just structures. This starts with re-asserting the basic cosmopolitan claim that we all share a common humanity. The solution for just war thinking starts with recognizing that aggressors and defenders are both in need of *post bellum* goods.[50] Then this truth must be forced into every decision about war. Benevolence is the linchpin for such a shift in deliberation. Essentially what it is does is restore the enemy's worthiness, something that the new realism has made vague concerning terrorism and the future of Iraq.

This shift in deliberation requires compassion. Benevolence goes nowhere without it. The sort of broad global thinking necessary to engage terrorism is incomplete otherwise. The suffering of others must move us to pity. And their condition must cause us to fear suffering itself since a reversal of fortune could put us in the same kind of misery. Pity (and the lack of it) reveals our conception of flourishing and brings on motives for action.[51] Such motives help us to re-specify justice and to recognize the possibility of compassion and benevolent duties. Compassion changes our imagination about what is politically possible.[52] Again, these are the things benevolence brings to just war thinking. The net result is a theory that is vastly more prudential and accurate because it

[50] M. NUSSBAUM, *Kant and Stoic Cosmopolitanism*, in *Journal of Political Philosophy* 5 (1) (1997), pp. 11-13. (*De Officiis* I.89 on dignity for the defeated.)

[51] M. NUSSBAUM, *Compassion: the Basic Social Emotion*, in *Social Philosophy and Policy* 13 (1) (1996), pp. 35-38. Also see her *Human Functioning and Social Justice: In Defense of Aristotelian Essentialism*, in *Political Theory* 20 (2) (1992), p. 237 on compassion or pity (*eleos*) as a painful emotion based on the belief that another person's sufferings are not trivial, nor their fault, and could happen to us. It forces us to admit vulnerability and humane treatment of others. For recent criticism of her theory see M. WEBER, *Compassion and Pity. An Evaluation of Nussbaum's Analysis and Defense*, in *Ethical Theory and Moral Practice* 7 (5) (2004), pp. 487-511.

[52] M. NUSSBAUM, *Compassion*, p. 56. Nussbaum compares it to John Rawls' "original position" in politics and distribution.

not only decides if wars are licit and validly fought but measures those decisions against a variety of peace-building criteria, and it does this from virtues within itself. In short, a just war theory in accord with global ethics.

6. CONCLUDING WITH AN IMAGE

Compassion, benevolence and cosmopolitanism guide just war thinking to an 'originary position' from which it can function more accurately. Such a program of emotions and re-thinking is what is needed to correct the excesses of intentionality and justification that are part and parcel to the traditional framework of justifying war. Inserting benevolence into the just war vocabulary is one step in a larger process of renovating the theory, though from a theoretical standpoint this is the indispensable first step in curbing the tendency to default to realism under the name of justifiable warfare. This plan of correction proposes a rather liberal view of humanity and virtues so as to bring about a more conservative approach to the process of deliberating combat, in other words, to hold to a sound justification and a more cautious reading of the physical and moral realities that terrorism has placed before us. Albeit, this is only an outline, but enough to put us back in the opera house with the last seconds of *Khovanshchina* playing, with troops rushing on stage, unable to reverse the moral tragedy that their leaders have forced on them. Ethicists and war professionals should want to pull back the curtain before it falls and re-write the score and change this ending. They shall have to write in the voice of compassion from the very first note. For those who choose to compose in the just war tradition, theirs will be a reasoned mercy.

CLAUDE SELIS

Conditions For the Just War in a Time of New Conflicts

1. EMERGENCE OF THE CONCEPT

One might be surprised at the very existence of a concept of a 'just war' in Christian theology in view of the Gospel's ideal of non-violence.[1] Indeed, the first Christian writers held to this principle of non-violence,[2] preferring martyrdom to armed resistance. It was in fact St. Augustine who introduced the idea of a just war into theology.[3] He reasoned as follows: The earthly city is not an end in itself: it is merely preparation for the heavenly city. A disrupted, disordered, torn society could not be good preparation. Spiritual man can only develop in a 'tranquil' society where justice, order, and peace reign, but these values are fragile[4] and so must be defended. Thus, the use of force is justified to defend justice and order without which social life is not possible, the goal certainly being to restore peace. Non-violence that might promote an injustice could not be a good, and according to St. Augustine, justice becomes more important than non-violence. The first duty in the earthly city is to ensure justice so that peace will be its fruit.

---

[1] 'If anyone strikes you on the right cheek' (Mt. 5:38-40); 'for all who take the sword will perish by the sword' (Mt. 26:52).

[2] Thus, Tertullian in *de Corona* (in particular §11), written about 211, or Origen in his *An Exhortation to Martyrdom*, written in 235.

[3] AUGUSTINE in *The City of God* (to book 19), completed in 427.

[4] Augustine, like all Christians up to the 5th century and despite persecution, greatly appreciated the '*pax romana*' and was terrified by the fall of Rome in 410 to the Visigoth Alaric. He was clearly aware that the world was entering a troubled era. Certainly, in *The City of God*, which was a work written in direct connection with the fall of Rome, Augustine considered the earthly city to be less of value than the heavenly city but left no doubt that, as far as the earthly city was concerned, he was on the side of the Roman Empire.

St. Augustine did not create the concept of 'just war' but took it from Cicero[5] and gave it a theological justification. In the Roman mentality of the time, any war that could be justified by the greater interests of Rome and started according to certain rules was considered 'just.'[6] The Ciceronian concept, purely theoretical, represented an important step forward because it no longer placed the justness of war in relation to a state's particular policy but rather in relation to a moral imperative concerning the human race, an imperative to which the state itself had to submit. Moreover, in his campaign in Gaul, Julius Caesar is said to have assumed certain *ius in bello* principles of avoiding unnecessary acts of cruelty and harming only the enemy.[7]

The Germanic invasions and the feudal organization that would result left little room for reflection on political philosophy. Only a few people transmitted the Augustinian notion: Isidore of Seville[8] (7th c.), Pope Nicholas I[9] (9th c.), Bishop Rufin[10] (11th c.), Ivo of Chartres[11] and Abelard[12] (12th c.). It regained its place and was developed by the 12th century canonist Gratian.[13] Three reasons were considered admissible for war: driving back the enemy from one's borders, recovering property, and avenging injustice. Offensive war was clearly distinguished from defensive war, and defending one's allies was considered a duty. The only objective of

[5] CICERO, in *de Officiis*, written in 44-43 B.C., his last work. He argued that not confronting an injustice committed by others when possible is a mistake because it is allowing injustice to be done and is thus an attack on the human race. Augustine takes up this argument as a whole in his *Contra Faustum XXII, 74.*

[6] Verification whether Rome was bound by a treaty, peace proposals, declarations of war in due form, rituals of sacrifice, rituals of throwing a javelin in the enemy's direction, all fell under the guidance of the fetial clergy, who became true guardians of the treaties and the first corps of ambassadors.

[7] JULIUS CESAR, in *De Bello Gallico*, Book V, 19.

[8] ISIDORUS HISPALENSIS, *Etymologiarun*, Book 18, in PL 82, col.639.

[9] In his *Letter to the Bulgarians*.

[10] *De Bono Pacis* (1056).

[11] YVO CARNUTENSIS, *Decretum*, in PL 161, cols. 47-1022.

[12] ABELARDUS, *Sic et Non*, in PL 178, cols. 1339-1610 and especially 1608.

[13] GRATIANUS, *Decretum, Causa 23*, in *Corpus Iuris Canonici*, t.1, col 889, Leipzig, 1879.

war was to ensure that justice be respected or to re-establish justice between states where that has been violated for want of a body of law such as that which exists for private conflicts.

2. FORMULATION OF THE CONDITIONS

Thomas Aquinas (13th c.) brought about a certain systematization,[14] although in a still limited way and in a distorted context. The theme occupies only a small part of his work (two to three pages of several thousand). It is considered in the section on charity and not in the section on justice and is presented as a question of private conscience and not one of political philosophy. Of the four articles that constitute Question 40, two are of little importance and show a lack of political understanding of the issue. Despite his ancestry (Thomas Aquinas was grand-nephew to Frederick II), the political involvement of his family (the Lombards went down to Naples to defend the interests of the Empire), his position as a celebrated professor (he was, on this account, a guest of St. Louis), and the bellicose context of the time (aside from local wars, the Crusades had been going on for two centuries), Thomas seem to have been truly unfamiliar with what was happening. Nevertheless, what he would say, referring to Augustine and largely indebted to Gratian, would be entirely pertinent and at the opposite pole of the bellicose ideologies of the Crusades.[15] Three conditions are clearly advanced in the first article:

– Only a *legitimate authority* can validly declare war. This requirement aims at disqualifying all the 'private wars' between minor feudal lords (and *a fortiori* seditious leaders). It presupposes a superior authority (real independence of the nation concerned). In fact, as long as there is a superior authority (the emperor in relation to princes or vassals), the conflict should be determined by arbitration within the political entity.

---

[14] Thomas Aquinas, *Summa theologiae, Secunda secundae*, Question 40.
[15] Represented Pope Urban II, Peter the Hermit, Bernard de Clairvaux, etc.

– War can only be declared for a *just cause*, which limits it, in fact, to repairing an identifiable injustice (intentional, clearly attributable, objective, and of a certain gravity) and to defending against an unjust attack. Achieving an utopia is not, for example, included.

– One should keep to one's right intention, limiting oneself, therefore, to a return to peace in justice and should not seek to satisfy vengeance or to pursue related material advantages.

The novelty of the treatment of Thomas Aquinas of the concept of just war is not immediately apparent in the short text, but it is genuine and significant when one considers his work in its entirety. Indeed, for Thomas, reflecting on war no longer occurs in the context of ranking the earthly city inferior in relation to the heavenly city and where peace would only be a means or a condition for allowing the elevation of man to the City of God. Rather it is cast in the context of an autonomization of the *Res Publica* (provided the political power adheres to the Natural Law and is organized for the common good). Wars, unlike any other form of evil, are never the result of divine will but are the result of freedom and human autonomy (at the risk of its unfortunate consequences). Avoiding them, therefore, depends on the will of humans and, if avoidance is not possible, controlling them. The concept is thus completely secularized.

In the 13th century, too, the 'theory' of the just war would be enriched by a fourth explicit condition, that of *proportionality*, which was introduced by the canonist Raymond de Pennafort,[16] another Dominican. The principle or proportionality requires that one not commit a wrong that is greater than the damage that needs to be repaired and thus not to allow blind vengeance to run free or take advantage of the opportunity to satisfy other ambitions. It is a consequence, of a sort, of the condition of right intention. This is not to say that the principle of proportionality constitutes a right to wreak an equal number of wrongs as did the attacker but only the least possible (no unnecessary

---

[16] Raymundus de Pennafort, *Summa de casibus*, II, §§17 to 19.

wrongs to achieve a permissible objective, and thus the soldiers are not allowed to plunder or pillage). This 'principle of necessity' could have constituted an entirely distinct condition.[17] It would be taken up in the Geneva and Hague Conventions in the 19th century. Note that, with the principle of proportionality, there was already a tendency to slide into *ius in bello* (laws in war), while St. Thomas's three conditions held strictly to *ius ad bellum* (rights to war). Raymond de Pennafort's preference is characteristic of the concerns of a 'confessor'. No political philosophy is to be found here.

3. FORMULATION OF A POLITICAL THEORY

In the 16th century, in a very different context, a coherent synthesis of these conditions was made by Vitoria[18] for political reasons. The conquest of the New World and of the acts of violence against the Indians provoked fierce controversy in Spain. Theologians and canonists played a part in the public debate and affected the princes directly (hence the notorious Vallodolid controversy of Charles the Fifth of 1550-51). Some denied that Indians were human (hence, Sepulveda); others (like Bartholomew de las Casas, one of Vitoria's colleagues) defended them. Repeating St. Thomas's conditions sounded like disapproval of the Spanish conquests in the New World: American Indians had done no wrong to Spain and the lure of gold was certainly not a rightful intention. Nonetheless, in the context Francis I's war with France, these conditions could act as both guide and justification.

---

[17] It had already appeared in the *Letter to the Bulgarians*, cited above, of Pope Nicholas I.

[18] Francesco de Vitoria, 1483-1546, Dominican at the Spanish scholastic school in Salamanca, in his *Relectio de Iure belli (= de Indis II)*, of 1539 (complete edition: *Leçons sur les Indiens et le Droit de la guerre*, Geneva, Droz, 1966; translation in Vanderpol, *La guerre devant le christianisme*, Paris, 1911; extracts in French in MARTIN, *Vitoria et la leçon sur les Indiens*, Cerf, Paris, 1997 and particularly, in his comments on St. Thomas on Question 40 (Salamanca, 1932, Latin text only).

While it was implicit (or even explicit) in the writings of the early theologians and canonists (as well as institutions like the 'Peace of God'), Vitoria developed a fourth condition: the *principle of discrimination*, which distinguishes between civilians and combatants[19] (an *in bello* condition). This doctrine was not always clear in the 16th century. Occasionally, the distinction made was more between the 'innocents' (*innocentes*) and the 'guilty' (*nocentes*). The category of 'innocents' was sometimes reduced only to children, women, and the clergy. Conversely, the category of 'guilty' sometimes extended to include the entire enemy population or at least all those who were old enough to carry weapons (even if they did not fight). It is interesting that, according to Vitoria, the military/civilian distinction took precedence over all other kinds of discrimination (on the basis of race, language or religion). Similarly, at the state level, that it arose from another race or religion (e.g., Indian or Turkish) does not add to its legitimacy.

Moreover, in his comment on the second Thomist condition (just cause), Vitoria expands the field: it no longer concerns only strictly defensive war (defending oneself against a grave injustice) but possibly also 'vindictive' war (whenever the 'Law of Nations' is violated and even by a state that is not directly injured). The war becomes, according to Vittoria, the instrument of achieving law at the international level, given that war should be limited to this single function and should not act as a customary method for dealing with conflicts.

While the *secularization* of policy was a novelty with Thomas (the legacy that Vitoria forcefully repeats), with the Master of Salamanca came its *internationalization*. The only legitimate authority would be a supra-national or supra-state (and Vitoria expressly denies the papacy this role) because mankind as a whole, beyond the differences in race, language, culture, religion, territory, forms a single community (*communitas orbis*).

---

[19] Vitoria uses the terms *civis/miles*. His category *miles* is broad and in some places includes 'everyone who can bear arms'.

From this fundamental unity of mankind flow fundamental rights that arise from Natural Law, the concrete application of which is the Law of Nations. If there is no political authority, then it is Natural Law that is the authority. A state that, with right intention, takes the defence of Law of Nations to heart may, therefore, intervene in delinquent states. The existence of a plurality of states is not relevant to the problem – on the contrary, as they are a product of the Law of Nations these states are simply subordinate to the common good of mankind as a whole and, therefore, to Natural Law.

Similarly, unlike Thomas, who had formulated the problem of a just war in terms of personal morality,[20] Vitoria formulates it – appropriately – in the political terms of international relations. Nevertheless, considering it in terms of personal sin is not absent from Vitoria's reasoning. It is adequately placed at the level of personal involvement. In the event of a manifestly unjust war everyone, even the simple soldier, is obliged to refuse[21] to participate in it on pain of sin. If there is doubt, the simple soldier is relieved of all responsibility while those in charge have the duty to inform themselves on the justice of the war. The sovereign has no excuse. He alone may decide but must seek advice. If there is doubt, he may not engage in war. Moreover, according to Cajetan,[22] the cause has to be certain (anti-probabilism).

According to Suarez,[23] there are two more conditions that are to be added to the traditional list of conditions of just war:

[20] Question 40 is formulated as follows: *Utrum bellare semper sit peccatum* (is waging war always a sin)?

[21] This was a principle Antonin de Florence, OP, had already defended (1389-1459) in his *Summa theologiae.*

[22] TOMMASO DE VIO, OP, known as Cajetan, (1468-1534), otherwise a principal opponent to Luther, in his comments on Thomas Aquinas' Question 40.

[23] Spanish Jesuit (1548-1617), great Thomist commentator (acquainted with Vitoria's work) but having played a significant political role as advisor to and ambassador for the Pope (to refute James I of Scotland and also to the Portuguese viceroy)

– There must be *reasonable chance of success*,[24] so it is of no use to commit human lives, whether friends or enemies, to pure loss.

– War must be the last resort, that is, there must be no other way to repair the injustice and all other – non-violent – means have been attempted and exhausted without success. [25]

CLASSICAL CONDITIONS FOR A JUST WAR

ad bellum:

* *just cause* (St. Thomas)
* *right intention* (St. Thomas)
* *legitimate authority* (St. Thomas)
* *last resort* (Suarez)
* *reasonable chance of success* (Suarez)

in bello:

* *proportionality* (Raymond de Pennafort)
* *discrimination* (Vitoria)

4. THE RISE OF THE NATION STATES

The weakness in the conditions for a just war is that each state will always find sophists among its advisors to demonstrate that 'its' war is just so it will be 'just' for both sides simultaneously. In the context of the emergence of the nation state defined in function of features (race, territory, language, common history, religion, etc.)[26]

---

[24] In his treatise *de Caritate*, disp.13 *de Bello*, section IV, no. 10 volume 12, of his complete works (Latin text only). The French translation of this is given in *de Bello* in A. VANDERPOL, *La doctrine scolastique du droit de la guerre*, Pedone, Paris, 1935.

[25] This condition appears in Suarez's comments on St Thomas's 'just cause' (in *de Bello*). In fact, the principle had already been clearly expressed by Soto (1494-1560), another Spanish Dominican from Salamanca.

[26] For example, the *cujus regio, ejus religio* principle of the Peace of Augsburg of 1555 and the provisions in the Treaty of Westphalia of 1648.

– unlike the internationalist perspective – this meant the failure
and abandonment of the concept. Each state was considered independent, autonomous, and inviolable and the absolute master
within its borders. Each state was to behave as an individual, all
others being considered enemies or at least competitors in a kind
of political Darwinism *avant la lettre*. This led to the concept of
raison d'état (an expression suggested by Botero in 1583) that
would henceforth prevail and serve as justification for everything.
The very decision of the state (which corresponds to the first
Thomist condition) would be considered sufficient reason. Since
the 17th century, the 'national wars' engendered by this state of
mind have been several, long, massive, destructive, and cruel, more
so even than those of the Middle Ages.

It is significant that Grotius' treatise, *On the Laws of War and
Peace* (1625), the first in this new context, although inspired largely by Vitoria to create his Law of Nations, no longer takes up the
consideration of the conditions of the just war! Considered by the
textbooks on the history of law as decisive in the progress to the
definition of the human rights, this treatise bears witness in one
way to a great debacle: one can only try to defend a minimum of
rights of the individual caught in the snare of conflicts between
their respective states. Pufendorf (1632-1694), his disciple Wolff
(1679-1754), and Vattel (1714-1767) continued in this way and
formed the school called 'The Law of Nature and Nations', which
dominated throughout the 17th and 18th centuries. The nations
had definitively abandoned the idea of a 'just war'.

The Catholic Church[27] maintained the teaching but in a purely formal and repetitive manner. The reformed churches generally
became the national churches and rallied around the idea that a
raison d'etat was a sufficient condition. Even in the Catholic
Church, there were fiercely belligerent nationalist currents like
Gallicanism in France and Josephism in Austria. Perhaps because
of this, and after the Church had tried to 'colonize' the heart of

---

[27] The reformed churches took up the cause of the Law of the Nations, on
the one hand, and human rights, on the other.

the traditionally Catholic states in the 17th and 18th centuries,[28] the mistrust of the Catholic Church by the nation states intensified throughout the 19th century.[29] Thus, if the Catholic Church remained supra-national in sensibility, it was above all because of an institutional reflex of self-defence. The only theologian/canonist who renewed, at least partially, the theory of the just war in the 19th century was Taparelli d'Azeglio (1793-1862),[30] who advocated resorting to arbitration in cases of conflict between nations. This was not the pontifical arbitration of the Middle Ages (an idea taken up in the 19th century by the diplomat de Maistre[31]) but rather arbitration by a neutral and independent international court. A just war would be nothing more than international police operations under this authority (this idea was advanced in 1843). His work remained completely ignored in the textbooks of international public law but did have a direct and decisive influence on the political thought of Popes Benedict XV and Pius XI, who inserted the idea into their social encyclicals.

5. FORMULATION OF AN INTERNATIONAL LAW

At the end of the 19th century, the *ius in bello* underwent new developments.[32] The first resulted from the 1874 Brussels Conference.[33] Delegations from 15 European countries met at the invitation of Czar Alexander II of Russia, and the resulting declaration contained measures on issues as important as occupation in war, the definition of combatants, licit ways of harming the enemy,

[28] See: *Histoire de l'Eglise* [History of the Church], under the supervision of Fliche and Martin, Bloud et Gay, Paris, 1948, vol. 19, books 1 and 2.

[29] See: R. AUBERT, *The Pontificate of Pius IX*, vol. 21 by Fliche and Martin.

[30] In his treatise *Saggio teoretico di Dritto Naturale* (1840-3).

[31] In *du Pape*, 1819.

[32] R. KOLB, *Ius in bello, Le droit international des conflits armés*, Précis, Bruylant, Brussels, 2003.

[33] Preceded by the St. Petersburg Declaration of 1868 (not to inflict unnecessary suffering).

prisoners of war, the injured and the sick, the civilians, the parliamentarians, capitulations, armistices, and so on. The states never ratified the declaration, so it never went into force. It did, however, represent a significant advance in law. In 1899, Czar Nicholas II, Alexander's successor, called another conference, this time in The Hague, to follow up the 1874 Declaration and reduce the risk of war by reduction in armament. Twenty-six governments gathered and produced Convention I for the peaceful settlement of disputes as well as two Conventions on the laws of war, one for war on land (Convention II) and the other for war at sea (Convention III). These texts were ratified. The Czar again took the initiative to call a conference in The Hague in 1907, this time gathering 44 states together with a view to revising the Conventions of 1899 (thus Convention IV of 1907 revised the important Convention II of 1899). The third conference was scheduled for 1914 but could not take place. All these texts constitute the *Law of The Hague* concerning actors in war (the military). They have since then been further developed and are still applicable.

At the end of World War I, the political world launched the idea of a League of Nations, referring to philosophers such as Vitoria but more so to Kant and other philosophers of the Enlightenment. In the Catholic intellectual world,[34] this initiative raised much hope and revived interest in the just-war problem, but Pope Benedict XV marked it only with a polite declaration,[35] not because of any disagreement but because the Church had been expressly excluded from the debates by certain influential anticlerical members.

From the perspective of *ius ad bellum*, the Second World War left no doubt: the invaded countries had the law on their side, but this was of very little consolation. From the *ius in bello* perspective on the German side, while it was respected by the regular army, the very principle of the special corps (Gestapo, SS) was not to respect it. Nor did the Allies respect it (blind and massive bombings of entire villages, contrary to the principle of discrimination). Pope

---

[34] Y. de la Brière, S.J., R. Regout and A. Van der Pol, The Freiburg Group.
[35] In the *Pacem Dei Munus* encyclical, 1920.

Pius XII wanted to remain the 'guardian of the eternal principles of humanity and charity'[36] but was unable to be effective.

After the Second World War, the United Nations saw the light of day but on a 'contractual' basis between the independent and sovereign nation states. Thus it did not correspond to the supra-national 'transcendence' advocated by Vitoria. The Universal Declaration of Human Rights was adopted in 1948 and was supported in the years that followed by various states. It formed the basis of a true and general international law affecting the humanity of mankind. However, in Geneva in 1949, a convention was signed under the aegis of the Red Cross (having been preceded by several others since 1864 and complemented also by Protocols in 1977), this time on victims of war which formed what could be termed a 'Law of Geneva,' or 'Humanitarian Law,' thus reviving the *ius gentium* of Grotius.

Meanwhile in the Church, in the new context of the Cold War between the East and West and under the nuclear threat, the conviction evolved that wars could no longer be considered just and this because the condition of proportionality would be or risked being quickly overtaken. Grass-roots Christian movements opted for pacifism,[37] which encouraged Christian intellectuals to rekindle reflection on peace rather than quibble over the idea of a just war.[38] In 1963, Pope John XXIII published his encyclical *Pacem in Terris*, which dealt no longer with the notion of a just war[39] but rather with peace through development. In the context of the Second Vatican Council, the first preparatory text of the constitution

---

[36] See: R. COSTE, *Le problème du droit de la guerre dans la pensée de Pie XII* [*The Problem of the Law of War in Pope Pius XII's Thoughts*], 1962. One of the chapters (11) is unnecessary: 'La disparition de la guerre juste' [*The Disappearance of the Just War*].

[37] *Pax Christi*, for example, appeared in 1944.

[38] J. COMBLIN, *Théologie de la paix* [*The Theology of Peace*] Editions Universitaires, Paris, 1963; R. COSTE, *Théologie de la paix* [*The Theology of Peace*], Cerf, Paris, 1997 and his work since 1962.

[39] 'It is unreasonable to think that war is still a means for obtaining justice for the violation of rights' §127.

Gaudium et Spes, also known as Schema XIII (on relations 'with the contemporary world'), did make no reference to the theory of a just war, although it was still standard material in seminary textbooks. In the general session, some bishops wanted to reintroduce the concept, but it did not appear in the final text (adopted on 7 December 1965).[40] Thus, one can conclude that the Church consciously and voluntarily abandoned the notion. Pope Paul VI's *Populorum Progressio* encyclical of 1967 confirmed this position. Nevertheless, in 1992, in the new *Catechism of the Catholic Church*, prepared at the request of Pope John-Paul II, the concept reappeared[41] but without further justification or follow-up.

6. INTRODUCTION OF THE 'HUMANITARIAN RIGHT OF INTERVENTION'

It is astonishing to see its reappearance since the 1990s in political texts and even in military and strategic texts, particularly in the United States.[42] Even before the fall of the USSR but still during the Gorbachev era, a form of 'right of intervention' had been officially recognized (UN Resolution 43/131 of 8 December 1988). This expression is inaccurate. No state would ever sign such a resolution that violated the sacrosanct principle of national sovereignty. The objective of the resolution was thus more modest: to facilitate access 'to victims of natural disasters and similar emergency situations'. It is also true that its essence was found in these 'similar emergency situations' by which the authors implied identifiable or veiled genocide (Sudan, Ethiopia, etc.). Normally, the aid would be requested by the legitimate government (the USSR called for it in 1989 – the first – following upon an earthquake in Armenian SSR). A clause in the

[40] For the history of this text, see: D. DUBARLE, '*Le Schéma XIII et la guerre*', in '*L'Eglise dans le monde de ce temps*', coll. *Unam Sanctam* 65b coll., Cerf, Paris, 1967, pp. 517-570.

[41] Ref.: §2309.

[42] About 50 documents between 1990 and 2000, including M. WALZER, *Just and Unjust Wars*, New York, 1992.

resolution provided that, in the event of a breach, incapacity, or lack of goodwill on the part of the legitimate authority, any member of the UN could refer the matter to the Security Council and take initiatives even if the principle remained only one of negotiation with the legitimate authorities concerned. This situation arose during the Bosnian civil war (1992-1994) when the still legitimate government in Belgrade prevented or made difficult the transportation to Sarajevo and other enclaves vital supplies to the people trapped there. The UN took a step by providing for the use of force to carry out its resolution on humanitarian aid, while being careful to define strictly the mandate (humanitarian zones and corridors) as well as the rules of engagement. It appeared that the mandate and the rules of engagement were unsuitable for the situation, and one can still recall the absurd nature of the situation in which the UN contingents were placed. The UN demonstrated its weakness (defeat in itself, but also through the red tape). The USA again took the initiative, diplomatic (until Rambouillet) and military, while always assuring itself of UN backing.

Nevertheless, the conditions were created, from the American perspective, for no longer holding UN decisions in high regard and for returning to an independent American decision-taking logic. It was in this context that work on the 'just war' was again taken up and that the US, as a super power without competition, started to use it to give itself a course of action (or at least moral justification in the media, certainly as regards Western public opinion). If it acted by giving itself a course of action as a sovereign state, it could be said that the Just War Theory was being applied appropriately, which, because of its origins, comes under the 'examination of conscience' or, in more secular terms, an analytical framework that could assist wise political decision making.

7. THE RETURN OF 'PRIVATE' ETHNIC WARS

In the meantime and intimately linked to the logic of the blocs and the structural weakness of several states, a new kind of conflict started to spread (in Africa first) where, faced with ethnic demands, the state itself changed into a partisan clan (Liberia, Somalia, Sierra Leone, etc.). The result was complete deregulation of conflicts, none of the parties being concerned with regulation of any kind, duly signed or not, and unknown to the clans who, at any rate, did not want to be burdened with it. This was accompanied by the *deprofessionalised* character of the armed gangs and the very rapid transformation of the regular armies into equally anarchic armed gangs. Structurally, it was no longer a matter of conflicts between duly constituted states or even between one state and a rebel army but rather of many private conflicts between rival chiefs. In this context, the moral scruples of a justification by a Doctrine of the Just War had no place nor did a 'Law of the Hague' or a 'Law of Geneva', so patiently updated for over the last century. Any power (the UN or other) wanting to intervene between these parties found itself in a *dissymmetrical* position: it would be bound to respect the Conventions unilaterally (so that it would not contradict the humanitarian values in the name of which it came onto the scene), which constituted a strategic advantage for the illegal parties who acted without any such scruples. This legal dissymmetry thus proved unfavourable to the regular troops. However, the licit troops could rely on technical resources (communication, observation, armament, logistics, etc.) that constituted a military dissymmetry that was greatly advantageous. The reply of the illegal armed gangs could be of two types, avoidance of battle or techniques of resistance (resistance movements, sabotage, harassment, lone gunmen, etc.). One of these methods (suicide attacks) was not new but spread in a specific manner in these dissymmetrical conflicts. This sacrificial method has a tactical effectiveness that is relatively or completely limited but has immeasurable social effects (general poisoning of all social relations, colossal security costs, climate of terror, etc.). These resistance techniques (attacks, kidnappings, extortion of funds under threat, and other mafia-like tactics) were not, however, a total war, even if each episode or each act was undertaken with complete intensity (the intention to kill and to cause maximum damage).

These conflicts remained localized but were, however, contained but always to the advantage of the ends of the logic of the blocs and none were seen any longer as being able to degenerate into major nuclear conflict. At first (1990-2000), therefore, responsibility was removed from the international community and particularly from the great 'sponsors.' This *laisser-faire* reduction was, perhaps, intentional on the part of certain powers (long-term strategy for 'deterioration' of certain areas and of sapping competing powers, proliferation of military 'exercises,' and maintenance of the military-industrial complex). The potential of conflicts of this kind is still enormous and will not abate, were it only because of global demography. One should not, therefore, patiently wait for peace by reduction in the number of micro-conflicts (even though potentially very deadly) but from their political management by the 'sponsors,' the UN being radically impotent before the interests of the powers. The theoretical principle of resolving these impasses is simple but doubtless utopian: in politics, like in economics, it is necessary to abandon the logic of the zero-sum game (for me to win, you have to lose) and adopt the logic of a non-zero sum game (win-win).

In any case, in these new conflicts it is clear that the conditions for the just war have no force. Their strength even originates from their subversion, as all causes will be considered subjectively just. Being amoral, the actors will be indifferent to the honesty of intention. Being partisan by nature, there is by definition no legitimate authority. That which should be the last resort is, in fact, used as the very first resort with violence being considered direct and immediate means. Being without a global strategy and/or relying only on the energy of despair, the reasonable chances of success are not even assessed. The only thing that counts is the success of the present operation (maximum deaths and harm to the enemy). The principle of proportionality is spontaneously replaced by its opposite, the 'maximin principle'[43]:

---

[43] A term I take by analogy from Rawls.

maximum effects at minimum cost. Discrimination only plays a role in the friend/enemy distinction and in no way impacts the military/civilian distinction. It is replaced by the easiest or the most spectacular or the most symbolic target.

Should the intervening powers respect, despite everything, the conditions of the just war? If they intervene effectively as a third-party power, they are thus both the court of justice and the police force. The conflict is then to be evaluated from the perspective not of the Just War Theory but of international positive law (even if it means improving it by a true 'Law of Nations' since even the Universal Declaration of Human Rights only refers to individual rights). The armed intervention is thus to be conducted according to principles close to those governing the police in common law without conflicting with the principles of the social order and human respect that they seek to defend.

8. THE RETURN OF THE RELIGIOUS WAR

What was noted about dissymmetric conflict is, in general, valid for wars and acts of war perpetrated wrongly or authorized in the name of Islam or even more specifically as a *jihad* ('holy war').[44] The concept is not new, for it is as old as Islam itself of which it is not a fanatical aberration but a constituent and permanent element (except for a period of weakness between 1920 and 1980). What is new is its concrete activation in our contemporary context, which one had thought to be secularized, with the technologies now accessible, considerable financing, and efficient means of communication (which were never available during the European religious wars of the 17th century). Unlike the terrorist acts of the Muslims, but falling in the category of 'private wars' between clans in the 'wars of liberation,' the *jihad* has precise and well-known

---

[44] Declared as such by the competent religious authorities to defend or to spread Islam, as an imposition in one way or another on all Muslims with divine reward being certain.

rules.[45] On many points and despite its archaic vocabulary, they are not very different from the Western Conventions (*Law of Geneva, Law of The Hague*), except that religious discrimination is a decisive criterion. If one were to apply the Doctrine of the Just War as an analytical framework to the *jihad*, one could say that:

– The *jihad* is, in principle, a just cause since the religious motivation is the only one that can justify the holy war, and religious motivation is always just.

– The intention must remain right, that is, exclusively religious and thus not guided by material or power interests, even if these elements could be deserving secondary consequences.[46]

– The legitimate authority can only be a religious authority. Ideally, this should be the Caliph. Since the abolition of the Caliphate by Kemal in 1924, there has been no legitimate authority for the entire Islamic world and this has in effect resulted in a certain anarchy in the declarations of *jihad* and its control. Actually, several Islamic groups are militating for the restoration of the Caliphate.

– War must not be the first resort but resorting to war does not in any way incite the same scruples of conscience as does the doctrine of the just war. As it happens, submission to Islam should always be proposed before a declaration of war because the problem would be formulated otherwise if the population were ready to convert than with infidels, idolaters, or non-believers.

– As regards chances of success, the Koran provides that one must fight if one feels superior.[47] The commitment must be total,[48] but there is no obligation of result, as victory belongs to God alone.

---

[45] See the seven chapters devoted to Islam, including six by Islamic authors, in the voluminous enquiry into 'Les religions et la guerre' of 1986 commissioned by the (French) Ministry of National Defence (published by Cerf editions in 1991).

[46] Koran 47:35: 'Allah will not deprive you of the reward for your labour.'

[47] *Ibid.*: 'You shall not waver and surrender in pursuit of peace, for you are guaranteed victory.'

[48] Koran 8:60: 'Against them make ready your strength to the utmost of your power, including steeds of war, to strike terror into (the hearts of) the enemies.'

If one does not feel in a position of power, one can wait for better times and temporarily accept a compromise (*dar-el-suhl*).

This way of understanding the conditions of a just war contradicts international law on certain significant points, such as non-discrimination on the basis of religion and the principle of separation of religion and politics. *A fortiori*, the Islamic vision of the world is in total conflict with this law on even more, equally fundamental points: the will to recreate a homogeneous Muslim world completely purified of present and even of past non-Muslim elements, to re-establish the social inferiority of women, to re-establish the Sharia (law directly derived from a literal interpretation of the Koran, unlike the Fiqh, which is derived from the Koran by analogy), and a few other points in the programme. These points are in flagrant conflict with international law and should be pursued and sanctioned systematically by the courts. The problems are that these are not mere violations but violations committed in the name of another source of law, that of 'customary' law and that, from the Muslim perspective, international law is only Western customary law. The dilemma is serious: either we accept this ethnic-religious derivative and therein a failure of international law, or we take the means to compel respect for international law, even if it means redefining it (not in the sense of concessions to the ethnic-religious but with a view to defining that which is truly fundamental to the humanity of mankind beyond cultures and religions). In any case, we are situated at the level of a civilization debate and not, from the outset at once, at that of the 'just war.' It is curious that we have arrived here because, in fact, the governments of the Muslim nations have subscribed to international law. But the object of the Islamic religious groups is precisely to replace the 'impious' rulers with true Muslims who will apply only Muslim rules, and this, clearly, with the support of the popular masses, including those who emigrate. Indeed, this support was certainly 'worked,' and this work of the Islamic groups succeeded.[49] The spectacular Islamic attacks were,

---

[49] Unlike Catholic fundamentalism, which did not 'succeed.'

evidently, part of this 'work.' They gave back a sense of pride and efficiency to the Muslim world (some disapprove but there were never any mass protests); they accelerate the process of ethnic-religious concessions by the Western countries to the 'moderate' Muslims (whose Islamic objective is the same); they arouse the co-operation of traditionally left European anarchists (who find them a valuable ally for destabalizing the establishment). If a war is to be declared, it will thus not be in relation to these attacks but in relation to the entire process. It is an ideological war that will not be won with guns.

CHARACTERISTICS OF NEW CONFLICTS

- Five Important Points -

* reduced
* relocated
* dissymmetric
* deregulated
* deprofessionalized

9. PREVENTIVE WAR

Is it necessary to wait for an attack before reacting? As such, the question is wrongly posed and open to all kinds of deviations (and to reinforcing the vicious cycle of the logic of violence). As was noted, if there is an attack (objective fact carried out), the reaction must be in accordance with the law and force used within the limits of the law. The 'pre-emptive' (or 'interceptive') use of force (attack in progress) is clearly justified but not the 'preventive' use of force, which opens the door to all kinds of abuse[50] and deviations where emotional elements, manipulative mediatization, false information,

---

[50] O. CORTEN, *Le retour des guerres préventives, le Droit International menacé* [*The Return to Preventive Wars, International Law under Threat*] Labor, Brussels, 2003.

subjective and shallow analyses in bad faith, and so on are all too common place. This question is not new. Vitoria had considered it and concluded: "no one may be punished for a fault he has not yet committed." But it is also true that, in classic Christian morality, stopping someone from doing wrong, preventively, is permitted (the case of *occasio proxima*). It remains to be determined whether this principle, pertaining to private morality, can be extended by simple analogy to international relations. As in any doubtful circumstance, at least the principle of prudence would apply. Nevertheless, there would be no objection to a 'preventive war', albeit with non-military means, in the context and with the usual methods of information, legal directives, and legal protective measures.

In this respect, the new NATO doctrine, adopted in a climate of general indifference[51] and extending to the notion of security and no longer only that of defence, turns out to be very dangerous. The principle appears acceptable and does not seem offensive, but it surreptitiously includes the notion of prevention with all its possible diversions. We did not have to wait long for the 'security of energy supplies' (and other raw materials essential for industry or rare or very localized materials) to be invoked. The very mercantilist Grotius had already used it for the Dutch power (and even Vitoria for the Spanish power) in the name of a 'right of commerce.' From here, it is a small step to extend it to 'market control', and it is in this way that 19th century England understood it. International commerce has very often resorted to an armed force to defend its interests (beginning with the Teutonic Knights in the 13th century) or, at best, to enforce respect for the conventions of international commerce. It will not be otherwise in our current era of effective and generalized globalization of commerce. This perspective can doubtless be defended in the name of access for everyone to Earth's common resources.[52]

---

[51] The anti-nuclear missiles provoked a colossal mobilization in the 1980s.

[52] This principle of 'universal destination of the Earth's resources,' essential to the Church's social doctrine, did not necessarily conflict with the system of private property (of individuals or Nations, acting as individuals) if the property is understood to be functional (and not 'ontological'), that is, open to the market.

We should keep in mind, however, that the Conventions we already have will prevent many conflicts. Instead, we should be thinking about the conditions for a *Just Peace*[53] rather than those for a Just War.

10. THE PROBLEM OF A SUPRANATIONAL AUTHORITY

We recall Vitoria's reasoning according to which armed conflicts occur only because there was no supranational authority that could resolve them through arbitration. This is an old idea that was born in the Carolingian empire and kept alive for the benefit of the Holy Roman Empire. The papacy also claimed such authority for itself. Vitoria denied any super power (the Holy Empire) and any religious authority (the papacy) this power of arbitration since the religious 'consensus' had already been shattered at that time in Europe – hence Vittoria's 'modernity' (perhaps motivated at least at first by his Spanish nationalism). Since then, the idea was picked up by the Abbé de Saint Pierre[54] and by Kant[55] as well as by Taparelli in 1843. These ideas were involved in the founding of the League of Nations in 1920, which was conceived, however, on an internationalist rather than a supra-nationalist basis. Despite the failure of this model, this was still the basis upon which the United Nations Organization was founded in 1945. Skilfully neutralized, torpedoed, or colonized by one or another power or coalition of countries and voluntarily divested of any means of coercion, the institution has not yet proved very effective. Moreover, having been conceived as a forum of nation states, the UN does not allow 'peoples' to have a political forum. Failing that, these peoples,[56] if they believe they have serious reasons for dissatisfaction,

[53] Of which 'equitable commerce' is an essential element in addition to the fundamental civil liberties.
[54] *Projet pour rendre la paix perpétuelle en Europe* (1717) [Project for settling an everlasting peace in Europe].
[55] *Projet de paix perpétuelle* (1795) [Project for everlasting peace].
[56] Some analysts count 5,000, but fortunately, there are not 5,000 in conflict.

will then have recourse to violence to assert them. These peoples, not knowing borders (which are often artificial, often ignore history, and often have been imposed by powers that arranged them to suit themselves and to fabricate *casus belli* in reserve), frequently constitute cross-border problems (e.g., the Kurds) and are open to various kinds of manipulation. Theoretically, a simple institutional solution would be to create a second assembly: an assembly of the peoples, with no statutory recognition or voting rights but with the right to speak and the right to question, which could already defuse many ethnic problems.

The current notion of the Security Council was also inherited from an outdated historical situation and has paralyzed (and thus discredited) the UN as a means of resolving conflicts until 1990. Rather than debate an expansion, a completely different conception would be conceivable, more appropriate for managing conflicts: creating an *ad hoc* Security Council structure (for each conflict that has been or risks being declared) gathering all countries involved (militarily and/or by reason of shared borders). The countries in conflict would then each appoint a third power as an 'advocate' for its cause.

Moreover, to defuse the 'clash of civilizations' (it is not sufficient to deny them to render them nonexistent) since, at least for now, the Islamic civilization wants to present a homogeneous front and is positioning itself as the enemy to all others, a high court should be assembled, not from the powers (this would be accepting the condition of force as a condition of law) but from the 'civilizations.' Huntington's nomenclature is relevant (no persuasive argument has yet proved it wrong). It would have the competence to revise regularly the UN Charter, the Universal Declaration of Human Rights, and other legislative texts (since the world has chosen contractual law instead of natural law, it is necessary to see this logic through to the end[57]) and their authentic interpretation when there is a conflict. Nevertheless, the 'civilizations' would not exist to defend their perspectives but, according to the rules of Habermas's discourse, to lead

---

[57] Unless one day we start to consider a law of man based on anthropology.

a purely rational discourse beyond the characteristics of each in order to return to the very core of the common good of the humanity of mankind. More than Rawls's 'veil of ignorance' (in which the interest in objectifying problems is well observed), it would be a matter of the will to transcend the particular self to return to the universal (just as it can be the least harmful formulated at a given moment in history).

Meanwhile, the international community should be aware that, clearly, there are no human rights as one would have us naïvely believe. It is not enough that a text be signed by political representatives for them to be 'received.' Reception of law is a crucial element under penalty of falling into anomie. In any event, it would suffice for certain movements to return to religious law (like the Sharia) rather than having for 'inalienable' Human Rights being flouted with complete impunity. The solution in this respect is not war but, if we believe in law, the absolute necessity of criminally prosecuting each violation of International law, everywhere, every time. The appropriate legislative instruments exist (and can be improved). The institutions exist or can exist. The coercive means could be made equal to the task if the political will were present. Their reinforcement would cost much less in money and in human devastation than the current punitive or preventive wars (which do not settle individual interests).

11. CONCLUSION

The doctrine of the just war is no longer adequate. Reusing it in international policy can only be termed opportunistic and dangerous. However, like the 'wisdom of the nations,' it retains its relevance. Moreover, volunarily it can always act as a deliberative instrument for the individual conscience, it being understood that the satisfaction of one or another condition or of all the conditions produced no 'right.'

As Vitoria imagined, true supranational institutions are the solution to rendering null and void the recourse to the subjective and discretionary doctrine of the just war. The emergence of the nation states resulted in the failure of Vitoria's ideas. As long as we take on this notion according to which each individual defends 'his' interests, even as opposed to the general welfare interest, peace will not be possible.

As Thomas Aquinas advocated, governing the world should be secularized since any theocracy in the name of one particular religion is contrary to human freedom and is, by its very essence, bellicose. Nevertheless, it is only when a theocracy commits acts of war that it can be the object of a defensive war. For the rest, it must be combated by legal means, each time a law is violated.

But human rights should not become a secular religion for which the UN would be the Great Temple and its officials the priests. The law should remain a positive matter, not idealist, subject to rational discussion (and not simply by majority rule: numbers do not make truth or the law), and be without religious or ethnic privilege.

SELECT BIBLIOGRAPHY

(general, in French, on Just War)
BACOT, G., *La doctrine de la guerre juste*, Economica, Paris, 1989.
BATIFOL, Mgr. *et al.*, *L'Eglise et le droit de guerre*, Bloud et Gay, Paris, 1920.
BEAUFORT, D., *La guerre comme instrument de secours ou de punition*, Nijhof, The Hague, 1933.
CHENU, M-D, *L'évolution de la doctrine de la guerre juste*, in *L'Evangile dans le temps*, Cogitatio Fidei 11, Cerf, Paris, 1964, pp. 571-590.
COSTE, R., *L'évolution de la doctrine de la guerre juste dans la pensée de l'Eglise*, in *Le problème du droit de guerre dans la pensée de Pie XII*, Aubier, Paris, 1962, Chap.1.
DE LA BRIERE, Y., *Le droit de juste guerre*, Pedone, Paris, 1938.
DE SOLAGES, Mgr., *La théologie de la guerre juste*, DDB, Bruges, 1946.
HAGGENMACHER, P., *Grotius et la doctrine de la guerre juste*, PUF, Paris, 1983.
REGOUT, R., *La doctrine de la guerre juste de St Augustin à nos jours*, Pedone, Paris, 1935 (reissued: Scientia Verlag, Aalen, 1974).
VANDERPOL, A., *La guerre devant le christianisme*, Tralin, Paris, 1911;
ID., *La doctrine scolastique du droit de la guerre*, Pedone, Paris, 1919.

WIM SMIT

Beyond Paralysing Fear and Blind Violence
Terrorism, Counter-Terrorism and the Violation of Human and Civil Rights

Much has been written after the 9/11 attacks about terrorism and the actual threat of international terrorism. This sort of terrorism not only sets down a challenge for military and humanitarian strategies, it also challenges the centuries old just war tradition itself. Indeed, this is not the first time that just war thinking has been questioned and put under pressure. In the sixteenth century it seemed that it could be used as a kind of legitimation for religious wars. Two centuries later, with the rise of pacifist sects, like the Mennonites and the Quakers, the Christian use of violence was fundamentally questioned. And during the period of secularisation, the role of God, as well as the role of the Church in (international) political-military thinking has been put in doubt. The last time just war thinking seemed to be in trouble was in the post-World War II period when there was a proliferation of nuclear weapons.[1] While this tension between nuclear threat and just war thinking is still unsolved (and seems to be unsolvable), another fundamental question has arisen: Does just war thinking offer a sufficient answer to the terrorist threat, and more specifically, what kind of guidelines does it offer for counterterrorist strategies?

The purpose of this article is to analyse this present terrorist threat in terms of the challenges it brings to just war thinking. This article begins with a history of the just war tradition. Afterwards it moves to a discussion of present-day international terrorism and

---

[1] B.T. ADENEY, *Just War, Political Realism, and Faith*, Metuchen, NJ/London, The American Theological Library Association and The Scarecrow Press, 1988, p. 46.

then to a discussion that links possible counterterrorist approaches with the rules we find in the just war tradition.

1. A SHORT HISTORY OF THE JUST WAR TRADITION

1.1. From the first Christians to Augustine

Traditionally, for Christians, the topic of the use of violence has always been very controversial.[2] In the early Church, only few Christians took military service and only a few were convinced that it was possible to reconcile service to God with service to the emperor. On the other side, we see the mainstream conviction in Christian societies that it was impossible to reconcile both services. This was put into words by Tertullian (around 160 – 225) and Origin (around 185 – 254). They both strongly leaned upon bible quotations such as "You shall not kill" (Ex. 20,13) and the Sermon on the Mount (especially Mt. 5,38-39) in which Jesus teaches his disciples about the right attitude toward violence. Tertullian as well as Origin pleaded for the formation of a kind of Christian 'pious army,' and emphasised the strength of prayer.[3]

With the reign of Constantine (306-337) and the acceptance of Christianity as the state religion, the attitude of most Christians toward military service changed. The question no longer was: can service to God be reconciled with service to the emperor, but what kind of conditions and rules should be satisfied during battle? This revolution in Christian thought started with Ambrose, who wrote a critique on injustices under the reign of Theodosius (346 – 395),[4] and was later systematised by his pupil Augustine (°354), who can be seen as the founder of the just war tradition.

[2] G. BACOT, *La doctrine de la guerre juste*, Paris, Economica, 1989, p. 12.

[3] L.S. CAHILL, *Love your Enemies. Discipleship, Pacifism, and Just War Theory*, Minneapolis, Fortress Press, 1994, pp. 41-53.

[4] J.H. YODER, *When War is Unjust. Being Honest in Just-War Thinking*, Eugene, OR, Wipf and Stock Publishers, 2001, pp. 17-18.

For Augustine, just wars were only to be waged because of the injustice of another party. Such injustice forces the wise man to use violence, but always with an eye to the reinstallation of peace. "Peace", he writes in his *De civitate Dei*[5] (The City of God), "is the purpose that also is in view with the conduct of the war, even for them who are bent upon exercising their skills in war by leading and fighting". That does not mean for Augustine that peace as a motive justifies warfare. He only means that war is nourished by the hope for peace. He completed his view with three necessary conditions for speaking about a just war: (1) the basic attitude of love should be present, (2) war is waged by a legitimate ruler or a legitimate government, and (3) the actions undertaken should be just (no excessive violence, no disfigurement of temples, no revenge or atrocities…).[6]

It seems that Augustine did not have an aversion to violence though he saw the horror of warfare and did not look at war from a kind of romanticised point of view. In a letter in reply to Faustus the Manichean, he writes: "The real evils in war are love of violence, revengeful cruelty, fierce and implacable enmity, wild resistance, and the lust of power and such like (…)."[7] For Augustine it is clear that this kind of negative motivation should be punished, and certainly cannot be part of a just war.

A last important element in Augustine's just war thinking is that it is forbidden to fight out of self-defence. For him it is only justified to use violence when it is necessary to save the life of somebody else. In his eyes self-defence is the worst of all possible excuses to wage war, or any other kind of resistance for that matter.[8] As we shall see later, this is one of the elements that changed throughout the subsequent history of the just war tradition.

---

[5] A. AUGUSTINUS, *De stad van God*, XIX, 12 [Translated from Latin by G. WIJ-DEVELD. Original title: De *civitate Dei*.] Amsterdam, Ambo-Olympus, 2002, p. 957.

[6] B.T. ADENEY, *o.c.*, pp. 32-33.

[7] S.K. WALSCH & E.D. ASCH, *Just War. A Wadsworth Casebook in Argument*, Boston, Wadsworth, 2004, p. 66.

[8] S. DAVIS, *"Et quod vis fac": Paul Ramsey and Augustinian Ethics*, in *The Journal of Religious Ethics* 19 (2) (1991), p. 37.

1.2. An evolving tradition: from Thomas Aquinas up to secularisation

1.2.1. Thomas Aquinas

Thomas Aquinas (°1225) further developed the thoughts of Augustine in his *Summa Theologiae*. In his oeuvre, he only devoted a few pages to the topic of just warfare. Nonetheless, he succeeded in systematising Augustine's thoughts about war. The importance of Thomas lies not in a fundamental reform, but in the fact that he pointed the just war tradition in a certain direction. To see this, it is important to recall that Thomas positions his questions about just war between questions about sins against peace. As Johan Verstraeten noticed, Thomas does not ask: "Is waging war a sin?", but: "Is waging war *always* a sin?" ("*Utrum bellare sit semper peccatum?*"). This makes it clear that for Thomas there is a fundamental connection between pacifism and the just war tradition.[9] "Every desire is a longing for peace," he writes in imitation of Augustine's notion of *tranquillitas ordinis*. Real peace, he says, only exists when a balance is found between one's own desires and those of other people.[10] A bit further he describes three conditions that must be satisfied before a war can be said to be just: (1) war must be declared by an authority that defends the common good (for example, a tyrannical ruler cannot satisfy this condition), (2) war is waged because of a just cause, and (3) the underlying intention behind going to war should be to promote good and to avoid evil. But Thomas not only writes about the so-called *ius ad bellum* (conditions that should be fulfilled before going to war), he also goes into the subject of *ius in bello* (the rules for combatants during battle). Fooling the enemy, lying and breaking

---

[9] J. VERSTRAETEN, *De "Bellum Iustum"-traditie en het vredesdenken*, in R. BURG-GRAEVE, J. DE TAVERNIER & L. VANDEWEYER (eds.), *Van rechtvaardige oorlog naar rechtvaardige vrede. Katholieken tussen militairisme en pacifisme in historisch-theologisch perspectief*, Leuven, Universitaire Pers Leuven, 1993, p. 90.

[10] T. AQUINAS, *Summa Theologiae. A Concise Translation*, II-X-29, [Translated from Latin by T. MCDERMOTT. Original title: *Summa Theologiae*.] Allen, Christian Classics, 1989, pp. 359-360.

promises Thomas calls unlawful. Rights and agreements, he writes, should always be kept during warfare.[11]

Thomas added one remarkable aspect to Augustine's just war thinking. While Augustine could not accept any form of self-defence, Thomas acknowledged that self-defence indeed can be accepted, as well as the death of the attacker, but only when the intention of the defender is to defend himself against aggression (or to drive back the enemy). To justify his opinion on this matter he introduced the notion what we know today as the 'principle of double effect,' a notion much more complex than is often supposed, and rather often misunderstood in military circles concerning situations where non-combatants are hit by an attack. Moral theologians do not agree on the exact meaning of this notion either, but in general there is a kind of consensus about it. An excellent explanation can be found in Michael Walzer's famous work *Just and Unjust Wars*. He describes the 'principle of double effect,' applied to the example of warfare, as follows: "(…) It is permitted to perform an act likely to have evil consequences (the killing of non-combatants) provided the following four conditions hold:

• The act is good in itself or at least indifferent, which means, for our purposes, that it is a legitimate act of war.
• The direct effect is morally acceptable – the destruction of military supplies, for example, or the killing of enemy soldiers.
• The intention of the actor is good, that is, he aims only at the acceptable effect; the evil effect is not one of his ends, nor is it a means to his ends.
• The good effect is sufficiently good to compensate for allowing the evil effect; it must be justifiable under Sidgwick's proportionality rule."[12]

Nevertheless, we should not forget that the possibility of non-combatants being involved in war in Thomas's time was much smaller

---

[11] *Ibid.*, pp. 367-368.
[12] M. WALZER, *Just and Unjust Wars. A Moral Argument with Historical Illustrations*, New York, Basic Books, 2000³, pp. 152-153.

than nowadays with the use of non-discriminating weapons. So, we should not be surprised that the importance of the principle of double effect has increased throughout history. In any case, it is undeniable that with this principle Thomas put his stamp on later military ethics.

1.2.2. Later developments in the just war tradition and secularisation
A deepening of just war thinking took place in the second half of the Middle Ages. Theologians and canonists contributed to the development of the tradition by making it a systematic juridical instrument, and no longer only a religious and moral notion.

In the 14th and 15th century the just war tradition underwent no fundamental changes. Nevertheless, people like Honoré Bonet (°1340), who tried to develop a code for international law, and Saint Anthony of Florence (°1389), who added the principle of proportionality to the just war tradition,[13] made original contributions to just war thinking.

The most complete picture of just war thinking in the first half of the 16th century is found in the works of the Spanish Dominican Francis de Vitoria (°1480), and especially in his *De iure belli* (About the Laws of War). Vitoria was part of the Spanish scholastic school and was consulted by rulers from all over Europe. It is clear that he influenced several generations of theologians.[14] The idea that war is a legitimate means to correct an injustice, (even when the aggressor appeals to a just cause) opened the gate for the possibility of a 'just war for both sides' (on the level of subjective assessment).[15] In his just war thinking Vitoria especially emphasised the principle of proportionality and the principle of discrimination (which is designed to protect non-combatants). A few years later, another Spanish theologian, the Jesuit Francisco Suarez (°1548), added the notion of 'a reasonable chance of success' to the principles of the just war tradition. This means that there has

[13] G. MINOIS, *L'église et la guerre. De la Bible à l'ère atomique*, Paris, Fayard, 1994, pp. 180-181.
[14] G. BACOT, *o.c.*, p. 44.
[15] B.T. ADENEY, *o.c.*, p. 42.

to be a reasonable chance that a military undertaking will result in the restoration of justice and/or peace.[16]

The 17th century heralded the laicising of international law and war law. Religious-based just war thinking was no longer the dominant concept. The splintering of ecclesial authority brought on by religious wars, was followed by a need to find new juridical principles. In this new stream of just war related thinking, it was Hugo Grotius (1583-1645) who gave modern international law a 'foundation' with his work *De jure belli ac pacis* (About the laws of war and peace).[17] It was Grotius' ambition to develop a secular philosophy of war, one that was no longer connected with religion. In his thinking and due to his influence, *ius in bello* gained importance.

In Grotius' footsteps, the German Samuel Pufendorf (1632-1694) laid the fundaments of the *school for natural law and the law of peoples*. His successors were Christian Wolff (1679-1754) and Wolff's disciple Emerich de Vattel (1714-1767). In their works, the secularisation of the just war tradition was assured.

1.2.3. The nuclear era: the ultimate and ongoing challenge for just war thinking

In the second half of the twentieth century the just war philosophy was dominated by the destructive power of nuclear weapons. The sheer force of these weapons called into question the feasibility of both *ius ad bellum* and *ius in bello*.[18] The confusion increased in 1949 when the Americans lost their monopoly on nuclear weapons after the Soviet Union built its own nuclear arsenal. This led to the doctrine of a 'balance of terror' between these

---

[16] C. MELLON, *Chrétiens devant la guerre et la paix*, Paris, Editions du Centurion, 1984, pp. 103-105.

[17] H. WILLIAMS, *International Relations and the Limits of Political Theory*, Houndmills, MacMillan Press, 1996, p. 73.

[18] W.V. O'BRIEN, *Just-War Doctrine in a Nuclear Context*, in R.B. MILLER (ed.), *War in the Twentieth Century. Sources in Theological Ethics*, Westminster, John Knox Press, 1992, pp. 315-331.

arch-enemies.[19] This dangerous situation lasted until 1992 when Russia and the USA signed a treaty in which they agreed to reduce their nuclear arsenal by two-thirds. The nuclear threat continues all the more because not all nuclear arms are properly protected and accounted for and could perhaps one day fall into the hands of terrorists.

Given the awesome power of nuclear weapons, it comes as no surprise that the situation in the second half of the last century resulted in many important political, military and ethical contributions in which the nuclear threat was at least one of the topics. One of the most important contributions was, without any doubt, Paul Ramsey's book *The Just War*[20] (1968). In this work he developed the idea that nothing is wrong with the just war tradition, except that modern nuclear warfare is unacceptable in that framework. Such warfare is unacceptable not the least because it conflicts with the proportionality and non-combatant or discrimination principles (see *infra*). Ramsey also rejected the idea of a 'limited nuclear war' as was sometimes proposed in other works of that time. Nevertheless, it would be wrong to interpret Ramsey as a 'nuclear pacifist' if for no other reason that, throughout his writings, he dissociated himself from that theory.[21]

Ramsey met with much of approval among just war philosophers. His book set the tone for much of the literature about the (im)possibility of just warfare in times of nuclear weapons. Nevertheless, James Turner Johnson[22] objected that it was not warfare as such that was the point of discussion in a nuclear era, but the notion *supreme emergency* (see *infra*) which Michael Walzer coined in his book *Just and Unjust Wars*. Walzer's point of view was that

---

[19] R.J. REGAN, *Just War. Principles and Cases*, Washington, The Catholic University of America Press, 1996, p. 101.

[20] See: P. RAMSEY, *The Just War. Force and Political Responsibility*, Oxford, Rowman & Littlefield Publishers, 2002, 554 p.

[21] W. WERPEHOWSKI & S.D. CROCCO (eds.), *The Essential Paul Ramsey. A Collection*, New Haven, Yale University Press, 1994, p. 96.

[22] J.T. JOHNSON, *Can Modern War Be Just?*, New Haven, Yale University Press, 1984, p. 185.

it was acceptable to use all means to protect the basic values of a civilisation when it is threatened.

The Catholic Church also played an important role in the discussion of that time. In his encyclical *Pacem in Terris* (Peace on Earth), John XXIII (1958-1963) issued his vision on world peace. He did not place much emphasis on the centuries old just war tradition, but instead focused on peace – not so much as the work of governments and international institutions, but as the fruit of cooperation between peoples and respect for human rights.[23] Nevertheless, this did not mean that Pope John or the Church rejected the just war tradition. That tradition came back as an important source of inspiration for the Pastoral Constitution *Gaudium et Spes* (Joy and Hope), one of the fruits of the Second Vatican Council (1962-1965). *Pacem in Terris* and *Gaudium et Spes* had the same undertone: war can not be defended as an instrument of justice in an atomic era. This does not mean that this statement can be seen as the conclusion of ecclesiastical thinking about just war of that time. As Paul Ramsey wrote in his commentary on *Pacem in Terris*, it was more a kind of framework for further analysis.[24]

One last ecclesiastical document deserves some attention because it is often cited and commented upon – *The Challenge of Peace: God's Promise and Our Response*[25] (1983) from the American Bishops. In a very direct way, this document focused on the use of nuclear weapons and the nuclear arms race. It condemned the intentional destruction of cities and the population of a country. It also paid much attention to the correct interpretation of the

---

[23] J. DE TAVERNIER, *Van rechtvaardige oorlog naar prudent pacifisme. Het kerkelijke vredesdenken van 1963 tot heden*, in R. BURGGRAEVE, J. DE TAVERNIER & L. VANDEWEYER (eds.), *o.c.*, pp. 156-157.

[24] P. RAMSEY, *The Just War Theory on Trial*, in *Cross Currents. The Journal of the Association for Religion and Intellectual Life* 13 (1963), pp. 481-482.

[25] For the text of this pastoral letter, see for example: http://www.haverford.edu/relg/mcguire/Challenge1.htm (the text is complete, except for nr. 85-110).

Catholic just war tradition and understandably to the principles of proportionality and discrimination. Christians, the American Bishops wrote, have no other choice than to protect peace against aggression. They emphasised their respect for those who engaged in pacifist practices and 'active non-violence', but also referred to the words of Pope Pius XII that Christians have a responsibility to resist unjust aggression.

The Catholic Church has never ceased emphasising that the just war tradition does not exist to justify war, but to reduce the possibility of armed conflict, and the number of victims and the material damage that occurs when, unhappily, it does break out.

2. Ius ad bellum and ius in bello: The pillars of just war philosophy

Just war philosophy is a normative ethical theory derived from principles that should be satisfied before a nation can go to war (*ius ad bellum*), and principles that need to be taken into account when a war breaks out (*ius in bello*). In contradiction with what often is thought, especially in pacifistic circles, just war philosophy does not make it easier to go to war. On the contrary, like pacifism, just war thinking sees war as a sin. But on the other side it also recognises that situations can exist in which there is no other recourse but to take up arms to achieve peace. Below we will comment on the most commonly accepted principles of the just war tradition.

2.1. Ius ad bellum

a) Just cause:
Traditionally there are three reasons that are accepted before one can speak of a 'just cause.' First of all to restore justice after aggression has occurred, secondly to take back stolen property, and lastly to resist an ongoing armed attack. But this original

meaning is reduced to one in modern warfare: only defence against aggression is still seen and accepted as a just cause.[26]

b) Legal authority:

By definition a war is an armed conflict between nations. And within these nations only a designated legal authority has the right to decide to employ military means to undo a certain injustice – but only when it serves the common good. Gangs, terrorist groups or organisations and guerrilla groups are not seen as legitimately authorised to wage war.

But it is not always clear who represents the legal authority, certainly not in times of revolution. That is why the Catholic Church states that political authority loses its legitimacy when it violates human rights seriously and persistently. For the same reason, Christian Mellon does not write about 'legal authority' but '*competent* authority' instead.[27]

c) Right intention:

The notion of 'right intention' is integrally connected to the other principles of just war thinking. In essence, this principle means that the intention of waging war must be to undo evil and to bring about peace. Acts like rape, aimless destruction, plundering, etc. indicate an intention that is neither just nor sincere.

d) Proportionality:

The principle of proportionality implies that the good that is reached by military counter-measures is equal to or greater than the evil caused by the enemy. This principle directs those in charge of battle to avoid deploying soldiers for trivial reasons. It says that the weapons used must be in balance with the extent and the importance of the conflict.

In connection with this principle, it is important to elucidate the notion *supreme emergency exemption*. In his book *Just and Unjust Wars*, as well as in his more recent book *Arguing About War*,[28]

---

[26] B.M. KANE, *John XXIII and Just Cause for Modern War*, in *New Blackfriars* 80 (1999) 56-72, p. 56.

[27] C. MELLON, *o.c.*, p. 109.

Michael Walzer defends the so-called '*back-to-the-wall*' argument – a term Winston Churchill used to describe the British situation in 1939. The *supreme emergency* has two essential and necessary criteria: (1) a threat must be serious, and (2) imminent. Walzer says fundamental values must be at stake. This means that the victory of the other party signifies a human disaster for the victim nation. For that nation it is a choice between war or intolerable slavery or mass murder.[29] In these rare cases, and only in these cases, a defence using all possible means is morally acceptable. Another philosopher, John Rawls, agrees with Walzer's vision. In his book *The Law of Peoples*[30] Rawls integrates Walzer's position into his principles of social contract theory. Both authors share the view that we should be very careful in dealing with this solution. Both authors call for prudence,[31] as does James Turner Johnson.[32] All of these writers are aware that the notion of *supreme emergency* can lead nations quickly down a dangerous and very slippery slope.

e) A reasonable chance of success:

Of all the just war principles 'a reasonable chance of success' is surely the one principle that speaks for itself. Wars waged against an overwhelmingly superior power, are not acceptable within the just war tradition. This is a criterion that, as Ralph B. Potter writes, originates from "the moral ban upon suicide and the fundamental principle that political leaders are stewards of the welfare of the nation and the life of each citizen."[33]

---

[28] M. WALZER, *Arguing about War*, New Haven/London, Yale University Press, 2004, pp. 33-50.

[29] ID., *Just and Unjust Wars*, pp. 251-255.

[30] J. RAWLS, *The Law of Peoples*, Cambridge, Harvard University Press, 2002⁴, pp. 98-99.

[31] Walzer for example writes: "We should always be reluctant to grant such exemptions, for every exemption is also a concession to those who argue that justice has a price, which may sometimes be too high and which we need not always pay." (M. WALZER, *Arguing about War*, p. 37.)

[32] J.T. JOHNSON, *o.c.*, p. 57.

[33] R.B. POTTER, JR., *The Moral Logic of War*, in R.B. MILLER (ed.), *o.c.*, p. 207.

f) <u>Last resort:</u>

War as a last resort means that all peaceful means need to be exhausted before war is considered. Because with this principle there is a strict necessity to be able to 'justify' or legitimise war, the idea of a *preventive* war (waging a war to protect oneself against possible aggression *in the future*) is unacceptable. On the other side, within the same just war framework, pre-emptive war (militarily reacting to manifest signs of aggression or an acute aggressive threat) is acceptable.

The acceptance of pre-emptive military operations can sound surprising in light of the recent attack on Iraq. But it needs to be said that the actual use of the term 'pre-emptive war' by some Americans is closely tied to that war. They use the word to help justify military actions in Iraq even though there is no nation, least of all Iraq, that poses (or posed) an aggressive threat against the American State.

2.2. Ius in bello

When the *ius ad bellum* principles fail to prevent a war, the just war tradition offers rules that aim to limit warfare. These *ius in bello* principles act as a kind of prohibition against a total war. They form an ethical protective shield for soldiers and non-combatants alike.

a) <u>Proportionality:</u>

This notion of proportionality is narrowly connected with the same notion in the *ius ad bellum*. The principle has to do with what is acceptable in the use of military means, in comparison with the means used by the enemy. In contrast to the proportionality principle within the *ius ad bellum*, the same principle in the *ius in bello* refers to the deployment of non-discriminatory weapons (nuclear bombs, poison-gas, starvation…). According to this principle, such weapons are prohibited because the principle seeks to minimise the number of victims.

Immediately, it is clear that within the *ius in bello* the notions of 'proportionality' and 'discrimination' (see *infra*) are interwoven.

The death of non-combatants can only be acceptable when it is not the intentional consequence of an attack.

b) Discrimination:

The discrimination or non-combatant principle implies that unarmed citizens should never be a target in a war. This seems rather straight forward, but the reality of applying the principle is less sharp than seems at first sight. For example, take citizens working in a weapons factory. The factory is a legitimate target in a war, but the workers (citizens) are not. They are covered under the non-combatant principle. But most just war philosophers agree that the factory remains a legitimate target even when citizens are working in it because they are keeping the war industry going. This example shows that a seemingly unambiguous principle opens onto a much more complex reality.

2.3. Conclusion: about the relation between 'just war' and 'pacifism'

In essence, pacifism and just war philosophy, want to bring about lasting peace. The means and presuppositions of the two traditions are different, but in the end, they want to reach the same goal. In his book *Speak Up for Just War or Pacifism*[34] Paul Ramsey wrote about this: "Just war and pacifism do not share an equivalent rejection of violence. Pacifism's presumption is in favour of *peace* (or else peace and justice are believed never to conflict). Just war's presumption favours the defence of an ordered *justice* (which sometimes may not consist with peace)."

This is also emphasised by the recent attention from different just war philosophers for the so-called *jus post bellum,* namely, doing justice for the vanquished people after the war, and helping them rebuild their country. For those who dedicate themselves genuinely to peace, the *bellum iustum* is unfinished without an

---

[34] P. RAMSEY, *Speak Up for Just War or Pacifism. A Critique of the United Methodist Bishops' Pastoral Letter 'In Defense of Creation',* University Park, PA, Pennsylvania State University Press, 1988, p. 54.

effort to realise post-war justice. Except for the preference for non-violence, pacifism and the just war tradition have much in common. For example, they share common views concerning the protection of innocents, opposition to resorting to war out of vindictiveness or egocentric considerations or a crusader mentality, and the will to convince states to temper their use of violence.[35] As John Howard Yoder expressed it, pacifism and just war philosophy are on the same side in most of the debates about war.[36]

Pacifism is a colourful palette where the extreme end of the spectrum is the most visible – absolute pacifism. Nevertheless, there also exists a kind of mild pacifism that is not unwilling to give the political and military (international) reality its place in thinking about peace. This kind of pacifism comes close to just war philosophy, often even in the sense that there is hardly any difference between either perspectives. In this sense, the development of a 'pacifistic just war philosophy' which no longer sees killing as an absolute evil, but questions the 'natural right' of a nation's military self-defence[37] makes it possible to speak about a kind of continuum between pacifism on one side, and the just war tradition on the other.

As was clear from the discussion of the principles of just war philosophy, the most serious shortcoming of this tradition is the vagueness with which most principles are defined. When we apply them to the complex reality of international political tensions and military conflicts, we get a lot of room for some 'free' interpretation of the principles. Even so, these principles still offer an excellent starting point for moral reflection, though they sometimes are misused in propaganda, as was the case in 2003 in the prelude to the war on Iraq.[38] At such moments, it is the responsibility of

[35] D.R. SMOCK, *Religious Perspectives on War. Revised Edition*, Washington, United States Institute of Peace, 2002, p. 31.

[36] J.H. YODER, *When War is Unjust*, p. 69.

[37] B.T. ADENEY, *o.c.*, p. 93.

[38] On 10 February 2003 the American Theologian Michael Novak was invited by Jim Nicholson, the ambassador of the United States at the Holy See, to present his view on the just war philosophy concerning the Iraq case. Novak's

theologians, ethicists and lawyers to emphasise the correct use of the just war philosophy.

In any case, the just war tradition offers a moral frame of reference, a mirror for political and military decision-making. Objections against it, even when correct, do not undermine it. As a consequence, it loses neither credibility nor usability in deciding actual conflicts. Just war philosophy continues to offer valuable insights for achieving a lasting peace, when these principles are respected. If not, there will never be a real 'justified or justifiable war.' Bruno Coppieters writes: "No war should be seen as just (or legitimate) if one of the principles (...) isn't respected, or is over-ruled without any reason. This reason must have a moral character. No military necessity or political opportunity justifies exceptions to this rule."[39]

It will also be clear that the just war tradition is non-static. It adapts and corrects itself according to the times. A clear example of this is the revision of the opinion of Ambrose and Augustine that violence should only be used to help a third person against an unjust enemy, and not for self-defence. The history of just war thinking questioned that conclusion so much that self-defence is now a key element in just war theory. The tradition has shown itself to be quite resilient while being in tension with the insights of theologians, philosophers, ethicists and lawyers, in various contexts and times. What has resulted is a level-headed self-correcting

controversial opinion in which he took the American side, was printed in 'The National Review and at the website of the journal (See: M. NOVAK, 'Asymmetrical Warfare' & Just War. A Moral Obligation: http://www.nationalreview.com/novak/novak021003.asp). In this article Novak defines the war in Iraq as a preventive war, that he wrongly saw as acceptable within the just war tradition. Moreover, the rise of international terrorism did strengthen the power of Saddam Hussein in Novak's eyes "a hundredfold." He also emphasised the novelty of 'asymmetric warfare' in the 20th century, stated that the interests of the Americans went much beyond their oil interests, and emphasised that under the original Catholic doctrine of the *bellum iustum*, a limited and carefully executed war to change a regime – as a last resort – is a moral obligation.

[39] B. COPPIETERS, *The Right to Military Disobedience in Militarism, Pacifism, Realism and Just War Theory*, in *Professional Ethics* 10 (2, 3 & 4), p. 190.

theory. And this conception of the theory stands up well against those critics who say just war thinking is outdated or defunct.[40]

3. FIGHTING TERRORISM WITH ALL POSSIBLE MEANS?

"(…) [U]ntil September 11, over the preceding 33 years," the well-known terrorism analyst Bruce Hoffman writes, "a total of no more than perhaps 1,000 Americans had been killed by terrorists either overseas or even within the US itself. In less than 90 minutes that day, nearly three times that number were killed. To put those uniquely tragic events in context, during the whole of the twentieth century, no more than 14 terrorist operations killed more than 100 persons at any one time. Or, viewed from still another perspective, until the attacks on the World Trade Centre and Pentagon, no single terrorist operation had ever killed more than 500 persons at one time. Whatever the metric, therefore, the attacks that day were unparalleled in their severity and lethal ambitions."[41] No wonder this catastrophic and traumatizing event was often compared with the 1941 attack on Pearl Harbor.[42]

A strong reaction to the attacks was necessary, and after a short preparation in October 2001, Afghanistan was invaded, the Taliban regime was overthrown, al-Qaida training camps were

[40] In the discussions during the nuclear era, as well as today, while terrorism is a threatening factor in people's lives, this argument is used. As will become clear further on in this article the reality is more complex than was often is presumed at first sight because just war philosophy only offers partial answers to the specific situation of (the fight against) terrorism.

[41] B. HOFFMAN, *The Emergence of the New Terrorism*, in A. TAN & K. RAMA-KRISHNA (eds.), *The New Terrorism. Anatomy, Trends and Counter-Strategies*, Singapore, Eastern University Press, 2002, p. 31.

[42] See for example the theologian David Ray Griffin in the title of his book: *The New Pearl Harbor. Disturbing Questions about the Bush Administration and 9/11*, Northampton, Olive Branch Press, 2004, p. 254; and Henry Burke Wend who draws historical parallels between Pearl Harbor and September 11 in his article: *Pearl Harbor and the 11th of September: Some Historical Parallels* (see: http://www.boell.de/en/04_thema/960.html).

bombed and its members dislodged. Thousands of people were killed, but certainly after the invasion in Iraq, the world did not become a safer place. More than ever, terrorism is the highest priority on most national and international agendas, and the intelligence agencies underwent drastic changes. In this section we will focus on the fight against terrorism from different points of view. First of all we will discuss both the lack of and the necessity of a definition of terrorism. Secondly we will focus on the possibilities of fighting terrorism effectively and the recent initiatives from the US, EU, NATO and UN. Afterwards we will shed light on the violations of civil and human rights by US and EU initiatives.

3.1. About the impossibility and necessity of a definition

One of the most remarkable things about terrorism is that most people seem to be able to recognise and distinguish terrorist acts from most other criminal acts. But scholars seem to be incapable of developing a universally accepted definition of this phenomenon. In their famous and often cited book *Political Terrorism*[43] Alex Schmidt and Albert Jongman identified 109 different definitions of terrorism. Many more definitions have cropped up especially in the wake of September 11th.

There are four major reasons why no definition of terrorism has yet been found. The first two we find in Bruce Hoffman's book *Inside Terrorism*.[44] He notes first of all that, throughout history, especially since the French Revolution, the meaning of terrorism has been changing.[45] In 1793 and 1794 it was strongly connected with the '*régime de la terreur*' led by Maximilien de

---

[43] A.P. SCHMIDT & A.J. JONGMAN, *Political Terrorism. A New Guide to Actors, Authors, Concepts, Data Bases, Theories, and Literature*, Amsterdam, SWIDOC, 1988, p. 700.

[44] B. HOFFMAN, *Inside Terrorism*, New York, Columbia University Press, 1998, pp. 15-44.

[45] For the first reason, see also: W. LAQUEUR, *A History of Terrorism*, New Brunswick/London, 2002², pp. 6-20.

Robespierre (1758-1794), which was a reaction to the chaos and disorder immediately following the French Revolution. Terrorism meant anti-revolutionary (against the achievements of the French Revolution) and anti-governmental acts, executed by sub-national entities. Later in a second phase, during the industrial revolution, many far-reaching socio-economical changes resulted in the development of 'universal' ideologies like communism and Marxism. In this new ideological stream a new kind of terrorism emerged, one marked by the still familiar revolutionary and anti-state characteristics. The third phase of terrorism was connected to the growing restlessness in the Ottoman and Habsburg empires at the end of the 19th century. Organisations like the militant Armenian nationalistic movements came into action and led to the development of a variety of so-called nationalistic and separatist movements. In the 1930s its meaning changed again to include the Fascist and Nazist governments in Europe, and Stalinism in the Soviet Union. From that moment on, terrorism meant the abuse of power by the government of a certain country. After the Second World War, it would be referred to the violent revolts of the nationalistic and anti-colonial groups in Asia, Africa and the Middle-East. In the 60s and 70s terrorism was also used by nationalistic and ethnical-separatist movements, while in the 90s it mainly referred to narco-terrorism and the so-called 'grey area phenomenon' which threatened the stability of states by non-states and non-governmental processes and organisations. After the 9/11 attacks its meaning has shifted to the global scene. International terrorism is not a completely new phenomenon – it has its roots in the Middle-East at the end of the 70s – but it seems that 2001 was a breakthrough year for a new terrorist wave.[46] The

---

[46] In an often cited article David Rapoport argues that now we are witnessing the 'fourth wave' of terrorism. (D. C. RAPOPORT, *The Fourth Wave: September 11 in the History of Terrorism*, in *Current History* 100 (650) (2001), pp. 419-424. See also: D. C. RAPOPORT, *The Four Waves of Rebel Terror and September 11*, in *Anthropoetics* 8 (1) (2002), or: http://www.anthropoetics.ucla.edu/ap0801/terror.htm.

new terrorist attacks appear to be connected to political ideologies and take advantage of geopolitical instability, as in the Israeli-Palestine conflict for example.

The second reason is closely connected with the first one. Because there is a range of different kinds of terrorism (state terrorism, anarchistic terrorism, ethnical terrorism, political terrorism and religious terrorism), each with its own specific characteristics, it is difficult to formulate a definition that covers all kinds of terrorism.

The third reason it is difficult to define terrorism is that often there are political interests at play. The United States, for example, refuses to accept the consensus view which includes state terrorism to the definition. Undoubtedly this is due to its position in the Israeli-Palestine conflict. This seems to be another strong reason why it is unlikely that one day a kind of 'universal' definition of terrorism will be accepted. The only possible way out of this stalemate is for everyone to accept a very narrow definition. But the disadvantage of this solution is that certain forms of terrorism will be excluded, and as a consequence, this will limit the effectiveness of (inter)national counterterrorism efforts. On the other side, a broad definition will never be accepted in some political quarters, and as human rights organisations rightly fear, this will likely undermine human rights and lead to repression.

Fourthly, the concept of terrorism is essentially 'value ridden.' This means that it can never be defined in a completely neutral way. As a consequence, Marianne Van Leeuwen, Deputy Director of the *Clingendael Institute* in The Hague, knowingly observed that if "this thesis is correct, then it is impossible to capture 'terrorism' in universally accepted laws and rules."[47]

However, this does not mean that we should stop working for a broadly accepted definition. First of all, having such a definition in hand will enable us to punish terrorism-related or supporting conduct, like fund-raising. Secondly, "a definition is necessary for

---

[47] M. VAN LEEUWEN, *Confronting Terrorism*, in ID. (ed.), *Confronting Terrorism. European Experiences, Threat Perceptions and Policies*, The Hague, Kluwer Law International, 2003, p. 3.

establishing extraterritorial jurisdiction for such crimes, and for staking out the field where we want to give extra powers to public security and law enforcement agencies. On the one hand, we want to be protected against terrorism, but, on the other hand, we do not want to live in a totalitarian state."[48] The importance of this tension can be seen in the European Union's condemnation of the *US Patriot Act* as having made the border between counterterrorism and the violation of privacy too thin.[49] The same problem came to light in Great Britain where the Law Lords on December 16 2004 decided that the British anti-terror law violated the European convention of human rights. It did so because the anti-terror law allowed the government to imprison foreign suspects of terror for a certain time, without any accusation or trial. And thirdly, a definition of terrorism allows for a more or less clearly defined terrain for counterterrorism. That would refine the struggle and help toward harmonising national policies.

A new definition, even if it is widely accepted, will nevertheless not be the ultimate solution for the existing and persistent confusion between terrorism and freedom fighting. This centuries old dilemma has already been discussed many times in all kinds of literature on terrorism. One of the most clarifying contributions about this topic came from Boaz Ganor, the Executive Director of the *International Policy Institute for Counter-Terrorism*. In his article *Is One Man's Terrorist Another Man's Freedom Fighter?* he pointed out that the concepts of 'terrorist' and 'freedom fighter' are not

---

[48] N. KEIJZER, *Terrorism as a Crime*, in W.P. HEERE (ed.), *Terrorism and the Military. International Legal Implications*, The Hague, TMC Asser Press, 2003, p. 116.

[49] J. MONAR, *Die EU und die Herausforderung des internationalen Terrorismus. Handlungsgrundlagen, Fortschritte und Defizite*, in H. FRANK & K. HIRSCHMANN (Hrsg.), *Die weltweite Gefahr. Terrorismus als internationale Herausforderung*, Berlin, Berlin Verlag, 2002, p. 160. Despite criticism from the European Community, an opinion poll of Americans (on August 29, 2003) said a great majority thought the *Patriot Act* did affect their civil rights, but less than half of the people polled thought it went too far in restricting people's civil rights. (See: http://www.life-andliberty.gov/subs/s_people.htm)

mutually contradictory, but only differ essentially in the fact that terrorists deliberately involve citizens or non-combatants in their attacks. He writes: "By characterizing terrorism as a mode of operation directed against civilian targets, as opposed to basing the definition on the goals of the violence, we refute the slogan that 'one man's 'terrorist' is another man's 'freedom fighter'. This distinction between the target of the attack and its aims shows that the discrepancy between 'terrorism' and 'freedom fighting' is not a subjective difference reflecting the personal viewpoint of the definer. Rather, it constitutes an essential difference involving a clear distinction between the perpetrators' aims and their mode of operation. As noted, an organization is defined as 'terrorist' because of its mode of operation and its target of attack, whereas calling something a 'struggle for liberation' has to do with the aim that the organization seeks to attain."[50] Therefore Kumar Rama-krishna's conclusion "that al-Qaida is waging a guerrilla war [with a trans-national character],"[51] seems to be a misinterpretation of the real situation.

3.2. How powerless are we in the fight against terrorism?

With their military approach of the terrorist problematic, the US proved that terrorist organisations can be dealt a blow, and that it is impossible to destroy them totally. Active members of al-Qaida for example were chased and killed, and important training infra-structure and hiding-places were destroyed by bombs, but in the end at least two conclusions can be drawn. First, the most impor-tant leaders of the organisation, like Osama bin Laden, are still on the run, and perhaps more influential and dangerous than ever.

---

[50] B. GANOR, *Is One Man's Terrorist Another Man's Freedom Fighter?* See: http://www.ict.org.il/articles/researchdet.cfm?researchid=4 (p. 11) (26/12/2004).

[51] K. RAMAKRISHNA, *Countering the New Terrorism of Al Qaeda Without Generating Civilizational Conflict: The Need for an Indirect Strategy*, in A. TAN & K. RAMAKRISHNA (eds.), *o.c.*, p. 209.

They still issue threatening messages in the media and have taken on an aura of untouchability despite the impressive military forces deployed against them. This has made them into heroes and role models in the eyes of many. Second, after 9/11 and the search for terrorists all around the world, small terrorist cells arose, and it seems impossible to fight this phenomenon effectively with sophisticated military means and thousands of highly trained and armed soldiers. As Kumar Ramakrishna and Andrew Tan write: "In the process, the suicide terrorists made America's conventional and nuclear military muscle – and planned missile defence schemes – look, if not outright irrelevant, then at the very least, worryingly inadequate. Worryingly inadequate because surely the key lesson that the September 11 strikes reinforce is that, despite *prima facie* appearances, the central conflict in the world today is not between states competing for global hegemony. It is between secularizing, homogenizing and avaricious global capitalism on the one hand and ethnic and religious fundamentalism on the other."[52]

Fortunately many other effective counter-strategies exist. In their book *Trends in Terrorism*[53] Muller, Spaaij and Ruitenberg, three researchers of the Dutch *Institute for Security and Crisis Management* analysed a variety of possible counter-measures including the social-preventive, juridical, and international (economic and military). This is not the place to survey all of these possibilities, but it will be clear that not all of them are equally effective or morally acceptable. Diplomacy and negotiations with terrorists, for example, are often ineffective, and unjustified according to public opinion. In our eyes, the position of both George W. Bush and Tony Blair not to negotiate with terrorists who have kidnapped civilians and threatened their lives is right. First of all, it would be unacceptable for the well-meaning Iraqi people to withdraw the troops and abandon them now. Secondly,

[52] K. RAMAKRISHNA & A. TAN, *The New Terrorism: Diagnosis and Prescriptions*, in A. TAN & K. RAMAKRISHNA (eds.), *o.c.*, p. 3.

[53] E.R. MULLER, R.F.J. SPAAIJ & A.G.W. RUITENBERG, *Trends in Terrorism*, Alphen aan den Rijn, Kluwer, 2003, pp. 146-205.

it would give the terrorists *carte blanche* to kidnap and kill people in order to force a nation to do their will. Thirdly, it could possibly endanger citizens at home.

Despite the undeniable emphasis on a military strategy with a really limited effectiveness, as we will see in the following section, much has already been done to enhance the deployment of intelligence services, and bilateral and international cooperation in the fight against terrorism. In any case, there is little doubt about the conviction that this trans-national approach is not just a branch, but the stem of an effective counterterrorism policy. Nevertheless, we should not cherish high expectations, because all scholars agree that terrorism always, in one form or another, makes up part of the world political order, and that it will never be totally destroyed. There will always be somebody with power who isn't happy with the way things are going and who cannot be prevented from attacking our open societies.

This should not discourage us, because with effective national and international specialised organisations, we will be rather capable of reducing the number of terrorist attacks in the future. This reduction can come about only if we never forget that there is more to do in the fight against terrorism than developing repressive approaches. We also should obviate the causes and breeding grounds of the problem, the most important and challenging factor in the fight. In any case, we are convinced that no unilateral response will eradicate this threat. What is needed is a collective security system with bilateral and multilateral responses firmly supported and guided by the United Nations.

3.3. Beyond narrow borders: the necessity of international cooperation

While terrorism in the past had been mainly restricted to specific countries and regions, it has now become a trans-national phenomenon. "Terrorists," Adel Maged rightly observes, "enjoy the benefits of globalization: modern technology, easy access to information, free world-wide communication and free movement of capital." One trend, he goes on to say, is the shift from well-organised located groups to loosely organised, international networks of terrorists. Another trend is the change of motivation for terrorism from being primarily political to more religious or ideological. Clearly, this evolution and globalisation of terrorism requires global cooperation to combat it.[54]

It seems obvious that nations and various organisations should be joining forces against this phenomenon. Lamentably, such an international approach has been "easier said than done." The United States took a unilateral approach; NATO is still not sure of its role and contribution, and is still militarily reorienting itself. Europe seems much more like a 'roaring mouse' while the United Nations appears to be paralysed by its own internal organisation. But nobody can deny that each of them, is doggedly seeking new and more effective methods to fight terrorism. Below we will discuss their most important steps since the 9/11 attacks.

3.3.1. The United States

Did the American intelligence fail?[55] That question is everywhere in the post-September 11 literature, and the answer is mainly 'yes.' The terrorism expert Walter Laqueur tells us in his book *No End to War*[56] that the reality was much more complex. Certainly there was a failure of intelligence, Laqueur says. There were several serious terrorist attacks in the years prior to 9/11: the amateurish

---

[54] A. MAGED, *International Legal Cooperation: An Essential Tool in the War Against Terrorism*, in W.P. HEERE (ed.), *o.c.*, p. 161.

[55] In December 2002 the joint Congressional panel asked for an internal investigation by the Central Intelligence Agency about who should be held accountable for the failure of the intelligence service. Among those criticised in the report, was George Tenet, the former intelligence chief who, at the end of 2004, was rewarded a '*Medal of Freedom*' by President George W. Bush. (D. JEHL, *C.I.A. Report Finds Its Officials Failed in Pre-9/11 Efforts*, in *The New York Times* (January 7, 2005). See: http://query.nytimes.com/gst/abstract.html? res=F509 16F83A5D0C748CDDA80894DD404482

[56] W. LAQUEUR, *No End to War. Terrorism in the Twenty-first Century*, New York & London, Continuum, 2003, pp. 119-146.

attempt to blow up the World Trade Center in New York, the attacks on the Khobar barracks in Saudi Arabia, the bombing of the embassies in East Africa and, not least, the attack on the US warship *Cole*. But too little changed and not enough priority was given to Islamic terrorism and effective counteraction. Also, the blame should not be on the intelligence agencies alone since the media also collected and evaluated information on terrorist events. Of course this is a controversial point of view because it suggests that the media are giving terrorists a forum[57] when they broadcast their messages. So, it seems that there will always be a tension between too little and too much information about terrorism. Furthermore, research on terrorism was too theoretical. It appears that theories were more important than Middle East realities. "In such a climate," Walter Laqueur writes, "there is a strong incentive to put theoretical commitment before empirical observation. Even though this had been the source of repeated error, breaking out of this ideological circle was to run the risk of being denounced as a disciplinary naïf or a latent Orientalist."

After the 9/11 attacks, President Bush drastically changed US foreign politics. First he offered China new opportunities for economic cooperation, and turned a blind eye toward human rights violations when China wanted to become a member of the antiterrorism coalition. Secondly, he became very interested in the United Nations because he understood the potential power of that organisation in the fight against terrorism. Nevertheless, the UN was of interest only so long as it supported US politics. From the moment it no longer gave support, as was the case in the war on Iraq (March 2003), there was hardly any hesitation on the part of

---

[57] It was Brian Jenkins who wrote that terrorists want people to listen, not to be dead. But that was before the wave of international terrorism. Twenty-five years later he adjusted his opinion and concluded that there was a change in terrorist minds, and that there was a real danger that terrorists one day would use nuclear weapons. (See: B. JENKINS, *Will Terrorists Go Nuclear?*, Santa Monica, CA, Rand, 1976, pp. 6-7; and B. JENKINS, *Will Terrorists Go Nuclear? A Reappraisal*, in H.W. KUSHNER (ed.), *The Future of Terrorism*, Thousand Oaks, CA, Sage Publications, 1998, p. 249.)

the US to forge "its own 'coalition of the willing' – which looks more like a coalition of the coerced."[58] Thirdly, Washington enthusiastically accepted that NATO for the first time in its history invoked Article 5. But the Bush government quickly realised that NATO was divided, not in its support for the fight against terrorism, but in its compliance with American plans. The US saw that in the first phase of the fight NATO's help would actually slow down its military operations and it was clear that NATO had little to offer against terrorism, though it was potentially a strong partner in the aftermath of the Afghanistan and Iraq wars. Fourthly, Europe was not a partner of the US though there was a great deal of cooperation between America and individual European countries such as the United Kingdom, Spain and Poland. Nevertheless, despite the relations between America, NATO and UN, the blame for the lack of cooperation between America and Europe seems to rest in part with the divided European Community itself.[59]

The military battle against terrorism has not been a total success. Al-Qaida suffered enormous losses. The Americans hunted down militants and squeezed the organisation. But these actions inspired many new sympathisers to join al-Qaida and turned up new groups around the world.[60] This has increased the difficulty of fighting terrorism and underlines more than ever the importance of effective intelligence cooperation. These developments make it clear that even inside the US a new approach is needed. In the immediate aftermath of the attacks, the Rand Institute (an

[58] T.R. MOCKAITIS, *Winning Hearts and Minds in the 'War on Terrorism'*, in ID. & P.B. RICH (eds.), *Grand Strategy in the War Against Terrorism*, London/Portland, Frank Cass, 2003, p. 35.

[59] C. HACKE, *Die amerikanische Aussenpolitik nach dem 11. September*, in H. FRANK & K. HIRSCHMANN (eds.), *Die weltweite Gefahr. Terrorismus als internationale Herausforderung*, Berlin, Berlin Verlag, 2002, pp. 331-347.

[60] Peter Chalk noticed that al-Qaeda (literally the 'Base') has "an interlocking complex of overseas terrorist organizations and cells that is thought to link extremists in at least 40 countries." (P. CHALK, *Al Qaeda and its Links to Terrorist Groups in Asia*, in A. TAN & K. RAMAKRISHNA (eds.), *o.c.*, p. 108.)

important American research organisation focusing on national security issues) wrote that it was difficult – in fact impossible – to coordinate the activities of so many executive branch departments and agencies. "There is constant tension between the coordinator's enumerated responsibilities and limited means."[61] The American government seems to have learned its lesson so that by the end of 2004 the American Congress and President Bush were enacting the recommendations of the September 11 commission.[62] Among other things, the government approved "the largest overhaul of US intelligence gathering in 50 years."[63] The bill that Congress passed also led to the creation of a *National Counterterrorism Center* to coordinate terrorism intelligence throughout the government, the establishment of an independent *civil liberties board* to review the government's privacy policies, and the appointment of a national intelligence director to be responsible for all spy agencies within the Pentagon (including the *National Security Agency*) and other intelligence organisations, like the CIA and the FBI.[64]

However, it seems these decisions have sidelined civil liberties and human rights. Advocates of civil liberties opposed this bill because it granted new surveillance and anti-immigration powers that 'endanger constitutional protections.' The centralisation of the intelligence community's surveillance powers increases the likelihood of government abuses. For example, the expansion of wiretap authority can give rise to such abuses.[65] So much has changed since September 11.

---

[61] RAND, *Issue Paper. Organizing for Homeland Security*, Rand, 2002, p. 3.

[62] For the 9-11 commission report, see: http://www.9-11commission.gov/report/index.htm

[63] See: http://www.cnn.com/2004/ALLPOLITICS/12/17/intelligence.reform.ap/

[64] For the complete document of the intelligence reform, see: http://news.findlaw.com/hdocs/docs/terrorism/irtpa2004.pdf

[65] P. SHENON, *Accord Reached on Overhauling U.S. Intelligence*, in *The New York Times* (December 7, 2004). We will come back to the violations of civil and human rights in point 2.4.

3.3.2. Europe

After the terrorist attack of March 11 2004 in Madrid the European Council wrote a *Declaration on Combating Terrorism*[66] in which it said that it was "deeply shocked" by this attack. Just like the *European Security Strategy*,[67] this document identified terrorism as one of the key threats to EU interests. Therefore the Council called for the development of an EU long-term strategy to address all the factors that contribute to terrorism. It proposed legislative measures, the reinforcement of operational cooperation and the maximisation of the effectiveness of information systems. Moreover, the document also emphasised the importance of strengthening border controls and document security, the development of strategic objectives for a revised EU plan of action to combat terrorism, the obligation to share intelligence, the prevention of the financing of terrorism, the necessity of measures to protect transportation facilities and the population in general. It also recommended more international cooperation, and the establishment of the position of a counterterrorism coordinator.[68] This led to many (often already ongoing) initiatives, proposed in the first update of the EU *Plan of Action on Combating Terrorism*.[69]

But these documents did not express a really new attitude within the EU. Already even before September 11, Europe had a great deal of experience in fighting terrorism. Nevertheless, as Monica Den Boer, the *Managing Director of the Euopean Institute for Law Enforcement Cooperation*, correctly notices, these experiences with terrorism "have traditionally mainly – although not solely – been of the 'domestic type.' As a consequence, governments by and

---

[66] See: http://www.statewatch.org/news/2004/mar/eu-terr-decl.pdf (document dated: 25 March 2004).

[67] See: http://ue.eu.int/uedocs/cmsUpload/78367.pdf (document dated: 12 December 2003).

[68] This last demand was immediately redeemed with the appointment of Gijs de Vries to this position by Javier Solana, at the same meeting of the European Council of 25 March 2004.

[69] See: http://ue.eu.int/uedocs/cmsUpload/EUplan16090.pdf (This first update is from 14 December 2004. The document will be updated twice a year.)

large have approached anti-terrorist policies from a national perspective."[70] Indeed, with the experiences of the *IRA* in Northern Ireland, the *Cellules Communistes Combattantes* in Belgium, the *Rote Armee Fraktion* in Germany, the *Action Directe* in France, the *ETA* in Spain and the *Red Brigades* in Italy – to mention only a few – Europe has much domestic counterterrorist experience. Given that many of today's terrorist movements transcend domestic concerns, it has become increasingly important for the EU to develop a policy against terrorism across national borders.

Already some years before 9/11 there was a consensus among EU member states that terrorism was one of the main challenges of the Union. With the *Treaty of Maastricht* (1993) and the *Treaty of Amsterdam* (1999) Europe took big steps forward in inter-governmental cooperation in the fight against terrorism. The *Treaty of Maastricht* (especially in chapter VI) provides for the first time a legal basis for the fight against international terrorism in the EU, which was strengthened and expanded by the *Treaty of Amsterdam*. And as a result of the rapid development of EU justice and home affairs in the 1990's, the structural bases for the fight against terrorism at the EU level have improved considerably.[71]

But it is clear that European counterterrorism plans have accelerated since September 11. Some speak about the weeks between 20 September and 19 October 2001 as the 'month of transformation.' Since then decision-making about terrorism has advanced with several EU meetings and the widening of the mandate of several groups and institutions, like the *Task Force of Chiefs of Police*[72] and *Europol*, and the setting up of *Eurojust*, a cross-border prosecution unit,

---

[70] M. DEN BOER, *The EU Counter-Terrorism Wave: Window of Opportunity or Profound Policy Transformation?*, in M. VAN LEEUWEN (ed.), *Confronting Terrorism. European Experiences, Threat Perceptions and Policies*, The Hague/London/New York, Kluwer Law International, 2003, 185-206, p. 185.

[71] J. MONAR, *The European Response to 11 September 2001: Bases for Action, Performance and Limits*, p. 2-4. (Zie: http://tecn.rutgers.edu/cgcg/Presentations/ JHA-TERRORISM-NEWARK.doc)

[72] See: http://europa.eu.int/comm/justice_home/fsj/police/chief/wai/fsj_police-task_force_en.htm

officially adopted on 28 February 2002.[73] But perhaps the most surprising thing was the quick introduction of a *European Arrest Warrant*,[74] in only three months. It was expected to take several years.[75]

Europol is the abbreviation of *European Police Office*. Its objective is to improve the effectiveness and cooperation between the member states in the prevention of and fight against terrorism, unlawful drug trafficking, trafficking in nuclear and radioactive substances, illegal immigrant smuggling, trade in human beings and in motor vehicle crimes. But with actual and serious terrorist threats present, there is undeniably an emphasis on counterterrorism in Europol's activities. In its Convention[76] Europol describes its tasks in three parts. In the first part, it mentions facilitating the exchange of information between member states; obtaining, collating and analysing information and intelligence;[77] notifying the

---

[73] See: http://europa.eu.int/eur-lex/pri/en/oj/dat/2002/l_063/l_063200203 06en00010013.pdf

[74] The Warrant replaces the existing text: 1) the 1957 European Extradition Convention and the 1978 European Convention on the suppression of terrorism as regards extradition; 2) the agreement of 26 May 1989 between 12 member states on simplifying the transmission of extradition requests; 3) the 1995 Convention on the simplified extradition procedure; 4) the 1996 Convention on extradition; and 5) the relevant provisions of the Schengen agreement. (http://europa.eu.int/scadplus/leg/en/lvb/l33167.htm)

For the full text of the *Warrant*, see: http://europa.eu.int/eur-lex/pri/en/oj/dat/2002/l_190/l_19020020718en00010018.pdf.

[75] J. MONAR, *Art. cit.*, p. 18. Nevertheless, human rights and civil liberties organisations like *Statewatch* declared to be concerned about the speed at which the Council has agreed to this Warrant. They feel that too much attention went to the facilitation of investigations and prosecutions, and not enough to fundamental human rights, like the rights for suspects and defendants.

(See for example: http://www.statewatch.org/news/2001/oct/ewarrant.pdf)

[76] See: http://www.europol.eu.int/index.asp?page=legalconv (especially pp. 4-6.)

[77] It is important to notice here that experts from over 30 countries (all over the world) have established a network "that aims to make it easier to deal with criminals who have sheltered their illicit profits abroad." This *Camden Asset Recovery Inter-Agency Network* (CARIN) was a Dutch and Belgian initiative, with the cooperation of Ireland, UK, Austria, Eurojust, and later Germany. CARIN was launched in September 2004. This network must make it possible "to contact foreign colleagues in order to facilitate and speed up asset recovery operations." (http://www.europol.eu.int/index.asp?page=news&news=pr040923.htm)

competent authorities of the member states via the national units; to aid investigations in these states by forwarding all relevant information; and maintaining a computerised system of collected information. The second part is about the improvement of "the cooperation and effectiveness of the competent authorities in the Member States through the national units." This is done by developing specialist knowledge of the investigative procedures of the competent authorities and by providing advice on investigations; by providing strategic intelligence to assist with and promote the efficient and effective use of the resources available; and by preparing general situation reports. The last part deals with training the members of the competent authorities of all member states, the organisation and equipment of these authorities, the development of crime prevention methods, and technical and forensic investigative procedures.

It is clear that there is strong cooperation between Europol with the member states – also the most recent member states[78] – and with Eurojust[79] (see also *infra*) in combating organised crime. But the organisation went further in developing a network, even beyond the borders of the EU. In March 2004, for example, it expanded its cooperation by signing an agreement with the *United Nations Office on Drugs and Crime* (UNODC).[80] And earlier, at the end of 2002, together with the US, it signed an agreement which stated that they "are now able to fully implement the existing co-operation at a more operational level, to include the exchange of personal data."[81]

Eurojust is the judicial cooperation unit of the EU. It was established in 2002[82] to enhance the effectiveness of the competent

[78] See for example: http://www.europol.eu.int/index.asp?page=news&news=pr041215.htm

[79] http://www.europol.eu.int/index.asp?page=news&news=pr040609.htm

[80] http://www.europol.eu.int/index.asp?page=news&news=pr021220.htm

[81] http://www.europol.eu.int/index.asp?page=news&news=pr021220.htm

[82] The establishment was of course more complex than this. Elaine Krivel writes: "The European Council at the Tampere Summit in October 1999 determined that a judicial co-operation unit called Eurojust should be established. On

authorities within member states, dealing with the investigation and prosecution of serious cross-border and organised crime. Eurojust describes its task as: stimulating and improving the coordination between competent authorities in the Member States; taking into account any request emanating from a competent authority of a Member State and any information provided by any body within the framework of the Treaties; improving the cooperation between the competent authorities of the Member States, in particular by facilitating the execution of international mutual legal assistance and the implementation of extradition requests; and supporting the competent authorities of the Member States in order to render their investigations and prosecutions more effective when dealing with cross-border crime.[83]

As mentioned earlier, Eurojust closely cooperates with Europol, but the organisation also has strong connections with the *European Judicial Network* (EJN)[84] and with OLAF, the *European Anti-Fraud Office*.[85] It also works to develop a better awareness of its facilities and capacities, not only inside the member states, but also outside Europe. In its *Annual Report* for 2002[86] Eurojust indicated that Canada, Norway, Switzerland, Liechtenstein, the US and Japan had created contact points with it. It prepared itself, for example, for EU enlargement (1 May 2004) by introducing a system of 'godparents' to link candidate states to current Eurojust national members and by organising a seminar on Eurojust, as early as September 2003. It also sees the Russian Federation as an

---

December 14, 2000, the Council of the European Union established provisional judicial co-operation unit of Eurojust. Work by Eurojust began on March 1, 2001. On September 20, 2001, the Council issued a Decision on Terrorism. On December 15, 2001, the Council Declaration of Laeken indicated that Eurojust would be located in The Hague. And lastly by the Council Decision of February 28, 2002 (…) Eurojust was formally established." (E. KRIVEL, *The Evolution of Eurojust*, see: http://www.iap.nl.com/eurojust.htm)

[83] http://www.eurojust.eu.int

[84] See: http://europa.eu.int/comm/justice_home/ejn/index_en.htm

[85] See: http://europa.eu.int/comm/dgs/olaf/

[86] http://www.eurojust.eu.int/pdfannual/annual2002.pdf (p. 31)

important future partner in the fight against organised cross-border crime.[87]

The existing and further developing cooperation between the EU and the US is a hopeful and indispensable instrument in an effective fight against terrorism. Nevertheless, we must conclude that these cooperation initiatives do not reverse the fact that the US and the EU mainly do things their own way. Sometimes this leads to controversy, as with the acceptance of the Resolution on judicial cooperation by the European Parliament on December 13, 2001 where a categorical resistance to the US death penalty was expressed.[88] It is clear that fundamental differences of opinion like these will often make cooperation more difficult, but not necessarily undermine common initiatives and operations. What is much more threatening, for an effective fight against terrorism, is the fact that too many actors – on both the US and EU side – are involved, and that they bring with them overlapping competences.

3.3.3. NATO

Since the collapse of the USSR and the fall of the Berlin Wall (1989), NATO has been searching for a new profile and task. It seems to have found a new task in the stabilising and rebuilding of Afghanistan, and in a half-hearted contribution to the fight against terrorism. Nevertheless, NATO appears to be a victim of the ongoing Euro-American tensions. The EU and the US advocate different approaches to fighting terrorism, the US giving much more credence to military actions than the EU. It is very difficult to gather the member states of NATO around one concrete and effective plan on which they all can agree, and want to participate. That raises the often-asked question whether NATO still has a contribution to make in the world today.

After September 11, NATO responded quickly and in a determined way. In a declaration the same day it wrote that the Allies

---

[87] http://www.eurojust.eu.int/pdfannual/ar2003/Euj%20008%20Annual%20Report%20EN2.pdf (pp. 40-41)

[88] J. MONAR, *a.c.*, pp. 159-160.

stood united in their determination to combat the terrorist 'scourge'. "At this critical moment," the organisation stated, "the United States can rely on its 18 Allies in North America and Europe for assistance and support. NATO solidarity remains the essence of our Alliance. Our message to the people of the United States is that we are with you. Our message to those who perpetrated these unspeakable crimes is equally clear: you will not get away with it."[89] Two days later, in a joint statement, NATO and Russia declared to be "united in their resolve not to let those responsible for such an inhuman act to go unpunished. NATO and Russia call[ed] on the entire international community to unite in the struggle against terrorism."[90] This brought NATO and Russia closer together, and became a key point in NATO-Russia cooperation.[91]

In the meantime, on September 12, the North Atlantic Council met and agreed that the attacks were directed from abroad against the United States – a necessary conclusion to invoke Article 5 of the Washington Treaty. This Article states:

"*The Parties agree that an armed attack against one or more of them in Europe or North America shall be considered an attack against them all and consequently they agree that, if such an armed attack occurs, each of them, in exercise of the right of individual or collective self-defence recognised by Article 51 of the Charter of the United Nations,[92] will assist the Party or Parties so attacked by taking forthwith, individually and in concert with the other Parties, such*

---

[89] http://www.nato.int/docu/pr/2001/p01-122e.htm

[90] http://www.nato.int/docu/pr/2001/p010913e.htm

[91] http://www.nato.int/docu/update/2002/12-december/e1209a.htm

[92] See: http://www.un.org/aboutun/charter (Chapter VII) "Nothing in the present Charter shall impair the inherent right of individual or collective self-defence if an armed attack occurs against a Member of the United Nations, until the Security Council has taken measures necessary to maintain international peace and security. Measures taken by Members in the exercise of this right of self-defence shall be immediately reported to the Security Council and shall not in any way affect the authority and responsibility of the Security Council under the present Charter to take at any time such action as it deems necessary in order to maintain or restore international peace and security."

action as it deems necessary, including the use of armed force, to restore and maintain the security of the North Atlantic area. Any such armed attack and all measures taken as a result thereof shall immediately be reported to the Security Council. Such measures shall be terminated when the Security Council has taken the measures necessary to restore and maintain international peace and security."[93] In reality this means that the Allies "can provide any form of assistance they deem necessary to respond to the situation. This assistance is not necessarily military and depends on the material resources of each country."[94]

In addition, NATO came to an agreement concerning eight measures: (1) to enhance intelligence sharing and cooperation; (2) to provide appropriate assistance to Allies and other states that are or may be subject to increased terrorist threats; (3) to take measures to provide increased security for facilities of the US and other Allies; (4) to backfill selected Allied assets in NATO's area of responsibility, required to directly support operations against terrorism; (5) to provide over-flight clearances; (6) to give access to the US and other Allies to ports and airfields on NATO's territory; (7) to deploy elements of NATO's Standing Naval Forces; and (8) to deploy elements of NATO's Airborne Early Warning Force to support operations against terrorism.[95] This agreement became more or less concrete when in October 2001 operations *Eagle Assist* and *Active Endeavour* began. With the first operation, NATO Airborne Warning and Control Systems aircrafts were sent to help the US; and with the second, that started on 26 October, Standing Naval Forces were sent to patrol the Eastern Mediterranean.[96]

In its *Report on the Partnership Action Plan Against Terrorism*[97] from 23 June 2004, NATO made it clear that it focused on the development of practical cooperation (with for example opera-

[93] http://www.nato.int/terrorism/five.htm
[94] http://www.nato.int/docu/pr/2001/p01-124e.htm
[95] http://www.nato.int/docu/speech/2001/s011004b.htm
[96] http://www.nato.int/terrorism/index.htm
[97] http://www.nato.int/docu/basictxt/b040623be.htm

tions and exercises, and border security and management), extended participation (with regional cooperation), the improvement of the cooperation with other international institutions like the UN, and the improvement of support and mentoring mechanisms. All forms of cooperation are important aspects in the fight against terrorism. But one can ask if NATO did not overrate itself and bite off more than it can chew. We agree with Hans Frank,[98] President of the *Bundesakademie für Sicherheitspolitik* in Bonn, that in fact the direct fight of terrorism must not be seen as the task of NATO. Such a fight would overstretch the nature of the Alliance. Perhaps the future of NATO in its contribution to the fight against terrorism, lies in its roots: deterrence or discouragement. The prevention or solution of conflicts between states, should still be the main task of NATO.

This does not mean that there is no place for NATO in the fight against terrorism. It would be better and more effective if it focused on fewer tasks. It will always be an important mediator for the EU, the US, and Russia, and an indispensable partner for the UN. But NATO's tasks in fighting terrorism should be limited to protecting existing nuclear, chemical and biological weapons from falling into terrorist hands, assisting in border security, improving cooperation between the intelligence agencies of the member states, and maybe even the stabilisation of the Middle East,[99] to name but a few examples.

Only when NATO can resist the temptation to overload itself with tasks in the fight against terrorism, will it keep its credibility. Right now it seems to want to prove it has good reasons to exist, at any cost.

---

[98] H. FRANK, *Internationaler Terrorismus: Verändern sich die Sicherheitspolitischen Konstanten?*, in ID. & K. HIRSCHMANN (eds.) *o.c.*, pp. 295-310.

[99] U. WEISSER, *Dieveränderte Sicherheitslage. NATO und EU vor neuen Herausforderungen – Konsequenzen für deutsche Sicherheitspolitik und Streitkräfte*, in H. FRANK & K. HIRSCHMANN (eds.), *o.c.*, 2002, p. 87.

3.3.4. The United Nations

UN-experts have been discussing possible definitions of terrorism for more than half a century, and three Conventions (1963, 1970 and 1971)[100] on the topic have appeared, but it was only in the 70s that the UN really 'discovered' the problematic.[101] Many other Conventions[102] followed, especially leading up to 9/11. But van Ginkel adds a pertinent critical note: "Most of these Conventions were, sadly enough, drafted after specific terrorist attacks had occurred, and can therefore be characterised as repressive instruments. The most recent (draft) Conventions, namely on the suppression of financing of terrorism and on the suppression of nuclear terrorism are, however, of a more preventive character. Nevertheless, each of them is only applicable to a specific act of terrorism. By maintaining this approach, the international community will always risk not being on time to draft a new Convention for yet another kind of terrorist act."[103]

Immediately after the September 11 attacks, the Security Council strongly condemned the terrorist activities against the US and all other states in Resolution 1368 saying it "*unequivocally condemns* in the strongest terms the horrifying terrorist attacks which took place on 11 September 2001 in New York, Washington, D.C. and Pennsylvania and *regards* such acts, like any act of international terrorism, as a threat to international peace and security." Moreover, it called on all states "to work together urgently to bring to justice the perpetrators, organizers and sponsors of these terrorist attacks."[104] On 28 September the Security

---

[100] See: www.un.org/geninfo/faq/factsheets/FS8.HTM

[101] H.-J. HEINTZE, *Ächtung des Terrorismus durch das Völkerrecht*, in H. FRANK & K. HIRSCHMANN (eds.), *o.c.*, p. 71.

[102] For a list of these Conventions, see: http://untreaty.un.org/English/Terrorism.asp

[103] B.T. VAN GINKEL, *The United Nations: Towards a Comprehensive Convention on Combating Terrorism*, in W.P. HEERE (ed.), *Terrorism and the Military. International Legal Implications*, The Hague, TMC Asser Press, p. 213.

[104] *Resolution 1368 (2001), Adopted by the Security Council at its 4370th meeting, on 12 September 2001.* See: http://daccessdds.un.org/doc/UNDOC/GEN/N01/533/82/PDF/N0153382.pdf?OpenElement

Council approved another more comprehensive resolution – Resolution 1373. This responded to the September 11 attacks under Chapter VII of the UN Charter and reaffirmed the condemnations of Resolution 1368 while adding some specific tasks for states in the fight against terrorism like prevention and suppression of the financing of the terrorist acts, and the prevention of terrorist acts by exchange of information. Moreover, the document called for the increase of bilateral and multilateral cooperation in the fight against terrorism while non-cooperation can subject a state to international sanctions.[105]

The same Resolution 1373 asked for the establishment of a *Counter-Terrorism Committee* (CTC), a committee to monitor the implementation of resolution 1373 and report to the Security Council. The UN acknowledges that regional co-operation is fundamental to the fight against terrorism, but it also strongly encourages global activities in the fight against terrorism, and it is exactly the CTC that is charged with the increase of the "global co-ordination of activities and co-operation in the fight against terrorism".[106] Moreover it assists states with the ratification of the existing international conventions on terrorism,[107] and in dialogue with the *Office of the High Commissioner for Human Rights*,[108] keeps an eye on the interaction between counterterrorism strategies and tactics and human rights law.[109]

This brings us to another important task of the UN in the global fight against terrorism: concern for respecting human rights. This is an urgent matter for the UN after September 11. As mentioned above, the *Office of the High Commissioner for Human Rights* has placed a priority on the protection of human rights, "notably the right to life, and the question of protecting human

---

[105] http://daccessdds.un.org/doc/UNDOC/GEN/N01/557/43/PDF/N015 5743.pdf?OpenElement (especially, pp. 2-4)

[106] http://www.un.org/Docs/sc/committees/1373/contacts.html

[107] http://www.un.org/Docs/sc/committees/1373/conventions.html

[108] For more information about this Office, see: http://www.ohchr.org/english/

[109] http://www.un.org/Docs/sc/committees/1373/human_rights.html

rights in the context of counter-terrorism measures."[110] This concern is strongly supported by the UN Secretary-General Kofi Annan, who stated in a speech at a special meeting of the *Counter-Terrorism Committee* in March 2003: "Terrorist acts, particularly those involving the loss of life, constitute grave violations of human rights. Our responses to terrorism, as well as our efforts to thwart it and prevent it should uphold the human rights that terrorists aim to destroy. Human rights, fundamental freedoms and the rule of law are essential tools in the effort to combat terrorism – not privileges to be sacrificed at a time of tension."[111]

Annan and the Commissioner for Human Rights are not alone in their worries. Special UN experts stated at their annual meeting in June 2003: "The fight against terrorism had on occasion also been used as an excuse to cover up or justify other human rights violations, such as the suppression of opposition groups. There was also the feeling that there had been a regression with respect to certain non-derogable human rights norms, for example, court-sanctioned torture and failure to respect the requirements for the declaration of a state of emergency. Particularly disturbing in this regard were actions by states that had previously professed support for human rights."[112] Moreover, the *Digest of Jurisprudence*[113] states that legislation enacted pursuant to Resolution 1373 must be in conformity with the *International Convenant on Civil and Political Rights*,[114] and notices that the *Human Rights Committee*, which oversees this Convenant, is worried about the overly broad definition of the crime of

---

[110] http://www.unhchr.ch/terrorism/

[111] http://www.unis.unvienna.org/unis/pressrels/2003/sgsm8624.html

[112] ECONOMIC AND SOCIAL COUNCIL, *Report of the United Nations High Commissioner for Human Rights and Follow-up to the World Conference on Human Rights. Effective Functioning of Human Rights Mechanisms*, n° 27, p. 10. See: http://www.unhchr.ch/Huridocda/Huridoca.nsf/(Symbol)/E.CN.4.2004.4. En?Opendocument

[113] See: http://www.ohchr.org/english/about/publications/docs/digest.doc

[114] See: http://www.unhchr.ch/html/menu3/b/a_ccpr.htm

terrorism,[115] and measures taken against terrorism that exceed the limits of Resolution 1373.[116]

These concerns will be more relevant in the next section where we focus on the problem between fighting terrorism and respecting human rights. But we need to conclude here with some discussion about the relevance of the *International Criminal Court* (ICC). This court was established on 17 July 1998. (Its Statute was entered into force on 1 July 2002 and adopted by 120 states.) The ICC describes itself as "the first ever permanent, treaty-based, international criminal court established to promote the rule of law and ensure that the gravest international crimes do not go unpunished."[117] Following the *Rome Statute of the International Criminal Court*[118] the ICC has an enormous and multilateral co-ordinate responsibility to try genocide, crimes against humanity and war crimes cases.

Anyone who commits any of the crimes under the Rome Statute, is liable to prosecution by the Court. In this sense, it seems to us that cases of international terrorism, seen as offences against the world community, should be tried as crimes against humanity by the ICC. An important supplementary advantage of this approach would be that violations against presumed terrorists, like those we will discuss below, will probably disappear, though we are not very optimistic about that possibility. It is unlikely, for example, that the larger nations of the world will catch persons suspected of terrorist activities and immediately deliver them to

---

[115] HUMAN RIGHTS COMMITTEE, *Concluding Observations of the Human Rights Committee: Estonia 15/04/2003. CCPR/CO/77/EST. (Concluding Observations/comments)*, art. 8. See: http://www.unhchr.ch/tbs/doc.nsf/0/cc15536c13c4 c49ac1256d0100312a35?Opendocument

[116] HUMAN RIGHTS COMMITTEE, *Concluding Observations of the Human Rights Committee: Yemen 26/07/2003. CCPR/CO/75/YEM. (Concluding Observations/Comments)*, art. 18.
See: http://www.unhchr.ch/tbs/doc.nsf/0/83b4694b87b1f1abc1256c05002 53d65?Opendocument

[117] http://www.icc-cpi.int/about.html

[118] http://www.icc-cpi.int/library/about/officialjournal/Rome_Statute_ 120704-EN.pdf

the ICC. We can only hope this will become automatic, but in the aftermath of 9/11 it seems like a dream for the future. As Madeline Morris writes: "Currently, the prosecution of terrorism cases is pursued at the national level, largely in the targeted State. Given the underlying factors shaping this practice, this arrangement, as imperfect as it is, likely will (…) remain in place for the foreseeable future."[119] In any case, the UN needs to take its responsibility seriously and should persist in the promotion of the ICC as the central court for the trial of terrorists.

3.4. No other choice? Counterterrorism and the violation of human and civil rights

It seems now that as fundamental changes in intelligence and strategies in the fight against terrorism are implemented, human rights and privacy rules will likely be sacrificed. In this section we very briefly want to make some critical comments on US and EU post-9/11 intelligence reforms.

3.4.1. Post-9/11 security measures and civil and human rights critique in the US

On 26 October 2001, only 45 days after the attacks and with hardly a debate, the American Congress passed the *USA Patriot Act*.[120] Almost immediately the document was seriously criticised by defenders of civil and human rights. Especially Section 215, which provides access to records and other items under the *Foreign Surveillance Act*. With it, the FBI has accessed private medical and library records and secretly conducted physical searches or wiretaps on American citizens. The essence of the debate is about the violation of the *First Amendment* – which states that people have the

---

[119] M. MORRIS, *Prosecuting Terrorism: The Quandaries of Criminal Jurisdiction and International Relations*, in W.P. HEERE (ed.), *o.c.,* p. 146.

[120] For the full text of the *USA Patriot Act*, see: http://www.aclu.org/SafeandFree/SafeandFree.cfm?ID=12251&c=207.

right to practice the religion of their choice, freedom of speech, free press, a right to gather in public to protest, and otherwise express their views in a non-violent way, and that people have the right to appeal to the government for or against policies that affect them, and the *Fourth Amendment* – which protects the right of people to be secure in their persons, houses, papers, and effects, against unreasonable searches and seizures.[121]

In February 2003 a second piece of legislation – the *Domestic Security Enhancement Act of 2003* or the so-called the *USA Patriot Act II*[122] – leaked out even before it was released. The sequel gave the government "broad, sweeping new powers to increase domestic intelligence-gathering, surveillance and law enforcement prerogatives, and simultaneously decrease judicial review and public access to information."[123] An additional problem in this document was the further limitation of the 'public's right-to-know.'[124] As a memo of the *American Society of Newspaper Editors* (ASNE) stated, this document was the continuation of "the disturbing trend started by the Fall 2001 USA Patriot Act of Congressional erosion of civil liberties ranging from immigrants' rights, to the right to challenge secret evidence at trial, to the right to be free of intrusive wiretapping without the existence of a court-issued search warrant."[125]

But perhaps even more important is the *Intelligence Reform Act*[126] which came into force by the end of 2004. This act brought about

---

[121] M. GEIST & M. HOMSI, *The Long Arm of the USA Patriot Act: A Threat to Canadian Privacy? A Submission on the USA Patriot Act to the B.C. Information and Privacy Commissioner*, 2004, p. 10. (See: http://www.mgblog.com/resc/Geisthomsipatriotact.pdf)

[122] For the full text of the *USA Patriot Act II*, see: http://www.dailyrotten.com/source-docs/patriot2draft.html.

[123] C. LEWIS & A. MAYLE, *Justice Dept. Drafts Sweeping Expansion of Anti-Terrorism Act*, see: http://www.public-i.org/dtaweb/report.asp?ReportID=502

[124] http://www.ombwatch.org/article/articleprint/1324/-1/163/ (See also in: *OMB Watcher* 4 (3) 2003.)

[125] http://www.asne.org/index.cfm?ID=4348 (p. 1)

[126] For the full text of this reform, see: http://news.findlaw.com/hdocs/docs/terrorism/irtpa2004.pdf.

far-reaching reforms of the intelligence services. It is very controversial because it declares that if the government says that someone
is a terrorist and a flight risk, the defendant must prove that he or
she is not. This "turns the presumption of innocence on its head,
since in criminal cases, the Constitution requires that defendants
do not have to prove anything in order to enjoy freedom."[127]
Another problem with this act is that there is an emphasis on an
intelligence-centered approach, much more than on law enforcement. This is in the line of the post-September 11 rhetoric of intelligence and prevention. As civil liberties lawyer Kate Martin wrote
in an article earlier the same year: "There is every reason to fear
that the Administration's insistence on describing the domestic
counterterrorism task as an 'intelligence' one is a back door effort
to construct a new approach that would allow the use of 'intelligence' and military methods against individuals, including citizens,
found in the United States and fully protected by the Constitution."[128] Analysing the *Intelligence Reform Act*, we must conclude
that Martin's conclusions are right and that the Bush administration did indeed opt for the 'intelligence paradigm.' This has enormous consequences for the way the intelligence agencies will work.
The costs of this reorganisation will be enormous, it will work inef-
fectively and, not the least, there is a great danger that this way of
working will focus on communities much more than on dangerous
individuals. But it has already been proved that this not only leads
to violations of human rights, it also blinds the eyes of the intelligence agencies to what is really going on.

Before September 11, racial profiling was known to be wide-
spread. President Bush promised that he and his government
would end it. An important step in this direction was taken with

---

[127] A.P. NAPOLITANO, *Our Liberty Under Siege*, in *The Baltimore Sun*, December
29 (2004). See: http://www.baltimoresun.com/news/opinion/oped/bal-op.patriot
29dec29,0,7430011.story?coll=bal-oped-headlines

[128] K. MARTIN, *Domestic Intelligence and Civil Liberties*, in *SAIS Review* XXIV
(1) (2004), p. 13. See also: http://www.saisreview.org/PDF/24.1martin.pdf

the *End Racial Profiling Act*[129] sponsored by Senator Russell Fein-
gold and Representative John Conyers on June 6 2001. But with
the events a few months later, this act fell into oblivion and new
measures in the fight on terrorism were accepted. From that
moment on, the federal government focused on Arabs, Arab
Americans, Muslims, Sikhs and South Asians, and again took
racial profiling for granted. In a report[130] against racial profiling,
the *Leadership Conference on Civil Rights Education Fund* condemned this trend. It exposed new forms of profiling in the anti-
terrorism context and called attention to "detaining and deporting
[of] Arabs and Muslims who are uninvolved in terrorism; and the
singling out of young Arab men for questioning based on nothing
other than their ethnicity."[131] But on 26 February 2004, a new
End Racial Profiling Act[132] was proposed in the House of Representatives, and in September of that same year, *Amnesty International* put pressure on the American government by publishing its
document *Threat and Humiliation*.[133]

One last example of the violation of human rights we want to
discuss concerns the torture practices of the detainees at Guantanamo Bay and the Abu Graib prison. In the course of 2004
and 2005, horrible photographs of ill-treated prisoners reached
a broad public. Sleep deprivation, beatings and chaining seemed
to be the most 'common' practices even though they are clearly
contrary to the *Geneva Convention*[134] (1949) and the *Convention*

---

[129] See: http://www.aele.org/s989.html
[130] LEADERSHIP CONFERENCE ON CIVIL RIGHTS EDUCATION FUND, *Wrong
Then, Wrong Now. Racial Profiling Before & After September 11, 2001*, p. 48.
(http://www.civilrights.org/publications/reports/racial_profiling/racial_profil-
ing_report.pdf)
[131] *Ibid.*, p. 5-6 (quotation), report pp. 22-28.
[132] See: http://www.theorator.com/bills108/hr3847.html
[133] AMNESTY INTERNATIONAL, *Threat and Humiliation. Racial Profiling, Domestic Security, and Human Rights in the United States*, New York, Amnesty International USA, 2004, p. 50.
(See: http://www.amnestyusa.org/racial_profiling/report/rp_report.pdf)
[134] See: http://www.unhchr.ch/html/menu3/b/91.htm

Against Torture and Other Cruel, Inhuman and Degrading Treatment or Punishment[135] (1987). But not only do these photographs throw light on the humiliation of detainees, released prisoners told horrifying stories about what happened to them.[136] In addition to these former prisoners, human rights organisations such as *Human Rights Watch* (HRW) and the *American Civil Liberties Union* (ACLU) also complained about these violation of human rights. The ACLU accused the CIA of categorically withholding records concerning wrongdoing in Iraq.[137] HRW also wrote critical reports[138] about the state of human rights, especially in Guantanamo Bay. And, after its own investigation[139] *Human Rights First* – the former *Lawyer Committee of Human Rights* – even demanded "a comprehensive, independent 9/11-style Commission investigation with similar powers and authority."[140]

In December 2004 an e-mail directed to senior members of the FBI was detected in which a reference was made to an Executive Order "that permitted military interrogators in Iraq to place detainees in painful stress positions, impose sensory deprivation

---

[135] See: http://www.unhchr.ch/html/menu3/b/h_cat39.htm
[136] See for example: http://www.statewatch.org/news/2004/aug/guantanamo-statement.pdf; or
http://observer.guardian.co.uk/print/0,3858,5120738-102285,00.html
[137] See: http://www.aclu.org/SafeandFree/SafeandFree.cfm?ID=17224&c=206
[138] See among others: http://hrw.org/backgrounder/usa/gitmo1004/gitmo1004.pdf; http://hrw.org/english/docs/2004/11/05/usdom9615_txt.htm; http://hrw.org/english/docs/2004/01/09/usdom6917_txt.htm;
and http://hrw.org/english/docs/2004/09/15/usdom9350_txt.htm (letter to Secretary Donald Rumsfeld).
For an extensive report on human rights abuses of detainees after September 11, see: HUMAN RIGHTS WATCH, *Presumption of Guilt. Human Rights Abuses of Post-September 11 Detainees*, New York, 2002, p. 96.
[139] See: HUMAN RIGHTS FIRST, *Ending Secret Detentions*, New York, 2004, pp. 14-15; and the earlier report LAWYERS COMMITTEE FOR HUMAN RIGHTS, *Assessing the New Normal. Liberty and Security for the Post-September 11 United States*, 2003, 126 p. (especially pp. 49-72)
[140] http://www.humanrightsfirst.org/us_law/after_911/PDF/9_11_3rd_anniversary.pdf (p. 7)

through the use of hoods, intimidate them with military dogs and use other coercive methods."[141] And again it was HRW that, in the words of its executive director Kenneth Roth, demanded that President Bush give a full explanation of these and other similar events, and no longer hide behind simple denials.

These are only a few examples of civil and human rights in American post-9/11 politics. There is also the ill-treatment of immigrants, refugees, asylum seekers and minorities; violations of the right to privacy; erosion of the open government laws; biometric systems, possible abuse of passenger name records (PNR); and infringement of human rights within border control policies.[142] The above-discussed examples show that there is not only a tension between protecting (democratic) values in the fight against terrorism; they show that in this struggle some civil liberties and human rights are sacrificed. Therefore it was no surprise that the authors of the document *America's Challenge* are sympathetic with a wide-ranging response on terrorism, but at the same time warn: "[O]ur new security measures must be effective rather than merely dramatic, and must not destroy what we are trying to defend. (...) We believe it is possible both to defend and to protect core American values and principles, but doing so requires a different approach. It is too easy to say that if we abandon our civil liberties the terrorists will win. It is just as easy to say that without security there will be little room for liberty."[143] In this

---

[141] http://hrw.org/english/docs/2004/12/21/usint9925.htm

[142] See for example the analytic documents: INTERNATIONAL HELSINKI FEDERATION FOR HUMAN RIGHTS, *Anti-terrorism Measures, Security and Human Rights. Developments in Europe, Central Asia and North America in the Aftermath of September 11*, Vienna, International Helsinki Federation for Human Rights, 2003, p. 256; and LAWYERS COMMITTEE FOR HUMAN RIGHTS, *Imbalance of Powers. How Changes to U.S. Law & Policy Since 9/11 Erode Human Rights and Civil Liberties*, New York, Lawyers Committee for Human Rights, 2003, p. 111.

[143] M.A. CHISHTI, D. MEISSNER, D.G. PAPADEMETRIOU, J. PETERZELL, M.J. WISHNIE & S.W. YALE-LOEHR, *America's Challenge. Domestic Security, Civil Liberties, and National Unity after September 11*, Washington, Migration Policy Institute, 2003, p. 7.

case it is promising that on 16 April 2003 President George Bush appointed Daniel W. Sutherland to serve as the head of the newly established *Office for Civil Rights and Civil Liberties* (CRCL). This is a Department whose task it is to offer legal, policy and warrant reviews to the government, and to watch over equal employment opportunity.[144] Nevertheless, we will have to wait for the first real results of this Office before we can really evaluate its contribution to the protection of civil rights.

3.4.2. Post-9/11 security measures and civil and human rights critics in the EU and the United Kingdom

In a submission[145] to the *Group of Specialists on Human Rights and the Fight Against Terrorism*,[146] *Amnesty International* has pointed to some shortcomings in EU politics and documents concerning human rights in the fight against terrorism. In this document, *Amnesty* stated that many of our rights are at stake in the so-called 'war on terrorism': freedom of expression; freedom of association; liberty; privacy; confidential communications between lawyer and client; fair trial (including rights of people who are detained); not to be tortured or subjected to other forms of cruel, inhuman or degrading treatment or punishment; and to seek and enjoy asylum. But *Amnesty* especially complained about the vague and/or broad definition of terrorism, and the indefinite detention and questionable protection strategies for refugees, especially in the UK. They also criticised the extradition politics of the EU, and the significant weakness in the current system of human rights protection in the context of internal conflicts and situations of internal tension, because there is not an international mechanism to

---

[144] HOMELAND SECURITY, *Report to Congress on Implementation of Section 705 of the Homeland Security Act and the Establishment of the Office for Civil Rights and Civil Liberties*, 2004, pp. 11-14. (See: http://www.dhs.gov/interweb/assetlibrary/ CRCL-ReportJun04.pdf)

[145] http://web.amnesty.org/library/pdf/IOR610052001ENGLISH/$File/ IOR6100501.pdf

[146] The Committee had its first meeting in September 2004. For the document of this first meeting, see: http://www.icj.org/IMG/pdf/Steering_Committee.pdf

systematically monitor legislation and practice in emergency situations. Below we will briefly focus on the much-debated critique of the treatment of suspected terrorists in the UK.

Already in the first months after the approval of the *Anti-terrorism, Crimes and Security Act* (ATCSA),[147] human rights organisations complained about violations of human rights proceeding from the far-reaching 'liberties' of intelligence and police services within the Act. Mainly the indefinite detention without charge or trial of non-UK nationals under the new legislation was criticised. Not surprisingly, already in July 2002, eleven non-UK nationals challenged the lawfulness of the ATCSA because it violated their human rights. In any case, the power of the Act to charge a person with a criminal offence and convicting him or her without trial, was "inconsistent with the right to liberty and security of person, as guaranteed under Articles 5(3) and 6 of the *European Convention for the Protection of Human Rights and Fundamental Freedoms* (ECHR)[148] and Article 14 of the *International Covenant on Civil and Political Rights* (ICCPR)."[149] The results of these practices are offensive. In September 2004, after being imprisoned for three years, 'D' was released because he was no longer 'a threat to security.' He was "one of 12 foreign nationals being held without due legal process at top security prisons in the UK under the Anti-Terrorism Crime and Security Act (...)."[150] He was only the third of the detainees to be released. Not surprisingly also HRW complained about this arbitrary nature of detention under the ATCSA.[151]

---

[147] For the text of this Act, see: http://www.legislation.hmso.gov.uk/acts/acts2001/20010024.htm.

[148] For the text of this Convention, see: http://www.echr.coe.int/Convention/webConvenENG.pdf.

[149] For the text of this Convenant, see: http://www.hrweb.org/legal/cpr.html (http://web.amnesty.org/library/print/ENGEUR450122002)

[150] *Statewatch* 14 (5) (2004), p. 5.

[151] HUMAN RIGHTS WATCH, *In the Name of Counter-Terrorism: Human Rights Abuses Worldwide. A Human Rights Watch Briefing Paper for the 59ᵗʰ Session of the United Nations Commission on Human Rights*, 2003, p. 20-21. (See: http://www.hrw.org/un/chr59/counter-terrorism-bck.pdf)

Secretary of State for the Home Department David Blunkett understood the grave shortcomings of the Act and charged the *Privy Counsellor Review Committee* to conduct a review of the original 2001 document. This resulted in the *Anti-terrorism, Crimes and Security Act 2001 Review: Report*[152] that was released in December 2003. Nevertheless, almost exactly one year later, on December 16, a committee of the House of Lords released an extensive opinions document[153] that resulted from a complaint of nine appellants in 2002 challenging the lawfulness of their detention. In this document the Lords of the Committee indirectly affirmed the conclusions of human rights organisations.[154] But they also rejected the use of Article 15 of the *European Convention on Human Rights* by the government. This Article states that "in time of war or other public emergency threatening the life of the nation any High Contracting Party may take measures derogating from its obligations under this Convention to the extent strictly required by the exigencies of the situation, provided that such measures are not inconsistent with its other obligations under international law." The conclusion of Lord Nicholls of Birkenhead did not leave much room for interpretation: "In the present case," he concluded, "I see no escape from the conclusion that

---

[152] See: http://www.official-documents.co.uk/document/deps/hc/hc100/100.pdf

[153] See: http://www.statewatch.org/news/2004/dec/belmarsh-appeal.pdf

[154] See for example Lord Hope of Craighead who writes in his concluding article: "I would declare that section 23 of the Anti-terrorism, Crime and Security Act 2001 is incompatible with the right to liberty in article 5 of the European Convention on Human Rights on the ground that it is not proportionate, and that it is incompatible with article 14 of the Convention on the ground that it discriminates against the appellants in their enjoyment of the right to liberty on the ground of their national origin." (in HOUSE OF LORDS, *Opinions of the Lords of Appeal for Judgment in the Cause A (FC) and others (FC) (Appellants) v. Secretary of State for the Home Department (Respondent), X (FC) and another (FC) (Appellants v. Secretary of State for the Home Department (Respondent)*, 2004, article 139, p. 66.)

Parliament must be regarded as having attached insufficient weight to the human rights of non-nationals."[155]

Is this the price we should be prepared to pay in the fight against terrorism? In any case it is clear that any violation of civil or human rights is unacceptable and needs to be criticised and corrected. After September 11 the principles of political realism sneaked into global politics, especially into the fight against terrorism. But no matter how terrible and inhuman the enemy might be, militarist strategies are bound by moral norms and values. To neglect civil and human rights is to endorse the far-reaching and unacceptable realistic cliché that the ends justify the means.

"(…) [I]f we allow ourselves to be convinced that it is our ideals, not our actions, that are under assault, that, despite our enormous power, our very 'civilization' is at stake," the Executive Director of *Amnesty International* USA William Schultz writes, "then there are no limits to what we may do to defend ourselves and no limits on our allies, either. But if we take that route, we risk sacrificing those very ideals that most inspire the rest of the world (…)."[156]

4. CONCLUSION: TOWARD A TIME OF RENEWED WAR ETHICS?

The often-mentioned objection to just war philosophy that it has never prevented or limited a war is true. However, one might wonder about the consequences had the Church not held fast to just war principles and if it had not incessantly called attention to them.[157] Indeed, it is exceptionally difficult, if not impossible, to judge this in

---

[155] N. OF BIRKENHEAD, in HOUSE OF LORDS, *Opinions of the Lords of Appeal for Judgment in the Cause A (FC) and others (FC) (Appellants) v. Secretary of State for the Home Department (Respondent), X (FC) and another (FC) (Appellants v. Secretary of State for the Home Department (Respondent)*, 2004, article 81, p. 48.

[156] W. SCHULTZ, *Tainted Legacy. 9/11 and the Ruin of Human Rights*, New York, Thunder's Mouth Press/Nation Books, 2003, pp. 62-63.

[157] C. MELLON, *o.c.*, p. 130. See also: J.H. YODER, *The 'Just War' Tradition: Is it Credible?*, in *The Christian Century* (1991), p. 298; or http://www.nd.edu/~theo/jhy/writings/justwar/credible.htm.

an objective way. In any case, it is unthinkable that the just war tradition did not have some influence in the course of history.

The actual attitude of people toward the just war tradition is
undeniably ambivalent. On one side, this tradition is more than
ever used as a mirror, especially toward the outside world – for
example by both the Presidents Bush who used it as a means of
legitimation in public justifications of war activities. On the other
side, the just war tradition is discredited by the easy and free interpretation with which it is subject, and the ease with which it can
be misused. At least at first sight, it seems that the principles are
outdated, and have little to contribute to the fight against terrorism.
Just war philosophy addresses wars between nations, not the present situation between regular armies and shadowy international
terrorism. So we should not be really surprised that the principles
of just war philosophy seem outdated.

As we already noticed in the introduction, the current situation
where many peoples are facing the threat of terrorism is not the
first time that the just war tradition has been questioned. Bernard
Adeney described four earlier phases of pressure on tradition. This
means that the recent fight against terrorism, and the way in
which it is waged, can probably be seen as a fifth phase of critique. On the other side, to be completely thorough, we should
inquire into the appropriateness of the critique itself. First of all it
is necessary to emphasise that the just war tradition only deals
with nation-nation conflicts. But this does not mean that, in the
current situation, the tradition is outdated. There are still many
(ongoing) international conflicts where nations fight each other,
and in which the just war philosophy can help judge those situations. Also, as we will show below, even in the fight (not war![158])

[158] It is not because armies are deployed in the fight against terrorists, that we
may call it a war. We should avoid this kind of terminology because it gives terrorists a status they do not deserve. First, they are not uniformed and thus not
clearly distinguishable from ordinary citizens. Secondly, they are not standing up
for the common interests. Thirdly, they deliberately attack citizens. And fourthly, they only accept the rule that there are no limits in the way they fight: for terrorists the end justifies the means. So, calling it a war would not only elevate the

between soldiers and terrorists, certain principles of the just war tradition are still important – even though terrorists do not accept any kind of moral rule in their fighting.

Concerning *just cause* and the specific situation of the fight against terrorism, it is sufficient to say that it will remain an important indispensable principle in any kind of fight. It will never lose its importance. Certainly from the point of view of self-defence, it always seems justified to take action against the aggression of terrorists. But the massive use of military force seems questionable. Nevertheless, a military reaction doesn't exclude the deployment of other means, like agency services. It is the duty of a government (as the 'legal authority') to protect its citizens against (possible) terrorist attacks, and to react to these attacks when the government is incapable of avoiding them. At the same time, and as much, it is a moral duty for the international community, through the voice of the UN, to support governments against terrorism morally and, if necessary, physically. This presents the UN with an important opportunity to renew and regain its credibility and efficacy, which will require a reform of its internal structure and functioning – especially its decision-making.

'*Good intention*' can also be easily defined in this fight. It means that no underlying agenda may influence the decision to fight. For example, it is unacceptable that economic, or more specifically oil interests, should determine the conduct of the fight against terrorism. The one and only aim must be the protection of civilians against terrorist attacks now and in the future.

Both the principles of *proportionality* (in *jus ad bellum* as well as in *jus in bello*) give us more to think about. As we already said before, the deployment of soldiers is understandable and acceptable. Maybe this principle is not the most effective instrument in the fight against terrorism, but at least it is sometimes useful. In any case, the fight against terrorism is reason enough to deploy soldiers if it is necessary or helpful. Yet it is not so evident as in

---

status of the terrorists, it would call for a redefinition of the word 'war' as we understand it today.

regular nation-nation warfare how we should estimate what is proportionate in this fight. How, for example, do you measure the constant fear and indirect influence terrorism has on the economy, even years after an attack? And what can be called proportionate means when terrorists bring down two symbolic buildings and kill more than 3,000 people, and would surely do it again and again until they reach their goal, and with biological and nuclear weapons if possible? What can be proportionate to that? Similar dilemmas exist in nation-nation warfare too. This reminds us that the proportionality principle admits of subjective interpretation in either instance. What helps political and military leaders at this point is reason, prudence, the existing rules of war. These must be part of every decision to react to a terrorist attack.

Another problem that must be considered is the possible invocation of the *supreme emergency exemption*, or so-called *back-to-the-wall* argument. It is clear that the fight against international terrorism is an emergency, but to call it a supreme emergency means it threatens our fundamental existence, our civilisation, the basis of our values. It is clear that it would be an exaggeration to say that terrorist activities strike at the very existence of our civilisation. Without minimizing the problem, it is always good to remember that, throughout history, democracy has been strong enough to survive terrorist threats. Indeed, terrorism sows fear in the hearts of people, and deeply affects the economy, but this is not a strong enough argument to consider the deployment of all possible military means to fight it. That would be morally unacceptable. If the concept of the supreme emergency exemption is already a slippery slope, applying it to the fight against terrorism is a total violation of the most fundamental moral rules of warfare. Though terrorists do not accept any rules, and often use all possible means to reach their end(s), it is irresponsible to adopt the same attitude. Even in the kind of warfare where a regular army is confronted with a sub-nation group, soldiers have to keep in mind not to cross the moral lines of warfare. As a consequence, we can conclude that the specific situation of an army fighting terrorist organisations, will have characteristic features, but this will not change the army's ethical obligation to the moral rules of warfare and civilian and human rights. The immorality of the terrorist enemy never allows soldiers (nor intelligence agencies) to violate the most fundamental rules that count in nation-nation conflicts. In this sense the just war philosophy – although not uncritically adoptable in the terrorist situation – still counts as a guide in warfare.

The problem of proportionality in *jus in bello* can only be dealt with, when we examine at the same time the complexity of the *non-combatant* or *discrimination principle*. Both principles are closely connected, and it is impossible to speak about one without mentioning the other. In the fight against terrorism the non-combatant principle is one of the most important principles of just war philosophy. We already emphasised this earlier in connection with the growing complexity of warfare. As a consequence, there is an increased danger for civilians to be involved in warfare. Terrorist activities make this danger even greater. First, because civilians are intentional victims of terrorist actions, and because terrorists often live as 'ordinary' and inconspicuous people among other people in cities or villages. So, when military actions against terrorists are considered, it is possible that the operation will hit civilians. That is why in the fight against terrorism the *principle of double effect* (or as it often has been called with an almost cynical undertone *collateral damage*) will likely be invoked more than ever. Concerning the proportionality principle, it suffices here to say that not only non-discriminatory weapons are unacceptable, but also any intentional killing of civilians. Tactics against terrorists must exclude or at least minimize potential civilian deaths.

Two other principles are the *reasonable chance of success* and military action as a *last resort*. Not much can be added to either principle as we know it. But there are a few points worth mentioning. First, it should be said that the meaning of *a reasonable chance of success* will shift in the terrorist context. Traditionally it meant a reasonable chance of defeating the enemy and/or of (re)establishing peace. Peace, or the prevention of further terrorist attacks from a certain organisation, is still the purpose of the fight against terrorism, but it seems that 'success' should be redefined specifically from the point of view of that fight. This means that we should start from the presumption that terrorism will not and cannot be totally defeated. In other words, when we define success as the elimination of all terrorist attacks, it seems we will never reach our end. Even when we state that 'success' means that a certain terrorist organisation must be unable to organise and execute attacks, it seems that we will seldom reach that goal. From our point of view, a reasonable chance of success should mean a marked reduction in the power of at least one terrorist organisation to act. But this still leaves us with many possible subjective interpretations of the concept, and possible side-effects nobody can predict. A good example of this is the US military going against al-Qaida. Some people point out that many al-Qaida members were killed or disabled. We agree that al-Qaida has suffered great losses and seems less powerful than before. But what goes unnoticed is how these military actions have splintered the organisation, making it now much more difficult to fight by traditional military means. Does this mean that the action against al-Qaida was unjustified or irresponsible? The American army did what it could, and with remarkable results. But it is time now for the military leaders to withdraw as the main players in this fight. The time has come for the intelligence agencies to take up their role in a more effective way. They have the means to detect and round up smaller (portions of) terrorist organisations. Moreover, national and international strategies should be developed to remove the causes of terrorism.

The specific nature of the fight against terrorism also affects the principle of *last resort*. It seems to us that this principle cannot be applied to the specific situation of a military fighting terrorists. In part this is because terrorist organisations cannot be put under pressure by, for example, economic sanctions the way governments can. Moreover, it is impossible and morally unacceptable to make compromises with terrorists. To make a compromise would mean to capitulate to subgroups that only represent their own (undemocratic) will. Even if you wanted to negotiate with a certain terrorist group, it is seldom possible to contact the leaders. And a last point is that armies always react to terrorist attacks. They only come into action out of self-defence of the state and of the civilians they represent. Immediately after a terrorist attack, a country has no other choice than to react as soon and effectively as possible. Connected with the critique on this last principle, we should also mention that there probably will be a shift in the near future in the deployment of military forces in the fight against terrorism. As we discussed earlier in this article, it is unacceptable in just war philosophy to act preventively. It seems that the specific situation of the fight against terrorism will challenge this principle. Because the existence of any terrorist organisation can be an immediate threat, it must be possible to intervene decisively without the presence of a *smoking gun*. It would be morally unacceptable to wait until an attack occurred or until at least there was clear proof of a near attack.

As we tried to show above, the fight against terrorism is not war. Nor are just war principles without relevance for today's terrorist challenge. On the contrary, most of them still count as guidelines even in a fight between a state and a non-nation group. Intelligence and law enforcement agencies are bound to civil and human rights, and military actions even in these new situations – bound to the well-known principles of the just war tradition, which are strongly connected with human rights as well. So, the actual challenge of terrorism to just war philosophy should not be overstated. The just war tradition has survived many more difficult moments. This challenge cannot be compared with the dilemma of nuclear weapons, for example. And even though the tradition offers few answers in this case, it remains an integrated and respected body of thought for political leaders more than ever. This is due to an increased moral consciousness in public opinion, and the overwhelming presence of the media within these conflicts. In other words, just war philosophy is not just barely alive but stronger and more influential than ever.

To underscore this conclusion, it might be best to close with a citation from Michael Walzer, who wrote with a bit of euphoria:

"Perhaps naively I am inclined to say that justice has become, in all Western countries, one of the tests that any proposed military strategy or tactic has to meet – only one of the tests and not the most important one, but this still gives just war theory a place and standing that it never had before. It is easier now than it ever was to imagine a general saying, 'No, we can't do that; it would cause too many civilian deaths; we have to find another way.' I am not sure that there are many generals who talk like that, but imagine for a moment that there are; imagine that strategies are evaluated morally as well as militarily; that civilian deaths are minimised; that new technologies are designed to avoid or limit collateral damage, and that these technologies are actually effective in achieving their intended purpose. Moral theory has been incorporated into war-making as a real constraint on when and how wars are fought. This picture is, remember, imaginary, but it is also partly true; and it makes for a far more interesting argument than the more standard claim that the triumph of just war is pure hypocrisy."[159]

---

[159] M. WALZER, *Arguing about War*, p. 12.

FRED VAN IERSEL

Stopping the Murdering Martyr
Just War Tradition and the Confrontation with Ethical Asymmetry in Warfare

1. INTRODUCTION

In this paper I want to address different challenges to the just war tradition. The background of this paper is that the Roman Catholic Church is increasingly sceptical about the just war tradition, or at least about the way it functions.[1] As a Catholic theologian I want to defend the legitimacy of the just war tradition as an alternative between pacifism – the categorical rejection of war as an instrument of international politics, and bellicism – the categorical acceptance of war as a regular instrument of international politics.

Very often the Augustinian tradition to peace as '*tranquillitas ordinis*' and Aquinas' approach of peace as a fruit of justice are treated as opposed paradigms in the ethics of war and peace.[2] In

---

[1] Thus for example two publications of the *Dutch Roman Catholic Bishops Conference on the Ethics of War and Peace*. ROOMS KATHOLIEKE BISSCHOPPEN-CONFERENTIE VAN NEDERLAND, *Een kerk voor Rechtvaardigheid en Vrede. De actualiteit van 'Pacem in Terris' veertig jaar later*, Uitgave van de afdeling Pers en Communicatie secretariaat RK Kerk, Utrecht, 2003. (DUTCH RC BISHOPS CONFERENCE, *A Church for Justice and Peace*); ROOMS KATHOLIEKE BISSCHOP-PENCONFERENTIE VAN NEDERLAND, *Tot vrede in staat? Wij persoonlijk geloven dat dit mogelijk is. Herderlijk schrijven over gerechtigheid, veiligheid en vrede*, bisschoppelijke brieven nr. 34, Uitgave van de afdeling Pers en Communicatie secretariaat RK Kerk, 1996.

[2] A representative of the theological paradigm of peace through security is: G. WEIGEL, *Tranquillitas Ordinis. The Present Failure and Future Promise of American Catholic Thought on War and Peace*. Oxford/New York, 1987. A representative of the theological paradigm of peace through justice is: R. BURGGRAEVE, *De christelijk geinspireerde vredesethiek in het spanningsveld en rechtvaardige oorlog van*

166 FRED VAN IERSEL

fact, however, the moral dilemma between peace as fruit of justice versus peace as fruit of stability, seen from the perspective of the Catholic tradition to a very large extent, is a false one.[3] For, on the one hand, only stable and secure states can guarantee and enforce compliance to human rights. On the other hand, the legitimacy of a stable state is unthinkable without the recognition of human rights by that state. At a factual level, if the doctrine of state's sovereignty could be erased from the mind of political leaders, this would not per se reduce the type of gross violations of human rights to which humanitarian intervention tries to respond. A reconciliation between state sovereignty as a political value and human rights is needed.[4] Therefore, the key dilemma with regard to the future of warfare is not about state's sovereignty versus human rights. It is about the way the fifth commandment – Thou shall not kill – should be interpreted in a specific situation.

2. Six strategies for handling dilemmas relating to killing in warfare

In my opinion, there are six ethical strategies to deal with moral dilemmas related to killing by the military in the context of a war.

1963 rot heden, in ID., J. DE TAVERNIER & L. VAN DE WEYER (eds.), *Van Rechtvaardige Oorlog naar Rechtvaardige Vrede, Katholieken tussen militarisme en pacifisme in historisch-theologisch perspectief*, Leuven, 1993, pp. 253-274. A good, synthetic survey of tendencies in the Catholic Social Doctrine of War and Peace from *Pacem in Terris* till 1992 is offered by J. DE TAVERNIER, *Van rechtvaardige Oorlog naar prudent pacifism. Het kerkelijke vredesdenken van 1963 tot heden*, in R. BURGGRAEVE, J. DE TAVERNIER & L. VAN DE WEYER (eds.), *Van Rechtvaardige Oorlog naar Rechtvaardige Vrede, Katholieken tussen militarisme en pacifisme in historisch-theologisch perspectief*, Leuven, 1993, pp. 153-183.

[3] See: F. VAN IERSEL, *The Ethical Basis for European Security*, in W. PALAVER (ed.), *Peace in Europe, Peace in the World*, Justitia et Pax Dokumentation no 3, Vienna, September 2002, pp. 143-160.

[4] R. FALK, *Sovereignty and Human Dignity. The Search for Reconciliation*, in H.J. STEINER & P. ALSTON (eds.), *International Human Rights in Context. Law. Politics, Morals.* Oxford, 2000[2], pp. 581-584.

The first strategy found both in practice and ethics is to redefine values. A classical example of this is the fifth Commandment of the Jewish and Christian Bible: "Thou Shall not kill." Nowadays this commandment very often is interpreted as a truly universal prohibition to kill, meant for all kinds of situations. But if we take into account the original meaning,[5] we have to face the fact that it did not refer to killing in wartime situations. Pacifist interpretations of the Fifth Commandment neglect the relevance of texts such as Ex. 2: 12 (Moses kills an Egyptian), and Ex. 17: 8-16 – the paradigm of just wars, namely the war of self defense against the Amalekites. Or, what may be even more important is Jethro's advice to Moses in Exodus chapter 18. This passage can be interpreted as a plea for a constitution for the recently liberated people to regulate their internal relations. I am convinced that originally the Fifth Commandment referred to murder in a civilian sense and to the prevention of lynching.

Through the Jewish prophetic tradition and the influence of Christianity, the Fifth Commandment has been universalised. It was the resistance of early Christianity against Roman idolatry that stimulated universal interpretations of the Ten Commandments. Besides, Christianity opposed the idolatry of the Roman Empire. In fact this was an effort to secularise the self-idolatry of Emperors who demanded absolute obedience also from their soldiers. Opposition to this Roman idolatry stimulated a culture of political and military abstinence in early Christianity. Meanwhile the early Christian community recognised the temporal power of an occupying force as St. Paul did in his Epistle to the Romans. All of this fit into the current eschatology of early Christianity: if the Messiah's return is expected within a short period of time, then it makes no sense to try to gain temporary, political and military power, even more so when the legal authorities persecuted Christians in several periods. Instead, the Church itself

[5] See: B.T. VIVIANO, *De christen en de staat volgens het Nieuwe Testament en binnen de vroege kerk*, in *Internationaal Commentaar op de Bijbel*, bd. I, Kampen 2001, pp. 361-364; see: J.F. CRAGHAN, *Exodus*, in *Internationaal Commentaar op de Bijbel*, bd. I, Kampen 2001, especially pp. 494-495.

was developing into a truly universal body of Christ in which ethnic identity plays no dominant role. Of course, the process of universalisation does not prevent Christians from getting into moral dilemmas. Instead it provokes moral dilemmas since conscription was obligatory in the Roman Empire. It provided a basis for Christian pacifism in later periods of the Church's history.

Still, originally, the Fifth Commandment was not about a prohibition to go to war. Instead it was a prohibition with a range of relevance in the civil sector: a prohibition of murder. And indeed sometimes these insights may help politicians who decide to go to war and soldiers who do the actual killing to make a distinction between killing and murdering. It may make sense to approach the Fifth Commandment in a hermeneutical way, thus softening the moral dilemmas related to killing as an instrument to protect innocent civilians.

The second strategy is to define a hierarchy of values. Through such a hierarchy some dilemmas can be solved because some values appear to be higher than others. Those values that are best related to core tasks have a higher place in the hierarchy of values. In other words, the centrality of the value is defined. This implies the need to develop a hierarchy between four key values that are at stake in case of humanitarian intervention: respect for sovereignty of states as a matter of justice in international relations versus human security of civilians as a matter of compassion. It is important to realise that the moral dilemmas related to humanitarian intervention are dilemmas of a 'third party' not directly involved in an armed conflict. Moral dilemmas are the dilemmas of a guilty bystander. These dilemmas only make sense if the bystander has the political and military power to actually do something about the gross violations of human rights. This perspective has been expressed by the Vatican Secretary of State Angelo Sodano, who on August, 6th in 1992 said: "…it is a sin of omission to remain silent and not to make every possible effort – using the means that international organisations can offer – to stop the aggression toward defenceless populations." He then invoked the right and duty of humanitarian intervention "in order to disarm someone who wants to kill...not so as to favour war, but to prevent it."[6] In the case of humanitarian intervention the sin of omission is a bystander's sin. Already as Ambrose of Milan said: "whoever does not combat the injustice threatening his neighbour, is as guilty as the one who actually commits it."[7] In this respect, the sin of omission, a sin of the bystander, is a variety of the Church doctrine on the *occasio proxima*. The notion of *occasio proxima* implies that powerful bystanders should not permit a moral evil to occur; if so they share the guilt when the evil actually occurs. Cardinal Sodano's statement seems to express the insight that humanitarian intervention implies a paradox: killing to prevent war may be justified under specific circumstance.

Thus redefining a hierarchy of values demands a choice between ethics of conviction (*Gesinnungsethik*), in which priority is given to the bystander's conviction that killing is forbidden, and an ethics of responsibility (*Verantwortungsethik*), in which priority is given to the intended result, namely, the protection of civilian population. Ambrose's approach is in the ethics of conviction. This presupposes access to political and military power and, as such, is typical for any 'post-Constantine' type of Christianity, in which Christianity is an important factor of legitimacy in a state. Complimentary to this strategy of redefining a hierarchy of values is the possibility to determine how the different values are interrelated. The more the values are interrelated, the higher their priority should be. In the case of humanitarian intervention the 'right to life' is recognised as a human right. Article 3 of the *Universal Declaration of Human Rights* (UDHR) states: "Everyone has the right to life, liberty and security of peace." This is stated immediately after the confirmation that all human beings are born free and equal in dignity and rights (art. 1 UDHR) and that everyone is entitled to all the rights in UDHR (art. 2 UDHR). The

---

[6] Cited in: U. COLOMBO SACCO, *John Paul II and World Politics: Twenty Years of Search for a New Approach 1978-1998*, Leuven, 1999, p. 49.

[7] AMBROSIUS OF MILANO, *De officiis ministrorum* I 36/178, Migne, Patrologia (series) Latina (MPL) 16, Sp. 75.

position of article 3 UDHR suggests that the right to life and
security has the highest priority. It is the basis of all other rights.
This of course is logical. The other human rights only make sense
if life is guaranteed. However this does not solve the dilemma, it
only sharpens it. It appears that humanitarian intervention brings
on a moral dilemma under article 3 for the intervening nation:
who has priority? Does priority go to the right to life and security of the threatened population, or the right to life of the threatening party? Formulated in this way it seems that the result of this
second strategy comes close to the result of the first. For one might
as well ask: is it allowed to kill to prevent murder?

The third ethical strategy for handling moral dilemmas is to develop a 'rule versus exception mechanism'. This mechanism implies
that values such as the prohibition to kill are accepted as valid, but
that there are exceptional circumstances where they do not apply.
It also implies that the values that are upheld gain in status. As a
consequence, it becomes possible to resolve moral dilemmas. A good
example of this is the prohibition of killing. Any civilised culture
will accept that non-violent conflict resolution strategies should be
normal. War, even for reasons of self-defence, should be exceptional. Of course, in such a 'rule versus exception' mechanism it is very
important that the definitions are clear and that competent
authorities make the distinction. In fact, the just war tradition can
be thought of as an ethical method for handling the 'rule versus
exception mechanism.'
    The fourth strategy for handling moral dilemmas related to
killing by the military is to reallocate these dilemmas from validity issues to application issues. By this I mean the following: Suppose a culture or religion embraces the value 'the right to life,'
which indeed is a human right. Then this culture or religion can
be sure that it will meet many moral dilemmas related to killing.
Now instead of discussing the validity of the principle itself, the
people in this culture or religion may ask themselves: 'when exactly
do I kill?' This way of handling dilemmas also applies to soldiers.
Imagine that we are a heavily armed peace keeping battalion

watching two conflicting parties in combat. Our mandate only allows us to use our weapons for self-defence. Imagine further that these rival parties are creating a massacre. Now suppose that we do not intervene. Are we morally co-responsible for the massacre? When exactly are we co-responsible for the killing: if we do intervene militarily or if we do not intervene? Don't we actually kill when we do nothing at all? This is what I mean by the reallocation of the moral dilemma from issues of validity to issues of application. Whatever we do, we recognise the validity of the principle that killing our fellow human beings should not be done. But the question remains: when do we apply it properly?

From this perspective the nature of the bystander's dilemma is different from the earlier approaches. The question is no longer if we are allowed to justify killing, but how our factual involvement with killing in confrontation with genocide, should be dealt with. This approach puts into question the presuppositions with regard to the human condition as a basically peaceful one and of human history as a context in which true peace can be fully realised. The question: 'when exactly do we kill?', shows us the way to an Augustinian approach to the role of violence in human nature and in history. In Augustine's approach violence has a threefold meaning. It is a symptom of sin; it is the 'ultimum remedium' (last resort) – to regain justice and peace against the power of sin; and it is also the legitimacy of violence as radically anti-messianic because the true peace is yet to come in the Kingdom of God. The avoidance of the question "When exactly do we kill?" appears to be the expression of a misunderstanding of the depth of sin. It underestimates the human condition as basically sinful by nature through original sin, and it overestimates the possibility of overcoming violence during human history. Instead, we should accept the presupposition that every man by nature and by his role in history and society participates in the consequences of the power of evil. The hope for a peaceful world is valid, but it is different from optimism about the human capacity to let non-violent solutions for armed conflicts prevail here and now. It should include the transcendent dimension of the heavenly peace.

From this insight it is not a large step to the fifth ethical strategy for handling moral dilemmas related to the military. This implies taking into account the indirect effect of actions. In fact a large part of military ethics, like medical ethics, can be understood as elaborations of the principle of the indirect effect. As Michael Walzer has worked it out, this principle of double effect consists of four steps.

a. Consider whether the objective of the action is morally acceptable. If it is not, stop the action.

b. Ask if the direct effects are justifiable. They are if, for example, the targets are military stock of an enemy in a combat situation.

c. Ask if the intention is right. The intentions are right if the negative effects that occur are in no way intended. In other words, the negative effect may not be purpose nor means.

d. The indirect effects are proportionate compared to the objective and the direct effect.[8]

The principle of indirect effect is an elaboration of the principle of proportionality derived from *ius in bello* as part of the just war tradition. It is specifically useful when it comes to handling moral dilemmas. For these dilemmas always occur when it is no longer possible to realise what is morally good and the only question left is: what is morally acceptable or justifiable, given the fact that the morally good is no longer reachable? The application of the principle of indirect effect thus presupposes the prudence to recognise a dilemma as forthcoming out of a non-ideal situation that is nevertheless real and unavoidable.

This principle of indirect effect is not just an academic finding. It has been and is very influential in military and also in medical practice. For example, it has had and still has influence on the development of weapon techniques, and on military strategy at the level of the selection of targets. It can be especially very useful during the planning stage of military actions. Of course this is

---

[8] M. WALZER, *Just and Unjust Wars. A Moral Argument with Historical Illustrations.* New York, 1977, p. 153.

more the case if step (d) provides the basis for step (b), that is, if one has a right intention. This then should be expressed in the weighing of foreseeable indirect effects. If the right intention is being disjoined from the actual planning of an action, this will pave the way to war crimes. Another function of the principle of indirect effect is related to the evaluation of military actions. It is very helpful to define the degree of moral responsibility for the effects of any action.

Conducting warfare implies a license to kill. However, in fact any legal killing by the military can be regarded as an indirect effect of an attempt to eliminate the adversary as a military factor. Thus understood, military killing in itself is not intentional in the sense that it directly aims at killing. In practice, this distinction perhaps is too subtle. Still it is an important principle for military planning and for military training to recognise that killing as a dimension of the military professions is not so much an intention in itself as it is a failed attempt to eliminate the adversary as a military factor. Taking this attitude implies that any victory also brings forth a loss. This attitude is expressed by the Chinese philosopher Lao Tse when he stated: "If there is to be a combat, let him win who most regrets the fighting."[9]

With regard to humanitarian intervention the principle of indirect effect can be applied as follows. It might be the intention of the intervening party to stop acts of murder against civilians. But what are the effects of the intervention? Will the indirect effects – the killings needed to stop the murdering – be proportionate? I think a fair moral argument requires that this question is not only posed to the act of humanitarian intervention, but also to the abstinence from humanitarian intervention. The Red Khmer's genocide on the civil population of Cambodia or the genocide between Hutu's and Tutsi's in Rwanda were not followed by humanitarian intervention. The unintended, indirect effect of this omission was a further escalation of violence.

---

[9] L. TSE, *Tao the King*, saying nr. 69.

Of course ethics should be resistant to a mere calculus of victims. Indeed, ethics is not about statistics. But an early humanitarian intervention in Cambodia or Rwanda could have possibly contributed to the avoidance of millions of casualties. These cases also clarify that the possible effectiveness of humanitarian intervention is very much dependent on early action, i.e., intervention in an early stage of conflict. Thus, humanitarian intervention illustrates a dilemma between two criteria of the just war tradition, namely the chances for success versus the exhaustion of peaceful means as preconditions for starting combat. In the cases of Cambodia and Rwanda, any attempt to first try more peaceful means to stop the genocides would have been counterproductive. The chance for success in stopping the genocides should have had priority.

The sixth ethical strategy for handling moral dilemmas related to military intervention goes even beyond the 'rule versus exception mechanism' and beyond the principle of the indirect effect. In the case of wars or acts of war, what is in question is the Supreme Emergency Exemption.[10] To put this in a clear way, this is a mechanism for consciously and willingly and temporarily putting aside certain values. Thus it can be legitimate to use illegal means and to commit acts of war that would be qualified as war crimes in other circumstances. For example, both the American philosophers Michael Walzer and John Rawls put forward that the military can be put in a situation where a strict application of the principle of indirect effect would risk universal values in an irreparable way. There are cases, Rawls writes in his last book, the *Laws of Peoples* (1999), in which this principle can and should be put aside.

According to Rawls, we should put aside our principles when the continuity of the democratic constitutional state system is threatened. In Rawls's approach the Supreme Emergency Exemption basically is a matter of self defence of a democratic nation-state.

---

[10] See: M. WALZER, *Just and Unjust Wars*, p. 251 and J. RAWLS, *The Law of Peoples*. London/Cambridge MA, 1999, p. 98.

In fact we see a possible justification for what has become the National Security Strategy. This strategy implies the concept of preventive war with the intent to safeguard the system of democratic constitutional states against the terrorist threats and the threats of authoritarian and totalitarian regimes. Rawls's approach to the legitimacy of military intervention against totalitarian states (specifically his acceptance of the Supreme Emergency Exemption) in fact smoothes the way for the justification of the preventive war. It is precisely this concept of the preventive war that the Vatican had opposed during the first Gulf War against Iraq.

Preventive war has nothing to do with humanitarian intervention. As Cardinal Sodano stated during the presentation of the Pope's declaration at the occasion of World Peace Day 2003, preventive war is not a part of the vocabulary of the United Nations. One may add: the effects of the war against the regime of Saddam Hussein may be good in terms of humanitarian relief, but these effects are only indirect. The intervention was undertaken because of the threat that regime posed to international peace and security, because of the risks of the use of weapons of mass destruction and because of suspicion of cooperation with al-Qaida. These motives may have some legitimacy (although in itself they are not enough to justify this war ethically because of the close relation of these motives with the Supreme Emergency motive and the negligence of international law through the intervening states. But most of all these motives are different from valid motives for humanitarian intervention.

Early military intervention against a genocide as part of humanitarian intervention is only to be considered as humanitarian intervention if it is not directed at safeguarding the political system of the intervening power.[11] Humanitarian intervention requires that military action be aimed at bringing about a stable society for the rival parties, and that it manage itself for the sake of the societies and states in a conflict. This 'altruistic' intention – the regard for

---

[11] Thus also: J. RAWLS, *The Law of Peoples*, p. 89ff.

the fate of civilians – explains exactly why true humanitarian intervention seldom occurs. The modern example of ethical humanitarian intervening is that of Tanzania against Idi Amin's Uganda, even though the humanitarian motives of Tanzania were combined with the need to deal with the destabilising effects of refugees fleeing into Tanzania.

3. JUST WAR AGAINST TERRORISM?

As we just saw, the just war tradition implies the position that war can, under certain circumstances and conditions, be a legitimate moral option or even a moral obligation. Also the approach of this tradition is an alternative between political realism which excludes normative arguments from international relations and their theory, and legalism which adheres to international law as the main source of legitimacy for the use of force. Ethics should be seen as a foundational, complementary, and transforming factor in international politics and international law. It cannot replace the legal or political dimension, nor be replaced by them.[12]

In practice I think that the just war tradition is a useful instrument to ethically judge whether or not, for example, humanitarian intervention[13] should be undertaken. It may also specify the realm of self-defence in the sense of article 51 of the UN Charter. In the context of the National Defence Doctrine of the USA

[12] A. TORNO, *La Moralita della Violenza. Considerazioni sul Male della Storia.* Milano, 2003.

[13] The official advisory committees Adviescommissie Mensenrechten (ACM) and the Commissie van Advies inzake Volkenrechtelijke vraagstukken (CAVV) gave the following definition: "The intervention, by a state or a group of states, through the use of force or the threat of such use on the territory of another country by reason of occurring gross violations of human rights, without any foregoing authorisation by the Security Council," in ACM & CAVV, *Het gebruik van geweld voor humanitaire doeleinden,* The Hague 1992. An elaboration can be found in: A.H.M. VAN IERSEL & TH. A. VAN BAARDA (eds.), *Militaire Ethiek. Morele dilemma's van militairen in theorie en praktijk.* Budel, 2002, pp. 144-149.

within which the notion of preventive war is developed, I think that a proper application of the just war tradition leads to the rejection of this doctrine. Regarding combat against terrorism, I think the term 'war' is not correct. Instead, terrorism should primarily be considered and treated as criminal activity.[14] Only if a country is willingly hosting terrorist bases, the combat against this country to get rid of these bases may be considered as warfare.

Against this background I now want to answer the other questions posed by the organisers of the seminar.

3.1. A short description of the tradition and development of the just war concept with its nuances and difficulties

I think the recent challenges to the just war tradition can be further typified by answering the following seven questions:

A. What exactly is an adequate formulation of each criterion?

An adequate formulation of the criteria is necessary. The main contemporary issues are first the definition of the just cause (e.g. putting an end to gross violations of human rights), and second, the spelling out of legitimate authority (state versus UN Security Council).

Among just war theorists there is consensus that stopping gross violations of human rights or genocide is a legitimate cause of war. More specifically this means that the just war tradition can be 'transferred' into humanitarian intervention. Also self-defence under article 51 UN Charter is accepted as a just cause. In the case of the combat against terrorism there is no such consensus. This is because that there is no consensus about the definition of terrorism, and no consensus on the question of whether combat against terrorism can properly be called a 'war.'

The question concerning legitimate authority divides ethicists into two camps: the idealists who proclaim that the UN Security Council is the legitimate authority, versus the 'realists' who regard

---

[14] *Ibid.*, pp. 149-179.

such a role of the UN security Council as desirable but presently not feasible and who therefore tend to accept single states or alliances as legitimate authority.

Another issue is the criterion of 'the last resort.' Exactly when are the peaceful means in an escalating conflict exhausted? Should not this criterion be specified? Which peaceful means should be used anyway before the use of force could be justified? Are there also cases, such as rapidly escalating ethic conflicts, in which no peaceful means are obliged as a precondition for the legitimate use of force to stop the escalation?

Last but not least: the criterion of proportionality is not quite so clear as it seems. Is it really true that human suffering as a consequence of war, can be measured. Can it be circumscribed in a statistically exact manner? I doubt it. I do so, not because I think that there are no quantitative aspects about human suffering. There are. But because in the context of a war, or preparation of a war, it is very hard to find exact, objective, facts and figures. Exactly what is the military balance before a war? Can data about casualties in a war be trusted? Can televised images of a war be trusted by a public that tries to come to an ethical judgment?

I think that facts and figures with regard to the military balance before a war are to a very great extent a matter of taxation, of prudent estimation, but not of hard-core statistics. And the same is valid for the damage to people and properties during a war. Even parliaments find it difficult to judge what really has happened, let alone the general public. I would therefore say that the decision to go to war can be legitimised through the proportion of human suffering caused by the enemy only in a very limited way. These statements contain prudent judgments that should be presented to the public with some reservation.

With regard to the legitimate authority there is a controversy between realists and idealists. The former accept the ideal of a strong UN but recognise this as utopia only, the latter think the UN can and should function as the sole competent authority immediately, an attitude resulting in legalism.

B. What exactly are the theoretical relations between the just war criteria?

– The main issue here concerns the consistency and hierarchy of the just war principles? An example of this problem this is the hierarchy between the 'chance for success' versus the 'last resort' criterion. What if a military intervention can only be effective or proportionate if it is executed in an early stage of escalation of a conflict? Should the 'last resort criterion' then be put aside, or can it be argued that it cannot be put aside, but applied as an early exhaustion of 'peaceful means?'

– A specific problem derived from the *ius in bello* is that it has different status in law and ethics. In the context of international law any party in an armed conflict must comply with the *ius in bello* principles. The validity of these principles is not dependent upon the *ius ad bellum* principles. In ethics, however, a party conducting an illegitimate war should be stopped even if the illegitimate war is conducted according to the *ius in bello* principles. Thus the moral meaning of compliance to the *ius in bello* is different from the legal meaning.[15]

– Basically all criteria of the just war tradition are no more than an elaboration of the Golden Rule in its minimal variety: do not treat the other conflicting party in a way that you do not want to be treated yourself by this party. The Golden Rule can be found in almost all world religions – which is not the same as saying that its content and validity are derived from religious truths – but it has an even wider acceptance in several types of humanistic ethics. The Golden Rule, I think, is integrated into world religions because it is true, not the other way round. This is not very remarkable, because the Golden Rule itself may be more a procedural than a substantial principle in its demand that one take the other's party's perspective and act accordingly.

In confronting ethical asymmetry in warfare, as in the case of 'murdering martyrs' (suicide bombers and the like), the conclusions derived from the Golden Rule are somewhat ambiguous. Is there a unilateral moral obligation towards people who do not

[15] *Ibid.*, pp.103-112.

respect the integrity of their own and other persons' lives? In other words, is there a kind of deontology implied in the just war criteria, even when they are to be applied to human beings that do not respect them? I think there is, for two reasons. First, the defence against terrorism is about the future of civilisation. This civilisation, or at least its basic values, should be upheld during its defence, otherwise the battle against terrorism will make no sense. Secondly, all warfare should be conducted in such a way that the military action is directed towards a post-war peace, including a process towards a just and stable peace and towards reconciliation between rival parties. This is not only a matter of moral obligation, but also a matter of self-interest for the conflicting parties.

C. Should not there be rules for the proper application of the criteria?

Can the abuse of the just war tradition by pacifists who already 'know' that any war is unjust be prevented? Also, can the abuse of that tradition by politicians who have decided to go to war and who only need a checklist to justify an already taken decision be prevented? My plea would be to integrate a fair use of the criteria into the criteria themselves, which implies a demand for integrity. Perhaps theoretically a fair use is presupposed, but in practice it is not. In my opinion the just war tradition is only taken seriously if a critical stance is taken on pacifist judgments against war and bellicose positions which regard war as a standard instrument in international conflict.

D. Do we need a just war tradition embedded in a theory of justice in international relations?

The just war tradition seems to imply a concept of justice, yet the criteria appear in completely different theories of justice. What does this mean, and what consequences does this have for the status of the criteria? Are they in fact perhaps heuristic instruments, or perhaps a method?[16] Or should the criteria only be accepted in a discussion

---

[16] F. VAN IERSEL, *On the Future of the Just Defence Tradition*, in B. WICKER, *Studying War No More? From Just War to Just Peace*, Kampen, 2003, pp. 74-90.

under the precondition that they are integrated in a comprehensive theory of justice and security in international relations?

It would be absurd to regard the criteria of just war as valid, if it were impossible to give them a plausible foundation. This will not be easy because of the pluralism of ethical theory. This pluralism gives food to ethical relativism, and this relativism in turn, is a dangerous context for the just war criteria since it turns them into a source of legitimacy of any war of any party in war. Perhaps it is enough to regard ethical theories as expressions of ethical cultures, and to recognise an intercultural validity of the criteria, which at least gives them a truly universal character at a factual level.

E. Does the just war tradition have a relationship to the international law?

On one hand, ethics can be seen as a foundation of international law. For example, it may be argued that treaties should be observed (*pacta servanda sunt*): a moral rule supporting the function of international law. On the other hand, ethics can have a complementary role, especially when international law is less developed or is not fit for new circumstances. For instance, in the context of UN peace operations, the legal status of the mandate or its rules of engagement is not always clear. Are they political instructions, are they binding in a legal sense, or are they morally obliging?

There is even a third option here: according to many specialists of international law, this law prevails over ethics. It might well be said that international law does not recognise the tradition of just war as such. It only accepts a limited concept of self-defence under article 51 of the UN Charter. Does this mean that the function of the just war criteria should be limited to the application of article 51 of the UN Charter? I think the answer should be 'yes' when considered apart from the specific case of humanitarian intervention, which I consider to be not a war, but a military action similar to war.

F. How should the just war tradition be related to politics?

Political and military power seem to be a precondition to put ethics into effect. Is the fact that power is a precondition for the effectiveness of ethics a chance or a challenge for the validity of normative ethics?

Let's ask Max Weber's help in solving this problem. He makes an ideal typical distinction between an ethics of responsibility (*Verantwortungsethik*) above ethics of conviction (*Gesinnungsethik*). In the first one, the moral meaning of a human act is being defined by its consequences (effects, success or failure), in the second the value is defined by the values expressed in human acting as a process. The distinction, Weber says, is not a real one, but only an ideal typical one. Nevertheless, in my opinion, the question as to which approach is more suitable is largely dependent on the context. In his essay *Politics as Profession* Weber shows that in a political context, the ethics of responsibility should prevail except when the personal integrity of the politician is at stake.[17]

With regard to military ethics, I think that we should be happy that normative ethics is embedded in power relations. It is not for nothing that in his early writings Max Weber uses the words *Verantwortungsethik* and *Machtsethik* (Ethics of Power) as synonyms. Indeed, if a state has power it should be judged not only by how it – or key persons in it – intends (or intend) to use it. On the contrary, the effects or results of the use of power do matter even more in a military context. This is about life, death, and killing. I think the just war tradition in fact presupposes a type of ethics of responsibility. It implies the willingness to prepare for war and acts of war in such a way that casualties are reduced to a justifiable minimum. Mistakes can be made in planning or execution of plans, but the intention to prevent unjustified casualties demands the willingness to maximise the anticipation of effects of one's own acts.

If politics has a role as precondition for a useful ethics of responsibility, the opposite is true as well. Politics cannot be fully separated from ethics. Politics is about values and about

---

[17] See: A.H.M. VAN IERSEL, *Op zoek naar een gewetenloze politiek. De tegenstelling tussen gezindheidsethiek en verantwoordelijkheidsethiek in het denken van Max Weber in het licht van de tegenstelling tussen conscientia en prudentie* (Thesis, Nijmegen, 1982).

working with values in an environment where not all values dominate. Politics can be defined as a "combat for values."[18] Exactly therefore values should give orientation to politics in a double sense. They need to be leading in the process of political choices with regard to the combination of ends and means, and they should deal with the fact that no open society is completely homogenous with regard to values. Any political option should include rights of political minorities and their value systems.

G. What exactly is the role of reason in the just war tradition?

In Western tradition the just war tradition seems very 'rational.' It seems to be a matter of systematic application of criteria to a specific case. Nevertheless, I dare say that there is no such application mechanism. Of course, everybody knows the newspaper articles in which authors present the criteria and their applications. But I am convinced that this is not the way in which decision makers really argue. I think that the criteria have a different function. They are helpful in the reconstruction of a moral argument, *ex ante* or *ex post*. In practice, prudence is more important than the mechanical application of criteria. Prudence is indeed a cognitive virtue with a moral status. This is according to Aristotle and especially Thomas Aquinas, and I think they are right about prudence being a cognitive competency or ability to judge things in a dynamic environment and to choose combinations of ends and means not by mechanical application but by gauging and assessing what is at hand. Its rational style is more Aristotelian than Kantian, due to the fact that prudent judgments are not a matter of deontology but of discovering the social reality and of choosing ends and means in such a dynamic context. In this way, the criteria are not a limitative approach but more a heuristic instrument for structuring our questions and making our moral arguments more balanced.

---

[18] A. VAN BRAAM, *Leerboek Bestuurskunde A*, Muiderberg, 1986.

3.2. The specific features found in the battle against terrorism and the feasibility of the classical concept of 'just war'

For Islamic terrorists, their combat in itself is a 'jihad' - a term that can be understood as 'holy war' or 'just war,' although it is a broader concept, especially in a properly religious setting.[19] Because Islamic terrorism is a highly visible sort of terrorism, the rise of Islamism threatens to discredit Islam, or even religion as such. Islamic authorities should respond to this by publicly rejecting suicide and willingly sought martyrdom, and by rejecting the attack of civilians as murder. If these acts are considered as acts of war they should be condemned as indiscriminate and disproportionate in the sense of the just war tradition.[20]

It will not be easy to work up to such public statements. One possibly fruitful way to such public declarations is 'intra-religious' dialogue or debate (between the different varieties of Islam) and inter-religious dialogue and debate (Christian-Islamic; Islamic-Jewish; Christian-Jewish). These dialogues should make it clear that the rights of religions do not provide a 'just cause' in the sense of the just war tradition. In this sense, it is a responsibility of the world religions to make the just war tradition function, paradoxically, by criticising specific acts of war. Of course I have no illusion that this will be enough to prevent any form of Islamic terrorism because precisely those groups who are preparing for terrorism are unfit for dialogue. Nevertheless, it is important to undermine the legitimacy of these 'murdering martyrs.'

Apart from the religious dimension of the perceived legitimacy of terrorism, I think it must be acknowledged that it is precisely the (perceived) reduction of the power gap between Islamists and non-Islamists that triggers terrorism that is causing the trouble. To put this in sharper focus, it is not the power gap between Muslim

---

[19] C. RAJEWSKI, *Der gerechte Krieg im Islam*, in R. STEINWEG, *Der Gerechte Krieg. Christentum Islam Marxismus*, Frankfurt, 1980, pp. 13-71; M.H. BELKHODIA, *Guerre et Paix dans lóptique de la traition musulmane*, in P. VIAUD, *La Religion et la guerre*, pp. 357-453.

[20] See: A.H.M. VAN IERSEL & TH. A. VAN BAARDA (eds.), *o.c.*

countries and the Western world in itself, but the diminishing of it that stimulates the grasp for even more power. The terrorists of 9/11 were all highly educated and already had their contacts and integration in the West. This is no coincidence! This view of things can be found in the Power-Distance-Reduction theory of Mauk Mulder,[21] and also in Johan Galtung's theory.[22] Formulated in the seventies of the last century, this view tells us that the shrinking of the gap between rich and poor will not decrease but increase the risk of armed conflict. By this I mean that the risk of terrorism is here to stay in a globalising world in which there is strife for international justice, especially for international distributive justice (a fair distribution of resources, goods and services among the world population). Galtung's paradox is that the greater the gap of injustice, the less chance that poor countries or their populations are a security risk for the rich countries.

I think we should not work for a world in which structural injustice is an instrument for security. Therefore, security risks are not only here to stay at a factual level, properly understood they should be here to stay – as a symptom of reducing the global power gaps. Of course by this I do not want to legitimise terrorism. On the contrary, I think that ethical behaviour towards terrorists or suspects should be asymmetric: give them what they do not give you, namely respect for their human dignity and corresponding rights, but check the legal use of their rights.

With regard to the battle against terrorism I would like to make some short remarks. In my opinion, terrorism should not be considered as warfare, but primarily as criminal behaviour. It is a concession to terrorists to accept the idea of a war conducted by them. This concession increases the legitimacy of their actions. The means used in this battle should be legal and they should be

---

[21] M. MULDER, *Het spel om de macht*, Meppel, 1972. This study elaborates the idea that power is addictive: once a 'power distance' is reduced, power does not become less attractive, but, on the contrary, it becomes more attractive and the hunger for power increases.

[22] J. GALTUNG, *Peace: Research, Education, Action*, Copenhagen, 1975.

under strict political control of governments with a proper demo-cratic mandate. In any case, the human rights both of suspects and of actual perpetrators should be respected. Because nobody is a terrorist before he or she actually commits an attack, the laws regarding suspects should be followed as long as prevention can be pursued. This may be complicated, but it is an obligation derived from the nature of a democratic constitutional state. In any case, the principle of proportionality should be upheld. It is part of the just war tradition and penal law alike.

3.3. About the justification of a pre-emptive approach

Preventive war can only be justified if its definition is clearly distinct from 'aggression' as it is understood in international relations (which indeed is not very exactly defined, but nevertheless, is more specific than a general theory of human aggression). If this distinction were a reality (and only then), preventive war could be considered accept-able. The reason is that the total amount of violence might be esti-mated lower than the amount of violence used in an armed conflict during a higher stage of escalation. In that case, the principle of proportionality could be applied in such a way that not only the force executed by one party would be weighed in the moral argu-ment, but the total amount of force of all parties participating in the conflict would be weighed. In such a calculus, an early, possibly preventive, deployment of force, could perhaps be defended.

3.4. The importance and role of the United Nations in the battle against terrorism

At a legal level each country has the right to defend itself in accor-dance with article 51 of the UN Charter, until the Security Coun-cil takes measures. The UN Security Council should not develop itself into a military alliance having a standing force. Instead it should accept the reality that states participate in military alliances. The UN should only try to influence these into functioning as regional security arrangements. In practice this rule will do, except in the cases of armed conflicts between non-state actors, such as inter-ethnic conflicts. In such cases international law, especially the Law of Peoples, is underdeveloped This lacuna creates a classical third party dilemma. State actors not involved in the conflict have a typical bystander's dilemma, whether or not to start a humanitarian intervention.

The wars against Afghanistan's Taliban regime and the regime of Saddam Hussein were real wars, but they are different. The war against the Taliban was a matter of self-defence. I think the war was justified because the Taliban hosted the hostile terrorist group al-Qaida, not by accident but as a matter of politics. The war against the Baath regime in Iraq was not directly aimed against terrorism. Its legitimacy was built around the threat of the regime against international peace and security, as provided by international law. It is significant that the regime did not visibly comply with UN resolutions. That fact in itself was a threat to international peace and security, especially with regard to the then plausible possession of weapons of mass destruction by the Baath regime.

The UN (i.e., Security Council) sometimes does not reach consensus. In that case no measures are taken and Article 51 is still valid as a framework for legitimate self-defence. The preventive war should be excluded from the concept of self-defence.

In Michael Walzer's and John Rawls' views on international relations[23] there can be a Supreme Emergency Exception, which implies a struggle for the continuity of the core institutions and values of the constitutional state.[24] In fact, this approach puts aside the very heart of the just war tradition. That is why this approach cannot be accepted. I state this in a rather firm way, because I fear the day that the preventive war is presented to us as

---

[23] M. WALZER, o.c., p. 251 and J. RAWLS, o.c., p 98.

[24] It is very tempting to read these notes as early defences of unilateral extra-legal war as a legitimisation of the preventive war in so far as it is directed to the continuity of the institutions of the USA. Of course this would be an anachronism. However, The Supreme Emergency Exception knows no limits, and logically speaking, no way back to civilisation.

a matter of Supreme Emergency. I think that war can be legitimate and ethically justifiable. But because I think so, I am very sceptical about any possible revival of the Supreme Emergency Concept. It puts aside what it wants to safeguard: the basic concept of war is a-moral.

3.5. Tomorrows peace: overcoming the scapegoat mechanism

None of these six strategies of moral argumentation is to be viewed as exclusively valid. Like the just war tradition as a whole, they should be used as methods of approaching problems, not as dogmas. It belongs to the nature of dilemmas that their solutions are not possible along the line of Christopher Colombo's egg. A multilateral approach to moral dilemmas provides the best chance for a balanced orientation towards humanitarian intervention.

Most of all, these strategies of handling moral dilemmas related to humanitarian intervention do not at all invalidate the prophetic approach of the Catholic Church towards war and peace. It is very important that Pope John XXIII and his successors have formulated the need to rethink peace in completely new terms. I would like to plead for a two-way evaluation. On one hand, his encyclical still provokes creative thought and politics with regard to war and peace. In fact, from the perspective of *Pacem in Terris* one might conclude that there is still no comprehensive ethics of non-violent conflict prevention. The instruments for non-violent intervention have not yet been optimised. On the other hand, *Pacem in Terris* may need a supplement in which a new approach is developed: a type of ethics suited to handle dilemmas related to peace operations (*ius ad pacem*), and their executing (*ius in pace*) amidst moral dilemmas. I think the Churches can be asked to develop a specific Christian contribution to military ethics for peace operations without denying any prophetic vision and ethics of peace.

To take a stand on genocide or 'murdering martyrs' always implies losing one's innocence. After the humanitarian intervention that did not come in Ruanda we should emphatically say "never again such innocence!"[25] For the Churches there is a huge task to rethink the theology of war and peace once more. The key issue will have to be how a prophetic vision can be combined with the renewed realism about the role of violence in man's nature and in history. I think the last thing the Catholic Church should do is to give up its tradition of 'just war.' Giving up this tradition would make it impossible for the Church to relate the radical Gospel of Peace to an ethics for a non-ideal world where responsibility is needed and must be elaborated into moral choices. Precisely strict interpretations of the just war give the Church instruments not to justify war, but to criticise it. Nevertheless, the acceptance of the idea of an ethics for a non-ideal world may in some exceptional cases also lead the Church to plead for humanitarian intervention, because of the lack of interest on the side of powerful third party nations. Such a plea does not oppose the prophetic task of the Church but is an elaboration of its task since prophets can be asked to interpret the signs of time. The Church can do this, provided she sees herself as being on pilgrimage in history needing to give moral guidance to world leaders about their military tasks through prudent judgments on contingent situations.

– Tomorrow's peace will integrate the paradigms of peace through justice (*pax opus justitiae*) and peace as a stable and secure order (*tranquillitas ordinis*).[26] If not, there will be either a world war or a worldwide backlash with regard to human rights within states.

– States will recognise the limits of any earthly peace. There will be no more political messianism. The world leaders will be open for a transcendent and eschatological power that truly secularises earthly power.

– Democracies will teach people the fruits of peaceful negotiations that will stabilise the zone of peace, built by democratic states.

---

[25] See: J. GLOVER, *Humanity. A Moral History of the Twentieth Century*, New Haven and London, 1999.

[26] See: F. VAN IERSEL, *The Ethical Basis for European Security*, pp. 143-160.

– Democracies will recognise the rights of minorities to exercise their human rights.

– International law will be reinforced,[27] supported by peace education.

– Tomorrow's peace will lead to the end of 'murdering martyrdom.' Martyrdom will regain its true meaning: of voluntary, nonviolent selfless suffering for a just cause. The true martyrdom, as it is understood in Jewish, Christian and Muslim traditions, is directed towards overcoming the scapegoat-mechanism instead of re-creating it.

– For tomorrow's peace it is necessary that secular states recognise the public role of religion instead of making religion into a private affair.

– Instead of stimulating 'murdering martyrs,' religions should focus on the dignity of the human person as living image of the living God and focus on the redemption of guilt, following the responsibility for peace. Sin is characterised by man's existential captivity not to do what he wants to do, and not wanting what he does. Religions have a dimension to add to the way moral dilemmas are experienced. Therefore religions should proclaim grace and forgiveness and stimulate conversion, in such a way that they pave the way for the overcoming of the scapegoat-mechanism.

---

[27] JOHN PAUL II, *Pacem in Terris: een permanente opdracht. Boodschap ter gelegenheid van de viering van de 36ste Internationale Dag voor de Vrede*, 1 januari 2003, nr. 6. (*Message for World Peace Day*, January 1sr, 2003, nr. 6).

Johan Verstraeten

From Just War Theory to the Ethics of Sustainable Peace and Conflict Resolution
A Reflection in Light of
the Recent War On Terror in Iraq

In a context in which the threat of terrorism has become one of the most important challenges to military leaders, policymakers and especially experts in the 'just war' tradition,[1] Carl von Clausewitz' magnum opus *On War* continues to be mandatory reading. In its opening paragraphs, Clausewitz demonstrates that war is not a game. Taken on its own, in its absolute sense, it is pure violence. It causes death and destruction and escalates to the extreme *unless* the wisdom of political rationality keeps the inherent tendency toward more violence under control. Only a war subjected to political rationality can be limited. But even in the case of prudent political discernment, it remains a dangerous reality, particularly when it is waged in a context characterized by vehement emotions such as the urge to take revenge after 9/11, hatred, frustrations and offended religious or national feelings. Vehement emotional undercurrents pour oil on the flames. They can transform a well-intended 'limited' war into an uncontrollable spiral of violence wherein a sustainable peace after the war is rendered impossible and where the absolute violence that is war's abstract nature ultimately becomes real.

The warning of Clausewitz is still valid in the context of the so-called war(s) on terror. It urges policymakers to see to it that the war they countenance as their political means of combating

[1] For a text-critical edition, see: C. von Clausewitz, *Vom Kriege. Neunzehnte Aulage. Jubiläumsausgabe mit erneut erweiterter historisch-kritischer Würdigung von Werner Hahlweg*, Bonn, Dümmlers Verlag, 1980. The references are based on J. Verstraeten, *Oorlog en politiek in het denken van Carl von Clausewitz*, Res Publica, XXVII (1) (1985), pp. 31-57.

terrorists and the regimes who support them does not become a catalyst in a process of escalating violence that would make our world more unsafe than ever before. A lack of prudence can lead to a situation in which the remedy becomes itself the cause of more evil. One of the best means for promoting such political prudence should be ethics. For centuries the just war theory, or more accurately the just war tradition, has fulfilled this role. Even today, on the occasion of the war in Iraq, just war arguments have played a crucial role. But did just war ethics really lead to more wisdom and prudence? Is it still adequate as an ethical framework for evaluating new problems such as terrorism or new developments in warfare?

The so-called 'just war theory,' which in fact is not a theory but a complex tradition, is quite paradoxical. On the one hand, it is an indispensable tool for a nuanced ethical reflection on the many complex aspects of wars and violent conflicts. On the other hand, it is also used by decision makers for the moral justification of their war policy. Particularly in the course of the twentieth century, 'just war theory' was repeatedly misused as a moral justification of violence and war for ideological purposes as well as the moral legitimization of real or potential massacres in which millions of soldiers and citizens were sacrificed for a 'good cause.'[2] This was

---

[2] For an historical analysis of the misuse of just war thinking during the 20th century see: J. VERSTRAETEN, *De bellum iustum traditie en het vredesdenken 1914-1964*, in R. BURGGRAEVE, J. DE TAVERNIER & L. VANDEWEYER (eds.), *Van rechtvaardige oorlog naar rechtvaardige vrede. Katholieken tussen militarisme en pacifisme in historisch-theologisch perspectief* (Kadok Studies, 15), Leuven, Universitaire Pers, 1993. See also: J. GLOVER, *Humanity. A Moral History of the Twentieth Century*, London, Pimlico, 2001. I consciously use the word sacrifice in this context as reference particularly to the first holocaust of Verdun. The poet Owen's text in which he reinterprets the sacrifice of Isaac by Abraham in Gen 22 (as disobedience of Abraham, who did indeed slaughter his son, an act that has been repeated throughout the whole of history) plays a prominent place in Benjamin Britten's War Requiem which is one of the most magisterial musical criticisms of war.

the case, for example, during the First World War when just war ethicists actively participated in the propaganda war between France and Germany.

During the Second World War, just war arguments were often (incorrectly) used for the justification of obliteration bombing and the destruction of two Japanese cities by nuclear weapons.[3] After the war, the '*fiat iustitia, pereat mundus*' argument of Gustav Gundlach became, to use the words of Böckenförde, Germany's most prominent philosopher of law, "the annihilation of the natural law doctrine on war."[4] It justified the possibility of an effective last-resort use of strategic nuclear weapons for the defence of the values of the free West against communism "even if the world would thereby perish."[5] According to Gordon Zahn such arguments allow only a single conclusion "it has become time to hide that theory away in the same drawer that contains the flat earth theory or geocentrism."[6] Others referred to the collapse of a paradigm[7] or to the post-just war age, to be replaced by the witness of the pre-just war age.[8]

---

[3] An exception to the factual misuse of just war arguments for the justification of obliteration bombing was the lucid and very critical article of John Ford, *The Morality of Obliteration Bombing*, in *Theological Studies* 5 (3) (1944), pp. 261-309.

[4] E.W. BÖCKENFÖRDE & R. SPAEMANN, *Die Zerstörung der naturrechtlichen Kriegslehre. Erwiderung an P. Gustav Gundlach S.J*, in *Atomare Kampfmittel und christliche Ethik. Diskussionsbeiträge deutscher Katholiken*, München, 1960, pp. 161-196.

[5] G. GUNDLACH, *Die Lehre Pius XII vom modernen Krieg*, in *Stimmen der Zeit*, CLXIV (1959) 7, pp. 1-14.
Böckenförde en Spaemann have criticized Gundlach's thesis as the 'destruction of the natural law doctrine on war.'

[6] G.C. ZAHN, *Afterword*, in T.A. SHANNON (ed.), *War or Peace? The Search for New Answers*, New York, Orbis Books, 1980, pp. 230-245

[7] E.J. NAGEL, *Methodisches zur Friedensethik*, in N. GLATZEL & E.J. NAGEL (eds.), *Frieden in Sicherheit. Zur Weiterentwicklung der Katholischen Friedensethik*, Freiburg/Basel/Wien, Herder, 1981, p. 230.

[8] E. EGAN, *The Beatitudes. The Work of Mercy and Pacifism*, in T.A. SHANNON (ed.), *War or Peace? The Search for New Answers*, New York, Orbis Books, 1980, p. 185.

But, despite the increasingly negative attitude towards the 'just war' in the 1960s and 1980s, the tradition remained alive and has even witnessed an unexpected comeback since the fall of the Berlin Wall in 1989. Ethnic conflicts, genocide and, not least, the vehement discussions about the two wars in Iraq and September 11th 2001, have brought 'just war' ethics back to the forefront as apparently indispensable moral framework for the justification of humanitarian or military interventions. The question is whether this factual comeback has also restored the legitimacy of the just war tradition. It remains an ambivalent framework.[9]

In this article I will show that a fundamental reinterpretation of it is unavoidable and necessary, and this for three reasons:

(1) Just war-arguments continue to be misused in public discourse and even 'revised' by some ethicists in order to justify national interests.

(2) This misuse is not a coincidence, but an unavoidable consequence of the complexity of this tradition and of its inherent conflict of interpretation.

(3) Classic just war thinking has no *ius post bellum* and fails to take into account the problem of sustainable peace building.

I will argue with reference to the second war against Iraq (2003), a war often justified as a response to terrorism.

1. RECENT MISUSES OF JUST WAR ARGUMENTS ON THE OCCASION OF THE RECENT WAR IN IRAQ

Just war theories are not simply useful and complex tools for abstract or academic ethical reasoning about war. In concrete war contexts and political discourse they become instruments of warfare as such. In an era in which manipulation of public opinion via the media has become an integral part of warfare itself (since

[9] Cf. J.T. JOHNSON, *Ideology, Reason and the Limitation of War: Religious and Secular Concepts, 1200-1740*, Princeton, Princeton University Press, 1975; and ID., *Just War Tradition and the Restraint of War. A Moral and Historical Inquiry*, Princeton, Princeton University Press, 1982.

politicians of democratic states need public support), the use of moral arguments for the defence of hidden national or particular interests is a permanent temptation. An outstanding example of this tendency is the justification of the second war against Saddam Hussein. In the months preceding the invasion, just war arguments were not only used to justify a 'pre-emptive' action but, in order to have them be more useful, some basic assumptions of the tradition were consciously reinterpreted in a way that was not really in accord with the theory as such.

1.1. Denial of the presumption against violence or war

The most striking example of the 'revision' was a clear denial of one of the most basic assumptions of just war thinking: its presumption against violence in general and war in particular.

The presumption against violence in general is so fundamental that some scholars do not hesitate to contend that the just war ethic has, in principle, more affinity with pacifism than with the holy war tradition.[10] Both share the same distrust of violence. Symptomatic of this distrust is the very definition of violence by Thomas Aquinas. For him, violence contradicts justice, because violence contradicts reason (*ST* I-II 6.4). As opposed to nature it is, by definition, disproportionate and irrational (*praeter ratio-nem*). Removing violence, or defending oneself or a nation against violence, is a restoration of the natural order and of justice. In this regard, justice is the 'indirect' way to peace, while love is the direct way (*ST* II-II 29). According to James Johnson, it is a "perversion of memory" and "one of the sad ironies of history" that the origin

---

[10] See my doctoral dissertation: J. VERSTRAETEN, *Tussen machteloos moralisme en amorele macht: de ethiek van de gerechtvaardigde verdediging. Een onderzoek naar de theologisch-ethische plausibiliteit en politique adequatie van de bellum justum traditie*, Leuven, unpublished Ph.D dissertation, 1987. The research results are summarized in J. VERSTRAETEN, *From Just War to Proportionate Defence: A Critical Reassessment of a Significant Tradition*, in J. SELLING (ed.), *Personalist Morals. Essays in Honor of Professor Louis Janssens*, Leuven, University Press, 1988, pp. 301-317.

of the just war theory, particularly the presumption against violence, has been so badly respected.[11]

The question now is, whether war is violence in the negative
moral sense of the word and whether, for that reason, there is
also a presumption against it. To answer this question, I will raise
two arguments for an original presumption against violence, and
re-assert the distinction between moral and pre-moral evil, a
crucial and neglected distinction in this discussion.

The first argument for the negative presumption is empirical:
war as a physical reality is not a good. It is a series of acts leading
to death and destruction. That does not mean, however, that it is
always and necessarily a *moral* evil or 'violence' in the negative
moral sense as described above. (In this regard we must acknowledge that natural law thinking never accepts that a *moral* evil be
used as a means to do good.) In the terminology of Aquinas'
interpreter Louis Janssens, it is a pre-moral evil, properly speaking. A 'pre-moral' evil can, in particular cases, become something
other than merely an unjustified act of violence. The same material acts of war (such as killing soldiers) can become, depending on
the case, an unjust revolution (*seditio*), a theft (*rapina*), a private
violent quarrel (*rixa*) – all of which are rejected by Aquinas –
while with a particular intention and in some circumstances war
can become a morally acceptable act, as for example, when the
intention of the act is the protection of life or institutional goods.
In the case where an individual is attacked and has no other alternative but to kill an assailant in order to protect his life, the physical act of killing is not 'violence' in the negative *moral* sense of
the word. Likewise, when a state must defend itself against an
unjust attack from an enemy army, the physical act of war is not
'violence' in that sense either. In his article on killing in self-
defence (*ST* II-II 64.7), Aquinas elucidates how the material act
of killing, which in normal circumstances is violence (a pre-moral
'evil'), is not morally qualified as violence but as justified defence,

---

[11] J.T. JOHNSON, *On Keeping Faith. The Use of History for Religious Ethics*, in
Journal of Religious Ethics 7 (1979), p. 113.

on the basis of the right intention which qualifies the act (*"morales autem actus recipiunt speciem secundum id quod intenditur..."*). The reason for killing is not revenge, or *lex talionis*, but to protect life, one of the most basic inclinations in nature. In other words, the moral character of the act of killing in self-defence is not determined by the injustice of the aggressor, nor by the physical act of killing (which is pre-moral evil), but by the intention to do what is in accordance with the most fundamental tendency of nature: *se conservare in esse* (cf. *ST* I-II 94. 2). Killing an aggressor is an unintended secondary effect of a well intended and objectively acceptable act. When Aquinas continues in the same question to talk about soldiers killing on behalf of public authorities, the presumption against the violence of killing (in the act of war) is still present: the direct killing of a person is prohibited, unless it is done for the sake of the protection of the common good (*refert hoc ad publicum bonum*). In both cases, the right intention is a necessary and not a sufficient reason since the act must also be in proportion with the moral end. When life can be protected without killing, then killing becomes immoral ("never use more violence than necessary").

The difference between the material acts of war (pre-moral evil) and its moral qualification via the intention is also what constitutes the difference between just war ethics and radical pacifism. *Radical* pacifists consider war *always* or in particular cases (for example, the nuclear pacifists) as a *moral* evil, while the proponents of just war ethics consider it first as a *pre-moral* evil, or in less accurate terms an *ontic* evil.

The second argument for the negative presumption is already implied in the previous one: war as a pre-moral evil [never moral evil!] can only be used to avoid a greater evil. According to John Langan, just war theory does not tell us something about the goods we intend to realise, but about the evil which events or policies urge us to commit in order to avoid a greater evil.[12]

---

[12] J. LANGAN, *The American Hierarchy and Nuclear Weapons*, in *Theological Studies* 43 (1982), pp. 456-457 [against J. McKenna, who wrote that for Catholics war is not the lesser of two evils, but of two goods].

When war become *morally* qualified as a justified act on the basis of a judgment about the right intention, proportionately it is not a *moral evil* and as such not an act of violence in the moral sense but a legitimate use of power (*potestas* or *potentia*). But even in that case, war remains an act or a set of acts which are 'violent' in the non-technical sense of the word.

In this regard, it would be wise for Catholic just war thinkers who refer to Thomas Aquinas the theologian, to keep in mind the warning of the philosopher Karl von Clausewitz against any sort of underestimation of the violent character of war: war is and remains, in itself (by absolute definition) a pure act of violence characterised by a tendency to escalation and violence which can only be brought under control by prudent political rationality (which is a rationality that takes into account the irrational aspects of war, such as sentiments of hatred and the emotions of the masses). Nothing is more dangerous and misleading than interpreting war as a 'good,' because that leads to misjudging its real (and violent!) nature. For that reason, the suggestion that waging a 'good' war against an empire of 'evil,' and euphemistic metaphors like nuclear umbrellas, smart bombs or smart nukes, clean wars, etc. must be absolutely avoided.

Symptomatic of the denial of the presumption against violence or war is the defence of the American war policy *vis à vis* Iraq by certain Catholic scholars.

In an article in *Origins*, the official journal of the North American Catholic Bishops Conference (NCCB), Michael Novak denies the presumption against violence. Although he describes the *situation* which leads to war as sinful, he does not interpret war as equally sinful. He, moreover, does not even distinguish, as Clausewiz and great American strategists like Osgood did, between war as an end and war as a means: "*Warfare under this teaching* [classic Catholic just war thinking] *is a morally appropriate political **end** and may be morally obligatory upon public authorities when circumstances dictate that **evil** must be stopped.*" And Novak continues: "*In the view of St. Augustine and St. Thomas, just war does not begin with a presumption against **violence**.*" A more nuanced argument is put forward by George Weigel in *America*: "*The just war tradition does not begin theologically with a presumption against war.*"[13]

Both authors contend that the starting point is "*the obligation of rightly constituted public authorities to defend the security of those for whom they have assumed responsibility.*" This is a correct reference to the criteria of just cause and right authority, but they both disregard the underlying proportionality reasoning, which starts precisely from the strong presumption against war as we have already articulated with regards to the question on killing in self-defence.

The negative presumption is clearly maintained by Aquinas in his question on war in the *Summa Theologiae* IIaIIae, Question 40, where he places war within a series of sins against peace (such as rebellion, private war and revolution). In that negative context his question is not "*Utrum bellare sit peccatum?*" (Is war sin?) but "*Utrum bellare* semper *sit peccatum*" (Is war *always* sin)? The presumption is clearly that war is evil (pre-moral evil in the terminology of Louis Janssens) and ought to be avoided. But in cases where there is a serious proportionate reason (just cause, supplemented by other criteria such as legitimate authority and a right intention) the pre-moral evil of war can be a justified form of defence rather than a moral evil as such.

The reinterpretations of Novak and Weigel minimise the negative presumption, and therefore run the risk of banalising the violent nature of war, a conclusion that is out of step with the thought of Aquinas.

[13] Cf. M. NOVAK, *An Argument That War Against Iraq Is Just*, in *Origins* 32 (2003) 36, p. 597; and G. WEIGEL, *The Just War Case for the War*, in *America* 188 (11) (2003), p. 8. Both authors who claim to represent Catholic thinking are much more inspired by the secular ideas of Honoré Bonet than by classic theologians such as Augustine and Thomas Aquinas or canonists like Gratianus. Cf. J.T. JOHNSON, *Ideology, Reason and the Limitation of War*, p. 67: "For Gratian and Thomas as well as for Augustine, war is something to be excused, something to be permitted Christians only as a final resort when all peaceful means have failed. But for Bonet (and this is one sign of his proximity to chivalric patterns of thought) war is much more; it is one of the good things God has given to his creatures."

1.2. A possible consequence of the denial of the original presumption against violence: the confusion between just war and holy war

While just war ethics has, in principle, more affinity with contextual prudential pacifism than with holy war thinking, the two wars against Iraq seem to have been inspired by an opposite interpretation. Just war arguments have been contaminated with political discourse, which means the very Pandora's box that the Treaty of Westphalia of 1648 closed has been reopened. Religious reasons for wars such as fighting for the truth against infidels, eliminating heretics and re-conquering the Holy Land were clearly accepted by the medieval proponents of the crusades. They were justified with sophisticated arguments such as those cited by Aquinas, who rejected the violent conversion of unbelievers and heretics but approved of severe punishments if they disturbed the public order, which was taken for granted because they were seen as 'guilty' (punishment of *culpa* as just cause).[14] Against those who misused the cause of religion as a justification for the Spanish *conquista* in Latin America, Francisco de Vitoria sharply rejected religious reasons for war. For him, only arguments based on reason can be accepted, not withstanding the fact that these arguments were also used to legitimate the *conquista* of Latin America, as is the case in the argument about the *bellum iustum ex utraque parte*. Despite the terrible wars of religion, Vitoria's rejection of religious reasons for war became one of the underlying ideas behind the peace treaty of Westphalia. Since then religious reasons have been excluded as just causes.

In the light of this historical development, it is disquieting that since the Gulf War in 1991, and particularly since September 11, the holy war has come back in political discourse, often in such a way that crusade language and just war discourse become intertwined. The explicit appeal to *jihad* by Saddam Hussein in 1991

[14] For an extensive study of Thomas Aquinas' theory on war, see: J. VERSTRAETEN, *Thomas van Aquino en de theory van de rechtvaardige oorlog*, Leuven, Cahiers van het Centrum voor Vredesonderzoek, 1984.

and by the terrorists today, as well as the mix of ethical and religious language in the discourse of both father and son Bush, have created a terrible confusion, not least concerning the very notion of *jihad* itself.[15] This reinforcement of the confusion between religious and reasonable reasons for war, radically contradicts, for example, the wisdom of American realists who had warned in the 1950s against the notion of ideological war and pleaded for the limitation of war to serving strictly limited political goals.[16]

1.3. The revision of the notion of defence

On the occasion of the debate on the legitimacy of the second war against Iraq, a third reinterpretation took place: viz., the stretching of the very notion of defence itself via concepts such as *preventive* war and *pre-emptive* war. Even worse is the confusion between the two.

A *preventive* war is a war to prevent possible aggression in the *future*. An historical example is the raid by the Israeli Air Force in 1981 against the nuclear reactor of Osiraq which Iraq had built with French assistance. The logic of this raid was clear: it was to prevent Saddam Hussein from developing nuclear arms and as such from threatening Israel. Although Israel tried to defend it as a 'morally supreme act of self-defence,' the raid was strongly condemned by the UN Security Council (Resolution 487).

---

[15] Jihad is not necessarily connected with war or violence, since in the oldest texts of the Quran the great Jihad is the inner fight against all that hinders faith. See: R. FIRESTONE, *Jihad. The Origin of Holy War in Islam*, Oxford, Oxford University Press, 1999; J. KELSAY & J.T. JOHNSON, *Just War and Jihad: Historical and Theoretical Perspectives on War and Peace in Western and Islamic Traditions*, Westport, Greenwood Press, 1991.

[16] Scholars like Henry Kissinger, George Kennan and Hans Morgenthau clearly argued against any sort of ideological warfare (cf. J.E. DOUGHERTY & R.L. PFALZGRAF, *Contending Theories of International Relations*, Philadelphia/New York/Toronto, J.B. Lippincott Company, 1971, pp. 65-99. An important work against ideological warfare is: R. OSGOOD, *Limited War. The Challenge to American Strategy*, Chicago, University of Chicago Press, 1957.)

A *pre-emptive* strike is a response to manifest signs of aggression or threats with aggression (such as massive troop concentrations, preparing missiles for launch, making dangerous chemical or biological weapons ready for use) which takes into account the potential victim's need to be nearly certain that initiation by the aggressor is imminent. An example could be a first strike against an imminent but not yet started launch of missiles by the enemy. According to Ramsey such 'pre-emptive' offensive acts can be justified as "a just initiation of armed force."[17] For Michael Walzer, however, the heart of the matter is not the imminent attack but the question whether there is a sufficient *"threat present."*[18] The two words are important: the threat must be real and verifiable, and it must be actual. Walzer contends that the first strike by Israel during the Six Day War (1967) was a justified 'pre-emptive' act. His analysis of that war leads, according to his method of developing theoretical insight from 'paradigmatic experiences' to the following rule: "States may use military force in the face of threats of war, whenever the failure to do so would seriously risk their territorial integrity or political independence."[19]

Supposing we agree with Walzer's rule and knowing now with almost certainty that Saddam Hussein had no weapons of mass destruction that could have posed a real and actual threat to the US in 2003 (the absence of WMD had been determined by experts before the war), it becomes extremely difficult to justify the intervention of the US and its allies as a morally acceptable 'pre-emptive' attack. In the absence of a real (and immediate) threat, the war shifted in fact from a (purported) pre-emptive war to a (real) preventive war. The justification of the war was not based on facts about weapons but on a firm (though inadequate) decision to prevent terrorists from attacking the US.

[17] P. RAMSEY, *The Just War. Force and Political Responsibility*, New York, Charles Scribner and Sons,1968, p. 68.

[18] M. WALZER, *Just and Unjust Wars. A Moral Argument with Historical Illustrations*, New York, Basic Books, 1977, p. 81.

[19] *Ibid.*, p. 85.

The fact that it has been an unjustifiable preventive war and not a pre-emptive action, can be confirmed by referring to *The National Security Strategy of the USA*, issued in September 2002. With regard to the struggle against global terrorism, the document declares that "we will not hesitate to act alone [the famous option of unilateralism], if necessary, to exercise our right of self-defence by acting pre-emptively against... terrorists, to prevent them from doing harm against our people and country."[20] At first glance this could be interpreted as a text about pre-emptive measures, but what follows leaves no doubt: "We must be prepared to stop rogue states and their terrorist clients before they are able to threaten or use WMD [weapons of mass destruction] against the US and our allies and friends."[21] This is preventive war language and as such it has more affinity with the raid against the reactor of Osiraq in 1981 than with Walzer's example of the Six Day War of 1967. It is very probable that this option for preventive action has been more decisive than the certainty about the presence of arms of massive destruction, a 'certainty' which before the war was not very probable given the serious doubts raised by experts.

All these arguments culminate in the conclusion that the invasion in Iraq of 2003 was not a pre-emptive, but a preventive war, and as such, it is clearly unjustified by both just war theory and international law.

But suppose there would have been evidence of WMD, could the war against Iraq in that case have been justified as a pre-emptive war? And is Walzer's acceptance of such pre-emptive strikes justified according to the just war criteria? The answer is not easy since it is impossible to give an unhistorical response. In the course of the history of the just war tradition, many ethicists have justified offensive acts. So for example most medieval authors accept war as *punitio* (punishment) and even sometimes *vindicatio* (revenge). The punishment of 'guilt' (*culpa*) is clearly one of

---

[20] The National Security Strategy of the United States of America, September 2002, p. 6. (http://www.whitehouse.gov/nsc/nss.html)

[21] *Ibid.*, p. 14.

Aquinas' criteria in the *Summa Theologiae* (II-II 40).[22] However, as a consequence of negative historical experiences, especially during the First World War, a definite consensus seemed to have been reached on the occasion of the Kellogg-Briand Pact, that only defence could be acceptable as reason for war. After the Second World War this became formalised in the Charter of the United Nations. Since then it has made history as the 'legalistic paradigm.' Article 2 of the UN Charter states that "*all members shall refrain in their international relations from the threat or use of force against the territorial integrity or political independence of any state, or in any other manner inconsistent with the purposes of the United Nations,*" a statement that was reinforced in 1970 when the UN added to it "*aggressive wars are crimes against humanity.*"

Defensive wars under certain conditions are not excluded: "Nothing in the present charter shall impair the **inherent** right of individual or collective self-defence if an armed **attack (French version:** *aggression armée***)** occurs against a member of the United Nations, until the Security Council has taken the measures necessary to maintain international peace and security." At first glance only a "response to an armed attack" is *sensu stricto* acceptable.[23] Two arguments can, however, be put forward in favour of broadening the notion of defence from 'response to armed attack' to 'pre-emptive defence'.

The first argument of Hugh Beach, refers to international customary law. Although he acknowledges that the idea of a pre-emptive strike "plainly goes beyond the terms of just war tradition," international customary law has long recognised that nations need not suffer an attack before they can legally take action to defend themselves against forces that present an imminent threat, but only on the conditions that the *Caroline* criteria are met: viz., the threat must be imminent and the nature of the response must be proportionate. In the case of

---

[22] For an extensive discussion of that problem see: JOHAN VERSTRAETEN, *Thomas van Aquino en de theorie van de rechtvaardige oorlog.*

[23] M. WALZER, *Just and Unjust Wars*, pp. 58-63.

Saddam Hussein, however, the principle became so stretched that, as we have seen, it became more a matter of preventive than pre-emptive war.[24]

A second consideration concerns the stretching of the notion of defence as a consequence of the reaffirmation by the Security Council, immediately after the events of September 11, of the right to self-defence against terrorism. Resolution 1368 declares that any 'act of international terrorism' is a 'threat against international peace and security' which justifies the readiness 'to take all necessary steps to respond.' The US government has stretched this interpretation of defence as the right to start an attack on terrorist bases in any country or on the government of a country if it had failed to prevent and punish such attacks. This became the moral justification of the war against the Taliban. 'Operation Enduring Freedom' was, however, not a pre-emptive act, since the terrorist attack of September 11 had already occurred.[25]

2. THE COMPLEXITY OF JUST WAR ETHICS

In the previous discussion of the reinterpretation of just war ethics in general and defence in particular, we have already implicitly suggested that what we have called 'misuse' is not a coincidence. It is a quasi-normal consequence of the complexity and ambiguity of the tradition as such. There is, quite simply, no single just war ethics or interpretation, but a plurality of approaches and conflicting interpretations. A brief reflection on another aspect of the just war tradition can demonstrate this, namely, the interpretation of the *ius in bello* principles of non-combatant immunity and proportionality.

---

[24] H. BEACH, *The Concept of 'Preventive War' – Old Wine in a New Wineskin* (paper presented at the CCADD International Conference, Bellem, Belgium, 29th August – 2nd. September 2003).
[25] *Ibid.*

2.1. Taken on its own, the principle non-combatant immunity seems to be beyond all doubt

It is clearly prohibited to kill civilians (defined as non-combatants or 'innocents'). Most scholars immediately qualify this to mean it is prohibited to kill non-combatants *directly*. This reference to 'directly' or 'intentionally,' opens the door to an acceptance of the killing of non-combatants as collateral damage, *praeter intentionem*.

A clear example of the stretching of the non-combatant immunity principle is Vitoria's justification of cannonades on cities in which soldiers and civilians are mixed: "*numquam licet per se et ex intentione interficere innocentem*"... "*per accidens autem etiam scienter licet interficere innocentes.*" When it is necessary to win the war, one has the right to kill innocents indirectly. A contemporary variant of the relativisation of the non-combatant immunity is Paul Ramsey's contention about counter-force nuclear war: "*Collateral civilian damage is certainly an unavoidable indirect effect and, in the technical sense, an 'unintended' result of something a nation may and should itself be conditionally willing and ready to do. The deterrent effect of which we are now speaking, is then, as it were, a direct effect of the foreseeable indirect effects of legitimate military conduct.*"[26]

One could object that the justification of a *per accidens* or *praeter intentionem* killing of non-combatants does not happen lightly. Taking the life of non-combatants indirectly is only acceptable on the condition that one takes into account the additional criterion of proportionality. The problem, however, is that proportionality is such a flexible concept that it can serve to justify almost anything. A brief survey of the different interpretations demonstrates its problematic character.

2.2. The many interpretations of the ius in bello proportionality

In contemporary just war ethics (since 1945) at least seven different interpretations of proportionality can be distinguished:

---

[26] Paul Ramsey, *The Just War*, p. 318f.

1. Proportionality as *lex talionis*: viz., the right or duty to use the same sort of weapons as the enemy. An example of this is the quite dubious interpretation of the war ethic of John Paul II by Gaby Verheggen. In his article he refers to a paragraph of the pope written on the occasion of the world peace day of 1982, which he cites as follows: "Therefore the Christians do not hesitate, to remember in the name of the essential requirements of justice, that nations do have the right and even the duty to protect themselves against an unjust attack and this with **proportionate means** (*mezzi proportionati*)." From this sentence Verheggen draws the incorrect conclusion that (and I quote in French to avoid any misunderstanding): "*De fait, le pape inclut les guerres nucléaires et bactériologiques parmi les guerres auxquelles l'exercice du droit de se défendre par de moyens proportionnés peut donner lieu.*"[27] This interpretation is manifestly a misrepresentation of the thoughts of the pope whose full text continues as follows: "Nevertheless, taking into account **the difference, so to speak by nature, between classic war and nuclear and bacteriological wars**, and taking into account the scandal of the arms race in the light of the needs of the third world, this right to defence, which is real in principle, does nothing else than reinforce the necessity that the international community should use efficient means of negotiation (...) War is the most barbarous and the most inefficient means to resolve conflicts."

2. *Proportionality of acts of war with regards to different levels of command* – A tactical act should be judged in the light of the tactical end, a strategic act should be judged in the light of the strategic end, and a political act should be judged in the light of the political end. This is, moreover, used in a very flexible way. One example is the scorched-earth tactic used by General von Manstein, who was not sentenced by the tribunal of Nürenberg, because the destruction of cities, houses, animals, fields and

---

[27] G. VERHEGGEN, *L'évolution de l'éthique de défense de l'église depuis la seconde guerre mondiale*, in *Veiligheid en Strategie/Sécurité et Stratégie* 4 (1) (1984), pp. 19-35. See particularly p. 32 and p. 34.

stocks, was, despite its cruel effect on the civilian population, interpreted as an unavoidable 'tactic' or manoeuvre to make the retreat from Russia possible. As a military officer he was not held responsible for the invasion, nor for the decision to retreat.[28] In this line of reasoning, proportionality is not related to the non-combatant immunity of the citizens of Russia.

3. *Proportionality as a sort of value Platonism* – This is the case in the *fiat iustitia pereat mundi* argument of Gustav Gundlach on the occasion of the discussion in Germany on accepting strategic nuclear weapons (5 May 1958). For Gundlach the right of defence of higher goods is so important that an effective use of these weapons must be considered as an extreme possibility: "Yes, even if the entire world would thereby perish, this would be no argument against our argumentation."[29] In this case, proportionality is interpreted as "the higher a value, the higher the price one has the right and duty to pay." Gundlach makes a complete abstraction from the real consequences on civilians.[30]

4. *Proportionality as a principle guiding limited war* – This is the definition of Robert Osgood who pleads against ideological warfare and for a return to the idea that limited war must be made possible. In this case one has the duty "to observe a rough proportion" between the limited political ends of the war and the means used in war. The means used must be 'commensurable' with the ends of war.[31]

[28] W.V. O'BRIEN, *The Conduct of Just and Limited War*, New York, Praeger, 1981, p. 182

[29] "Sogar für den möglichen Fall wo nur noch eine Manifestation der Majestät Gottes und seiner Ordnung (...) als Erfolg bliebe, ist Recht und Pflicht zur Verteidigung höchster Güter denkbar. Ja, wenn die Welt untergehen sollte dabei, dann wäre das auch kein Argument gegen unsere Argumentation."

[30] G. GUNDLACH, *Die Lehre Pius XII vom modernen Krieg*, in *Stimmen der Zeit* CLXIV (7) (1959), pp. 1-14.

[31] R. OSGOOD, *o.c.*, pp. 24-26.

5. *Economy of force* – This fifth variant is very similar to the previous one and is also described by Osgood: "In the light of this proportion between the dimensions of warfare and its susceptibility to political control, the importance of preserving an economy of force is apparent."[32]

6. *The supreme emergency argument* – According to this interpretation it is possible to tolerate what is not acceptable on the basis of the non-combatant immunity principle and this only in exceptional cases such as supreme emergency. Michael Walzer describes this argument as follows: "I have been more concerned to acknowledge that deterrence itself, for all its criminality, falls or may fall for the moment under the standard of necessity. But as with terror bombing so here with the threat of terrorism: supreme emergency is never a stable position. The realm of necessity is subject to historical change. And, what is more important, we are under an obligation to seize upon opportunities of escape, even to take risks for the sake of such opportunities. So the readiness to murder is balanced, or should be, by the readiness not to murder, not to threaten to murder, as soon as alternative ways to peace can be found."

7. *Proportion as right relation between the violence committed and the moral end that justifies the act* – This is Aquinas' interpretation of self-defence (*ST* II-II 64.7). The moral end that justifies violence is the preserving of life, or in the case of a state, the preservation of the common good. Means that are not in proportion with that end, such as using more violence than necessary for the preservation of life or the common good, are not acceptable. The Thomistic meaning implies that (a) we should never use more violence than necessary; (b) there must be a commitment to save life as much as possible (cf. the correct interpretation of the act with double effect by Michael Walzer); and (c) forms of violence that would endanger the ultimate end, the common good, are illicit. In this regard weapon systems that are so expensive that

[32] *Ibid.*

they lead to cutting the budget for education and poverty relief, are not acceptable. Military expenditures must be in proportion to other aspects of the common good rather than simply maintaining military security.[33]

Considering the very flexible uses of the criterion of 'proportionality' we can conclude, even if we acknowledge the fact that not all interpretations are accurate, that there is so much room for interpretation that with a sufficient dose of sophistication, almost any act overruling the rights of non-combatants can be justified.

3. THE LACK OF A 'POST CONFLICT ETHICS'

Last but not least, just war ethics almost never articulates the most important aspect of a war's justification, namely, the restoration of peace as its ultimate aim, the sustainable peace that is required after a conflict has come to an end.

Despite the rhetoric based on references to United Nations Security Council resolution 1441, the first war against Iraq (1991) is an example of a conflict that brought no peace and resolved virtually nothing save the restoration of the *status quo ante bellum* concerning the boarder line between Kuwait and Iraq. Saddam Hussein stayed in power and was kept in power by the decision of the allied forces to halt the war before he was eliminated. As a result, terrible atrocities were committed and tolerated against the Shiites and the Kurds, and infant mortality increased considerably. In a few weeks Iraq went from being a modern society with excellent infrastructure to a country "bombed back into the middle ages." The fact that a second war was perceived by US policy-makers as a necessity, confirms our judgment that the first war resolved nothing. The second war eliminated Saddam Hussein and his regime, but has left the country in complete chaos. There is not even minimal law and

---

[33] See my interpretation in J. VERSTRAETEN, *From Just War to Proportionate Defence: A Critical Re-assessment of a Significant Tradition*, pp. 301-317.

order since nearly every day some kind of terrorist attack occurs, and there is still no stable political power. The living conditions of the population have in no way improved. Furthermore, religious and ethnic tensions are unresolved.

These facts point up the greatest weakness of the just war tradition, which is without doubt its inability to deal with post-war situations. From European history we have learned that the total neglect of a future-oriented peace after the First World War and particularly the merciless revenge against Germany, paved the way for the success of the Nazis and the Second World War. Peace building in Europe after the Second World War, on the contrary, via the Marshall Plan, European Integration and different attempts to generate a spirit of reconciliation, has built sustainable foundations for a lasting peace between former enemies, whose borders have now become insignificant for EU members and who now share a common currency.

Recent research in the field of peace studies has produced some very interesting insights on the basic conditions for peace building,[34] for example, the role of truth and reconciliation commissions and

---

[34] We can mention a few of the most important recent contributions to the ethics of peace building: K. ASMAL ET AL., *Reconciliation Through Truth. A Reckoning of Apartheid's Criminal Governance*, Cape Town/Johannesburg, David Philip Publishers/Mayibuye Books, 1996; D. BLOOMFIELD ET AL., *Reconciliation after Violent Conflict*, Stockholm, IDEA Handbook Series, International Institute for Democracy and Electoral Assistance, 2003; R.D. ENRIGHT, *Exploring Forgiveness*, Madison, The University of Wisconsin Press, 1998; M. HAY, *Ukubuyisana. Reconciliation in South Africa*, Pietermaritzburg, Cluster Publications, 1998; R. MANI, *Beyond Retribution. Seeking Justice in the Shadow of War*, Cambridge, Polity Press (distribution: Oxford Blackwell), 2002; M. MINOW, *Between Vengeance and Forgiveness. Facing History after Genocide and Mass Violence*, Boston, Beacon Press, 1998; G. MÜLLER-FAHRENHOLZ, *The Art of Forgiveness. Theological Reflections on Healing and Reconciliation*, Geneva, World Council of Churches, 1997; EUROPEAN CENTRE FOR CONFLICT PREVENTION, *People Building Peace. 35 Inspiring Stories from Around the World*, Utrecht, 1999; R. J. SCHREITER, *Reconciliation. Mission and Ministry in a Changing Social Order*, New York, Orbis Books, 1999; R.S. APPLEBY, *Catholic Peacebuilding*, in *America* 188 (September 8, 2003), pp. 12-15. D.W. SCHRIVER, *An Ethic for Enemies: Forgiveness in Politics*, New York, University Press, 1995; M. VOLF, *Exclusion and*

the tension between the Nuremberg model and the South-African model (relevant for countries such as Chile, Argentina, Ireland, Bosnia, etc.). The tension between restorative justice and retributive justice is one of the interesting aspects of this conversation. Other studies have focused on the role of nation-building, religion, memory, narratives, trans-national organisations etc. Classic just war thinking seems to be immune to this literature, despite the fact that restoring peace is its basic justification, and despite the fact that a neglect of the logic of peace building can precipitate decisions to wage wars that are more an obstacle than a contribution to peace.

Only very recently have attempts been made to integrate the peace building literature into the just war tradition. An example is Michael Schuck's proposal for "a set of moral norms to govern the way we end war."[35] He pleads for three principles: First, the principle of repentance, which requires a sense of humility on the part of the victors for the suffering and death that was brought about even in a just cause. He connects this with an appropriate sense of mourning that is needed when one has killed even in a legitimate use of force. Secondly, the principle of honourable surrender which means the terms of surrender imposed ought not to demean the vanquished nor be punitive in intent. Thirdly, the principle of restoration, which requires, at minimum, that the victor removes the remaining instruments of war such as land mines, and imposes, at maximum, that the victor assist in repairing the opponent's basic infrastructure. Another suggestion for a *ius post bellum* is that of Brian Orend, who pleads for the following set of principles:[36] proportionality (a peace treaty must be fair

Embrace. A Theological Exploration of Identity, Otherness and Reconciliation, Nashville, Abingdon Press, 1996.

[35] K.R. HIMES, *Intervention, Just War, and U.S. National Security*, in *Theological Studies* 65 (2004), p. 141. Himes refers to M. SCHUCK, *When the Shooting Stops: Missing Elements in Just War Theory*, in *The Christian Century* 101 (October 26, 1994), pp. 982-984.

[36] B. OREND, *Justice after War*, in *Ethics and International Affairs* 16 (202), pp. 43-56. A summary of his argument is in K.R. HIMES, *Art. cit.*

and reasonable), publicity (particularly about the terms of the peace settlement), discrimination between leaders, soldiers and civilians with regards to culpability, restoration of violated rights ('rights vindication' but without revenge), punishment of decision makers who have waged an aggressive war, punishment of war crimes, compensation and rehabilitation.

In an interesting comment on Schuck and Orend, Kenneth Himes contends that a full restoration of the *status quo ante bellum* is in most cases impossible, but that there is nevertheless an obligation to establish a public order that satisfies basic human rights.[37] He also suggests that humanitarian intervention should focus more on the well-being of people than on punishing or vanquishing. With regards to the war in Iraq he pleads for "securing domestic peace through protection of civil liberties and human rights, as well as helping to organise police and judicial institutions so that the necessary social space is created for men and women to begin the work of restoring public life." There is also a duty to restore civil society, which means that the restoration of basic infrastructure must include more than the repair of roads, electricity and communication, but also a restoration "of the human infrastructure for peaceful communal life."[38]

In light of these very recent developments, it becomes urgent to rethink just war ethics fundamentally. It might even be useful to abandon the term 'just war.' This does not mean that the accumulated wisdom contained in the criteria of just war ethics and in the discussion of cases by scholars should be abandoned. On the contrary, some problems remain so complex that a sophisticated method of moral reasoning analogous with just war thinking is unavoidable: if one would totally abandon just war thinking, one would have to reinvent many of its ways of reasoning because the sort of problems they have treated continue to exist (for example nuclear deterrence and proliferation). It is nevertheless wise to stop speaking in terms of 'just war.' Much better would be an

[37] K.R. HIMES, *a.c.*, p. 155
[38] *Ibid.*, p. 156.

integration of some aspects of the moral reasoning of classic 'just war' into a more adequate '**ethics of sustainable peace and conflict resolution.**' This inclusive approach allows for other solutions to be considered apart from war or military means, and it includes the advantage of peace building and the *ius post bellum*.

The recent war in Iraq has given evidence of the fact that winning a war is much easier than building peace.

Finally, one must acknowledge that terrorism is a problem that requires another type of analysis than an analysis in classical war terms.[39] Apart from vague references to the non-combatant immunity and proportionality (problematic concepts as we have seen) the just war ethic really does not have very much to offer to this problem.

---

[39] C. COVINGTON, P. WILLIAMS, J. ARUNDALE & J. KNOX (eds.), *Terrorism and War. Unconscious Dynamics of Political Violence*, London/New York, Karnac, 2002; B.R. BARBER, *Jihad versus McWorld. Terrorism's Challenge to Democracy*, New York, Ballantine Books, 2001; and D.J. WHITTAKER (ed.), *The Terrorism Reader*, London/New York, Routledge, 2nd updated edition, 2003.

Alphart von Horn

Terrorism and a Future Concept of 'Just War'

1. Introduction

Since the 1990s, interventions in the internal affairs of other States have occurred regularly. These interventions have always been concerned with terrorism and human rights violations. Somalia, Bosnia-Herzegovina, Kosovo, Afghanistan and Iraq are the known examples. In all these interventions, the question is always raised: under what conditions and in what way are infringements of sovereignty legitimate? Until now, a satisfactory answer could not be given.

The Iraq war in particular has shown that the world will not allow itself to be regulated by the vision and wishes of the United States. A virtual religious mission in the mind of the evangelical American top leaders has led to a definite loss of reality in assessing the world situation and prevents the development of an effective, comprehensive, strategy against terrorism. Developing a strategy against terrorism is not confined to international law alone but requires ethics and morality all the more. A strategy for fighting terrorism has to be developed wherein the use of military force brings about not more but considerably less human suffering and material damage. This requirement however leads to a dilemma, for in the decision making process incompatible qualities have to be weighed against one another. A single general purpose strategy cannot therefore be formulated. However, at least the likely principles for a strategy **against** terrorism and **for** a just peace can be developed. That is the aim of my paper.

Before beginning my discussion, it is necessary from my point of view to touch upon the meaning of 'war' in connection with terrorism. I would like to make three points:

1. The main questions on the seminar 'The Challenges of
    Preventive Wars to the Concept of Just War' imply with the
    word '**war**' that terrorists are an enemy. Because of the nature
    of terrorism this is absolutely not the case. The traditional
    definition of war links 'co-operative' opponents and 'sym-
    metric' conduct of war. That is not applicable to terrorism.
    In combating terrorism in general one can only talk about
    the use of military force, or in short, about fighting terror-
    ism, but not about war on terrorism. This view has already
    practically been accepted internationally. In particular one must
    bear in mind that a war against terrorism automatically
    declares terrorists to be parties to the war and thereby to be
    legitimate combatants. President Bush's declaration of war
    on terrorism is therefore populist and wrong. It gives terrorism
    an unfounded moral and legal meaning.

2. Even the phrase '**just war**' is in my view misleading, for a
    war cannot in principle be justified, as there is no right to
    war. On the contrary, according to current international law,
    war is forbidden. The only exception to this is self-defence
    in the case of attack. A subjective assessment of an oppo-
    nent cannot and may not be the determining factor. This is
    especially apparent in the Iraq war. A war cannot therefore
    be called just because there are 'good grounds' for launching
    it, not when unverified intelligence is at issue. The descrip-
    tion 'justifiable' war seems to me to be more to the point
    and clearer.

3. The phrase '**preventive war**' is also in my view confusing,
    for it can be interpreted in more than one way. The phrase
    can have a negative character, if it has to do with an unjus-
    tifiable attack, and it can have a positive character if an
    opponent can only be repulsed in a manner that avoids a
    serious and imminent attack. I would therefore like to treat
    'preventive war' as a purely military-strategic phrase that
    describes the first phase of a war-like altercation without
    including in that phrase any moral or legal values.

I shall proceed in four stages in my discussion:

1. I shall start with a short description of the situation, then
2. describe the nature of terrorism,
3. followed by a description of the aims and possibilities for fighting terrorism and
4. finally develop seven principles for a strategy **against** terrorism and **for** a just peace.

2. THE SITUATION AFTER SEPTEMBER 11

The terrorist attacks of September 11, 2001 and the terrorist attacks in the wake of the wars in Afghanistan and in Iraq have perverted the image of Islam and severely shaken the feeling of security not only of Americans but also of the entire Western world. Since then there have been numerous further terrorist attacks around the world that have caused panic and feelings of anxiety. There is no doubt that this threat is real, so the question arises: are these acts of terror a planned campaign from a central authority or are they coming from fanatic individual groups?

Terrorism represents a new threat of global dimensions. It not only threatens states but also worldviews, religions, cultures and economic potentials. Terrorism means a dangerous internationalisation and privatisation of war. The time has come to reconsider our security policy and our ethical and moral conceptions of threat and war.

For the first time since the end of the Cold War, the Western world is again fearful of an enemy that represents a direct threat to life and limb. The history of wars has not yet come to an end, even if we would wish it to be so. It was wrong to cater to consumerism at the expense of the preventive security measures that address the new qualities of this threat. The world has not become safer. On the contrary, it is more insecure than ever because it has become far less predictable.

The media have painted an increasingly terrifying picture of the global terror organisation of al-Qaida. In response to this threat, US President Bush has declared a global war on terrorism, created a worldwide alliance against terrorism and, in the first steps, largely destroyed the Taliban regime in Afghanistan by military means. He has also defeated the regime of Saddam Hussein. He has called a number of other states, Somalia, North Korea and Iran, an 'axis of evil' and also threatened them with war. Last but not least, through reorgasization in early June 2002, he has created a new Homeland Security Department with 170,000 employees to more effectively organize the fight against terrorism in America.

The anti-terrorism campaign conducted by the United States and its allies against the Taliban in Afghanistan was met with the sympathetic understanding of many moderate Muslims. But the war against the Iraq and the US intention to wage war against other Arab states has been perceived as a continuation of the crusader's violence against the Muslim world. From the Muslim point of view, a process has been started at the global level that pursues the objective of suppressing and humiliating the Islamic states through the use of force. For many years now the story has been the same in Palestine. The terrorist attacks of September 11 have led to a worldwide solidarity between many states, including some Arab states, to fight terrorism. The question therefore arises whether this outcome was intended by Osama Bin Laden and whether this effect is not counterproductive for the Islamic cause. However, there is the possibility that the attack was not only designed to humiliate the United States but, more importantly, to provoke a counterattack against secularly governed Arab regimes. Thereby, in turn, weakening America and the other Western states and paving the way for the foundation of true Islamic kingdoms of God.

Four conclusions can be drawn from the terrorist attack of September 11 and the wars in Afghanistan and in Iraq:

1. The US has declared its retaliation for the attacks of September 11 and the global fight against terrorism to be a military problem. But it must be recognised now that it cannot solve all its

problems by military means even though it is undoubtedly the biggest military world power.

2. The Muslims themselves have been surprised by the tremendous effects of the attacks of September 11 and now believe that global terrorism is an efficient way to prevail against the West.

3. It is a fact that the Iraq war has led to a further expansion and amplification of terrorism. In the world there is not less but more violence than before. The US war against international terrorism must therefore be considered to have failed.

4. There is now the danger that we are getting into a spiral of uncontrollable violence and counter-violence worldwide. This spiral does not and will not help solve the problem of terrorism since it only fights the symptoms not the causes.

3. THE NATURE OF TERRORISM

3.1. Causes for Terrorism

From the Muslim point of view, it was the crusades that started the process of a permanent humiliation and powerlessness of Islamic states for which the West is to blame. What they considered to be particularly unjust and wrong was the Jewish occupation of Palestine. Since this occupation has been accepted and supported by many Western states, the West as a whole has been identified as an enemy.

Unlike Jesus Christ, Muhammad did not die as a religious martyr on a cross. Muhammad was both a political leader and the founder of a religion. He did not perform miracles but envisioned that Islam would be the world's sole religion. In spite of some successes in Arabic empire building against the resistance of the West, no progress could be made in the direction of a powerful Islamic world religion. That has created a feeling of humiliation and powerlessness. As a result, a large potential for impatience and despair has developed. In order to put an end to this feeling, and to gain power and influence, the Islamic world is counting on a 'holy war,' which, according to extremists and fundamentalists, also includes terrorism. Against this background, the attacks of September 11 are considered by Muslims as a potential end of their inferiority to the crusaders and the West.

The Western world must abandon its role of crusader, and change its attitude (which Muslims perceive to be one of disrespect and ignorance). Muslims, in turn, have to overcome their traditional inferiority complex. They have to face reality and stop considering everything Western as a threat. Such a change of attitude requires self-criticism on both sides so as to open a path to dialogue. This is a difficult political and psychological problem that can and must be solved by the United Nations.

However, it must be taken into account that Western states are also responsible for some of the causes of terrorism. Western states have waged many wars all over the world. They have changed existing states or established new ones by simply altering borders, and have established new democratic governments through the use of force. The motives for doing this have been a combination of ideals, economic advantages, and attempts to assert their own claims to power. The world economic order is the result of this Western policy which, as policy goes, is also the cause of many of the current tensions, crises, conflicts and wars. The non-Western world now fears that the West will continue to interfere in this way for the next 30 years due to its military superiority. This is the attitude ascribed to the United States and NATO in particular. It is quite understandable that some non-Western states are attempting to attain weapons of mass destruction in order to effectively deter America and the West from future interference. On the other hand, it is just as understandable that the United States is not at all willing to accept such a development since a terrorist attack with weapons of mass destruction would be a fatal threat to the West, not just a blow to its military world power. This is why the President of the United States has called such countries 'rogue states' or 'criminal states.'

3.2. Strategy and Methods

The power of terrorism is based on the idea that fear is worse than death. To frighten someone to death is more effective than killing him because a dead person cannot be frightened any more. Fear and permanent threat will wear down the enemy. Terrorism does not directly aim at the enemy's instruments of power but at spreading fear and insecurity so as to wear down the enemy psychologically, and thereby achieve success by indirect means. The targets of terrorism are symbolic in nature. Individuals too will be attacked if they are of symbolic importance.

Terrorism uses asymmetric methods of warfare. This asymmetry can have technical, psychological, ethical and strategic implications. A characteristic of asymmetric warfare is that highly developed nations are particularly vulnerable to it, and it takes relatively small efforts to achieve great effects. Terrorism strives to turn its disadvantages in terms of quality and quantity into an advantage. It avoids fighting the enemy on equal terms by deliberately adopting means qualitatively different from those of its enemy. Thus, it deliberately targets innocent people and neutral parties. Nor are Muslims spared. These attacks are characterized by insidiousness, cruelty and extreme cynicism. The strategy of terrorism relies on the fact that the ethical and religious scruples of the opponent will either lead them to inaction or too little action, or to an over-zealous use of force, thus putting them morally and legally in the wrong, either way causing their defeat. In either instance, terrorism considers itself the psychological winner.

Terrorism is further characterized by the fact that it cannot only be stopped by counter-violence or by giving in. This leads to the conclusion that he who fights more consistently and more relentlessly will have an advantage over a more irresolute opponent. And, in this respect, terrorists believe the odds are on their side.

3.3. Organization

Islamic terror organizations are a combination of ideology, politics, religion and financial resources that together form a highly dangerous critical mass. The cooperation between private sponsors and terrorists has led to a global privatization of terrorist wars. It is so that small terrorist groups have joined to form private holding companies under a single command and with an appropriate management structure. Different holdings finally merge into global networks whose leaders and sponsors pursue much wider goals than just the support of Islam in order to found the kingdom of God on earth. They are striving in particular for personal power and influence and, last but not least, for personal wealth. So, we must distinguish between state-organised terrorism and international terrorism. State-organised terrorism is the lesser problem since it can be countered by military means. International terrorism, however, involves autonomous terrorist cells difficult to identify, variously supported by particular states with specific purposes in mind, but independent due to the fact that they can count on being funded by dubious religious organisations, or through their own criminal activities.

The funding of terrorist organizations also comes from private businessmen. These sponsors of terrorism are mainly Saudi Arabian businessmen who are not only pursuing unselfish, religious objectives but also political, economic and ideological objectives. In the meantime, we have learned that the majority of Osama Bin Laden's adherents and supporters belong to the Islamistic Saudi Arabian opposition which has access to enormous financial resources, including worldwide influence and contacts. The fortunes of the al-Qaida organisation were recently estimated at billions of dollars, much of which is channelled to various terrorist groups through bogus firms.

The Saudi Arabian opposition wants to overthrow King Fahd and his dynasty since they are thought to be completely corrupt, too closely allied with the much-hated Americans, responsible for the desecration of Islam's holy places by the deployment of US forces, and thought to exert too much influence on the pilgrims who visit these sites. Should this opposition succeed, there will be the threat of an Islamic revolution with dramatic consequences for the West. It should be remembered that Saudi Arabia has the largest oil deposits in the world estimated at 255 billion barrels.

3.4. Ethic and Moral Aspects

Since September 11, terrorist attacks in Afghanistan and Iraq, and many other world-wide attacks prove that international terrorism is a grave and extremely serious danger. There is no reason to continue playing down or under-estimating the danger. The risk of further terrorist attacks must be reduced by all available means. This not only refers to an effective defence but also to an effective prevention. This will cause an ethical dilemma because, on the one hand, these preventive measures have to be as robust as possible and, on the other, no ethical principles must be violated. This is a different sort of dilemma than that faced by soldiers in war. In combat, civilians may be injured or even killed if they are accidentally in the vicinity. In terrorism, civilians are purposefully targeted, as when terrorists use them as shields for their own protection. Their intention is to cause death and injury to the innocent in order to exploit this for propaganda purposes.

By in large, terrorist activities are in stark contrast with their moral claims. Terrorists are obviously unable and unwilling to achieve their moral objectives by moral means. But ideologies and religion alone are not sufficient to make the world a better place. This objective requires more than economic and political power: appropriate infrastructures have to be made available. But terrorists are hardly versed in these issues, so they try to realise their goals by terrorism alone. But this strategy can never last. The achievement of terrorist goals can never provide a solution for real political and economic problems.

Due to their negative moral attitude and their readiness to use brutal force, it is rather unlikely that terrorists will ever be able to organise and rule a democratic society and a democratic state whose primary concern is the welfare of its citizens. Terrorists will always be authoritarian rulers and will therefore always try to abuse the welfare of the people for their own purposes. Depending on their objectives, terrorists can also be considered as freedom fighters. To distinguish terrorists from freedom fighters, the criterion of good and bad goals cannot be applied however. An action qualifies as terrorism when barbaric methods and procedures are used, regardless of whether they serve a good or a bad cause, or whether they are used by an inferior or a superior party.

4. Fight Against Terrorism

4.1. Objectives

The unparalleled effects of the terrorist attacks since 11 September have caused a dangerous radicalisation and increase in fundamentalism not only amongst the Islamic masses but the Islamic elite as well. For the first time since the crusades, the Islamic world feels that it can seriously threaten America and the West through terrorist activities. And that terrorism will win new adherents and supporters as a result of the West's exaggerated counter-measures against the Arab states is a foregone conclusion. Therefore, the fight against terrorism must not end in totally oppressing the Islamic world but must achieve a climate of tolerance and compromise instead. The Islamic world has to be developed into a peaceful and cooperative partner of the West.

In the past, it was possible to achieve a total victory and to dictate the terms of peace to the defeated country. Today, total victory is not possible any more due to the lethality of modern weapons. Present-day and future wars cause so much destruction, loss and suffering that democratic states can politically justify them only for a limited period of time. That is why, in the end, only a compromise can be realized, not a clear victory. This leads to the conclusion that the use of force must always be limited so as not to cause additional problems that are even more difficult to solve. The use of force can only be an appropriate means in the first phase of an operation and it will only be useful if there is a feasible plan for solving the problems that caused the use of force. Otherwise, the use of force will be counter-productive and must therefore be avoided. Terrorism is not only a problem of physical force but a psychological problem too. The defence against terrorism must therefore not only be limited to the use of force but must be comprehensive. This requires the integrated effort of different organisations and specialists such as secret service specialists, military and police security experts, psychologists, economic experts and politicians.

The fight against terrorism must pursue comprehensive objectives and must have a long-range horizon. Reconciliation is the most important requirement for a permanent and stable peace. But reconciliation, in turn, requires justice, tolerance, trust and the creation of a solid economic basis for the population. Such requirements cannot be fulfilled in a short time. The suffering brought on by terrorism and the retaliation that follows it, has aroused so much hatred and distrust, it will take a very long time, at least one generation, to heal these wounds. This makes any rapid solution to the conflict simply an illusion and, as a matter of principle, unsuitable. Nevertheless, politicians still pursue the illusion of a quick end, and repeatedly experience failure – as if they are unable to learn their lesson.

Part of the fight against terrorism requires that forces be directly employed against identified terrorist forces as well as indirectly against potential terrorist action. This kind of tasking must place individual terrorists and their organisations into situations where they will have to constantly fight against a full spectrum of governmental defences and security organizations operating simultaneously and at optimum effect. Though this approach seems self-evident, it is being implemented very hesitantly. The President of the United States has succeeded in this regard, but only after the attacks of September 11. The Europeans should have learned from that, yet there is every indication that they have not. They must resist the tendency to talk away the threat or to try and avert it by good behaviour instead of building up really effective security forces for the protection of its citizens which, by the way, is a requirement of most European constitutions.

Another anti-terrorist approach is to point up the ethical and moral depravity of terrorism. Terrorism must be seen for what it is, a criminal activity, highly immoral and dishonourable, and this perception must include the terrorists themselves and those who support them. After all, terrorists are not freedom fighters! To this end, the world's religions must be called upon not only reject terrorism but to condemn it outright. It is wrong to describe terrorism as a special kind of warfare. Terrorism deliberately relies on criminal methods far outside the international law of war, The Hague Convention and human rights. That is why it must be seen as a brutal crime, and the persons committing these crimes must be tracked down like criminals. Thus we must speak of fighting terrorism rather than merely defending against it. Any other expression would play down its character and objectives.

It must be assumed that the world will continue to solve its problems by the use of force. However, future weapons will make things different. Conventional weapons technology has achieved a lethality that has led to a form of deterrence similar to that of nuclear weapons. It is expected that violent confrontations in the future will be waged by means and methods qualitatively different from the present conventional ones. The war against Iraq has already shown that the so-called 'rogue states' have learned from the defeat of the Taliban and will employ terrorist methods offensively. It is doubtful whether the American forces and their allies will be able to sustain the Iraq war militarily and psychologically as the war continues to pass over to terrorist warfare, especially if terrorists begin to simultaneously target the population of their homelands.

Armed forces are undoubtedly able to fight large-scale terrorist actions, provide security and protection for the population, and pave the way for durable solutions, but they are unsuitable for sustaining these solutions. Military operations can only be seen as a transitional phase and must be immediately followed by stabilisation and consolidation measures that utilise civilian forces and means. However, it must be ensured that these assets are actually available prior to the deployment of military forces.

Counter-terrorism must not be limited to bringing an ongoing terrorist war to a conclusion. Its objective must be to prevent future terrorist wars as well. This is why defence forces must achieve a primary deterrent effect, namely, an operational efficiency which forces terrorist masterminds and their operatives to function at the highest risk of failure and loss of support should their plans fail. To defend against Islamic terrorism, it is essential to highlight its futility. Such deterrence must include the entire spectrum of military and civilian measures of reconnaissance, combat, damage minimisation and pursuit so as to cause terrorists to have to operate in an environment beyond their capacity. The same principles of conventional war fighting apply here, namely, seising the initiative from the terrorists, changing the situation so rapidly that they are unable to respond appropriately, narrowing their choices, forcing them to make errors. Anti-terrorism forces must therefore have an extremely short reaction time, high flexibility, and a wide range of engagement capabilities. Such capabilities are barely developed in military and civilian defence forces at present.

Prevention is a decisive component in the fight against terrorism and a credible form of deterrence. While deterrence is ethically acceptable, on the whole, prevention will cause ethical conflicts because such measures involve action against people who have not yet been proven guilty or who, for the time being, have done nothing wrong. A deterrence that includes a preventive component will always find itself on the ethical borderline. This is inevitable if the fight against terrorism is to be effective.

4.2. Strategies

In principle, we can distinguish two different strategies against terrorism – the European and American. Their essential differences are as follows:

In the American strategy, the armed forces in combination with the intelligence agencies play the main role. The goal of this strategy is to inflict such heavy losses on the terrorists that their struggle to survive obviates any possibilities for terror operations. Its disadvantage is that it drives new fighters and supporters into the ranks of the terrorists and thereby strengthens their staying power.

Its advantage is that it needs less financial and personnel resources and can be kept up for a long time. On the whole, it leads to a long conflict with heavy losses on both sides. This is exactly what has happened in the present Iraq conflict.

In the European strategy, the armed forces play their part for a limited time until relieved by police forces as soon as possible. This two-component strategy makes it more difficult for the terrorists to recruit new fighters and supporters because it achieves its aims without brutal force (which offends common Islamic doctrines). This strategy requires enormous financial and personnel resources, and it proceeds more slowly, making it more expensive. But it holds down the brutality and duration of the fighting. Altogether, this is the better strategy, though it must be said the Europeans are in no position to apply it since they lack the resources needed and have other interests.

4.3. Fight against the Causes

The causes of terrorism can only be overcome with intellectual and psychological weapons, not with purely military weapons. Similarly, in accord with Clausewitz we might say this is not the 'continuation of politics by other means,' but the 'continuation of war by other means.' A strategy against the causes of terrorism must at the same time be one against the psychology of terrorism. We must find out what is on the terrorist's mind and how we can influence it. We have to understand that people in desperate economics situations, those under oppression and persecution, will resort to violence as a last resort. The potential for terrorism can be reduced by alleviating these desperate situations. The objective of such a policy is not to buy the enemy's good behaviour, but to prevent them from turning to terrorism, which is far less costly than fighting a war as the United States is presently doing. But if this is true, then why is this approach not adopted more often? The answer is likely in our nature. Aggression, feelings of revenge and retaliation and the exercise of superior power are stronger than ethical and religious principles. It is probably primarily a matter of culture and education whether these strong feelings or intellectual principles will prevail. In this connection, it must be taken into account that in the evolution of man aggressiveness and the ability force have been major requirements for survival and they cannot easily be changed by education.

The reasons for a conflict must be seen in connection with the situation on the ground, which includes its specific cultural and moral conditions. In doing so, the same moral and ethical standards must be used as those applied in the crisis area and/or by the populations involved. To judge a situation only by one's own national standards, or by the standards of international organisations, will not lead to a lasting solution of crises and conflicts since the parties to a conflict will neither understand nor accept these standards.

The Islamic world cannot match the West in terms of technology, economic and military power, and will hardly be able to catch up in the future due to its religiously dominated leadership. However, the Islamic world has more to offer than the West in the areas of religion, culture and values.

Large parts of the Western world, especially the USA, have degenerated into fun-seeking, consumer-oriented societies that increasingly neglect their cultural achievements and the values underpinning and supporting their states. This is no example for the Islamic states. It is understandable that they refuse to accept Western influences in principle and especially this negative Western development. Still, the Western world, and Europe in particular, has highly-developed cultures that find general recognition also in other cultures. It is not enough, however, only to talk about the value of the Western culture, we must convincingly live by it. This implies that consumerism will cease to be the measure of all things, and in the future the proven traditional values will once again take effect.

The people of the West must recognize that they represent only a small proportion of the world's population and in the future will lose influence in social and religious fields. It is foreseeable that even its military superiority will decline, which means a global world order based on Western values and economic interests alone will not be possible in the future.

In the future, interests can only be met on the basis of a mutually fair balance of interests. From this follows that in the future a close and fair cooperation will also be required with the Arabic and Islamic states. Cooperation will automatically also remove some essential causes of terrorism. It is therefore not only reasonable and useful, but mandatory, to start a policy of fair cooperation with the Islamic states as soon as possible, instead of waging antiterrorism wars, which cannot be won. The Western world should not wait for the US, but should self-confidently seize the initiative in order to show the United States an alternative way into the future which is not based on economic and military superiority but on fair partnership.

4.4. Political Aspects

There are 46 Islamic states. None is a democracy. They all are more or less authoritarian and despotic. None of these countries accepts the concept of human rights. Islam does not distinguish between the private family and the public state. It does not know independent, responsible human beings, but only autonomous collectives. All citizens must subordinate themselves to the mullahs who have declared that they are the owners and guardians of the absolute truth.

It is an illusion to believe that Islamic states can be turned into Western-type democracies. Islamic states will never allow more democracy since this would secularise society and, as a consequence, curtail the power of the ruling religious leaders. That is why the Islamic states are also trying to prevent modernisation efforts. It would automatically encourage the establishment of democratic structures. However, this attitude will also lead to isolation and backwardness compared to the Western world. By adopting this approach, the Islamic states will throw away their chance of overcoming poverty and powerlessness through economic growth.

In spite of the US war on terror, the Islamic states have not reached a turning point in their religious and political goals. They fight against Western influences and particularly against more democracy. From the Islamic perspective democratic government would question the unity of religion and politics. For them, Islam is the only true and authoritative world religion and therefore politics must follow Islam and thus must not be separated from it. The members of the ruling religious elite of Islam especially do not want more democracy since the accompanying secularisation would deprive them of power. Thus, from the perspective of many Islamic states, Western influence represents a sure threat that even justifies terrorism. Therefore the effort by the Western world to democratise the Islamic states is a wrong approach.

A major weakness of Islam is the dogmatic character of the Koran that was developed 1400 years ago in a totally different era. The message of the Koran is backward-looking and opposed to progress because it inhibits believers from discussing its modernisation or adaptation. Since one's whole life is governed by the Koran, creativity and progress have no chance to develop. Creativity and progress are not compatible with the prohibition of independent thought and dogmatic ways of thinking. Strictly enforced Islam will therefore lead to social and economic deadlocks that will sooner or later give rise to undesirable developments and to the overthrow of the ruling classes. The most striking example in this regard has been the Soviet Union with the overthrow of its dogmatic communism and the most recent example of the Taliban in Afghanistan with their dogmatic Islamism. Iran could become a future example.

After September 11, once again, it has become painfully clear that Western governments are not capable of taking proactive measures against threats on the basis of 'learning by doing' but only by 'learning by suffering.' There is still a lack of conviction that the early implementation of risk precautions is better than subsequent risk management.

International terrorism is a new threat that is not directed against geographical borders of states or alliances but against Western religions, cultures, values and interests. That is why not the geographical borders of the Western world but Western religions, cultures, values and interests will have to be defended. This is a decisive qualitative change in security and defence policies, a change that, until now, has neither been understood properly nor implemented consistently.

Future threats will have new qualitative and global dimensions, which cannot be countered by an independent national security and defence policy any more. National security against international terrorism can only be ensured at the international level in cooperation with allies. This, however, can only be successful if all allies make a contribution in accordance with their economic and technological capabilities. At present, however, the political leaders still consider NATO as a community in which they will have a say, but if actions are needed, they can hide behind the strength of the other partners, especially behind the United States.

Today, only the US has a global ability for actions to limit the global risks of the international terrorism. Paradoxically, this strength is what the US is being criticised for employing. But also the Europeans have the economic potential to ensure a global capacity for action. What is missing here is a common political will as a result of national selfishness. Consequently, Europe unnecessarily puts at risk its security interest. It is a shame that Europe is unable to make an effective military and political contribution to the fight against the international terrorism side by side with the US. Therefore Europe can only watch idly while the United States, together with some willing nations, are making decisions which will then translate into military operations that will also have a severe impact on the future of the whole of Europe. It was wrong to believe that the USA would have to show consideration for a weak and undecided Europe. Also in the future the US will do what it considers it has to do and it will look again for the support of the 'willing' even if the UN does not agree.

Europe cannot compensate for its lack power and determination by criticising the behaviour of the United States. If Europe wants to influence the global decisions of the US it must develop into an important indispensable partner of the US. In this connection, it will not suffice to just have the same capabilities as the United States. Europe must develop complementary and new military capabilities that are not sufficiently available or not available at all in the US. Only in this way Europe can become an important indispensable partner that can have an influence on strategic decisions.

Another decisive deficit of the Western security policy is the recurring lack of planning for peace stabilizing measures after the military mission has been completed. For the solution of humanitarian, political, social, religious and economic problems not only must the appropriate civil means and forces be available, but also these means and forces must come into action. The employment of military forces will not make sense unless this requirement can be met. However, not all politicians are obviously familiar with this simple conclusion. Otherwise it can hardly be explained why a successful military operation is often followed by political helplessness; and why expensive and dangerous military missions drag on for years without finding solutions which can be realized.

Today, the internal security of a state can no longer be separated from its external security. To counter the risks of international terrorism, governments have to use all assets available. These assets comprise the whole of its military and police capabilities, to include the capabilities of territorial defence and disaster control. In the future, the security of a state cannot be considered as a national task. It must be seen as a common European a task. Both internal and external security must be seen as a whole and must be interlocked. For this purpose, a European security council provided with operational capabilities and responsibilities must be established. Recently, the first hesitant steps in this direction have been taken by the EU.

4.5. Military Aspects

The progress achieved in the war on terror until now has shown that the United States and its allies are not helpless in their fight against terrorism. Against the Taliban a military success was achieved, the dimensions of which were initially not expected. Countries that previously supported terror organizations now fear preventive strikes and try to cooperate with the United States against terrorism, or at least desist from openly supporting it.

But as a matter of principle, terrorism cannot be defeated in a war of destruction. While a war of destruction can knock out the combat elements, it cannot affect the ideas in the minds of the terrorist leaders. Terrorism accepts defeats but always makes certain that the masterminds and their ideas for the continuation of the struggle will survive. Therefore, the terrorist chain of command will always succeed in slipping away in time to save itself. This was the case in Afghanistan: the United States has not succeeded in destroying al-Qaida in Afghanistan totally. On the contrary, after the Iraq war al-Qaida reorganized itself and now operates a very effective terrorist resistance against the occupation troops.

Any sensible war policy must absolutely pursue the objective of achieving a lasting peace. This also applies to the fight against terrorism and requires holding open opportunities for an acceptable compromise to initiate a future reconciliation. When force is used it must always be kept in mind that its violent consequences should never block the road to compromise and reconciliation. This implies a qualitative and quantitative limitation of the force used and should ideally target only the operating terrorist, their leaders, supporters and fellow travellers, and spare as far as possible the civilian population not involved. The Western states (NATO included) do not have the capabilities to engage international terrorism with such high accuracy and selectiveness. The present conventional superiority of the armed forces is inadequate to fight terrorism because terrorism does not fight conventionally but asymmetrically. Even the United States is only partially able to fight an asymmetric war, and completely unable to face the moral dimensions of such a war.

The fight against international terrorism in urban terrain requires new technologies and precision weapons with pinpoint accuracy, able to minimize collateral damage while disabling combatants without killing them. The use of such weapons will require the development of appropriate tactics, techniques and strategies. European, and even American, armed forces are far away from such developments. In cooperation with their allies, today's armed forces are optimised for defeating an enemy that uses similar, symmetrical, military procedures and principles. What terrorism relies on is the exact opposite. Terrorism knows neither front lines, international law of war, nor human rights. Terrorists attack unexpectedly by using asymmetrical qualities and extremely brutal force. In doing this, they rely on their extreme brutality to traumatize their enemies and thereby prevent them from responding rapidly and effectively.

Privately available new technologies are of greater advantage to the terrorists than to the national defence organizations. For the terrorists, money for new technologies is not a problem because they only need relatively small sums, whereas government organizations depend on appropriated funds and have to overcome bureaucratic obstacles in good time. As a rule, the democratic states will only make available the required funds if the political pressure is strong enough. Usually this is only the case when it is already too late.

From previous conflicts we have learned that it is imperative to employ special ground forces to fight terrorism. Only on the ground can the resistance of other land forces and other hostile organizations be definitely crushed. In addition, this is the only way of defeating once and for all the remaining terrorist and criminal organisations after a military confrontation. If, for military reasons, ground troops cannot be deployed, it will not be possible to deploy police forces and humanitarian relief organizations for establishing a durable peace. The conflict will thus continue at a lower level. Only those who can move safely on the ground will be able to pursue effective humanitarian, political, social, religious and economic objectives.

However, the employment of land forces has its limitations if the enemy fights covertly. In this case, large-scale land operations will not make sense since they would only lead to a protracted war of attrition that is impossible to win on foreign soil even for great powers. If the enemy fights covertly, success can only be achieved by commando forces having superior information, capabilities, time, space and technology due to their high degree of specialization and optimization. The success of the fight against terrorism depends decisively on a lead in information about terrorist intentions and plans. The main problem here is an almost infinite number of targets that can be attacked by terrorists. Past experience has shown that terrorists select targets in certain situations according to a patterned strategy. Therefore, it is quite possible to filter out certain targets in certain situations with sufficient probability.

General-purpose forces will not suffice to defeat terrorists, irregular forces, partisans and organized crime. Military forces must be specialized to perform both infantry and police tasks. An example of this type of force is the *Multinational Specialized Unit* (MSU) that has been very successful for many years in all KFOR operations against non-military forces and organized crime. The decisive advantage of these civil-military detachments is that they are capable of rapidly switching between two tasks and roles, such as, the role of infantrymen who have combatant status and are equipped with heavy infantry weapons, and the role of anti-terrorism policemen who are authorized to arrest and to conduct investigations in support of police operations. These civil-military detachments are either composed of specialized military personnel or specialized policemen. Although the outcome will not be the same due to their different backgrounds, it will at least be similar.

Therefore, it is futile to carry on endless discussions on whether the responsibility should lie with the Ministry of the Interior or with the Ministry of Defence. What is of vital importance for the success of an operation is to have uniform operational command and control. In the first phase of an anti-terrorism campaign, this must be ensured by the armed forces and later on by the civil authorities. What must be prevented above all is that terrorism takes advantage of a dispute about responsibility and the resulting unsuitable compromises.

4.6. Ethical Aspects

Terrorism is a particular way of using force that is morally reprehensible. It must be rejected outright in view of its barbaric methods and procedures. That is exactly why the fight against terrorism must not cause cruelties similar to those inflicted by terrorists. To apply the principle of the Old Testament 'an eye for an eye, a tooth for a tooth' would be counterproductive here. Such behaviour will only arouse more hatred and thus increase the willingness to use force. However, the cruelties of terrorism always bring a constant risk that the parties who have fought fairly so far, will be induced to use barbaric methods and procedures as well. The reasons for this are emotional in nature such as revenge and retaliation but also the desire to prevent friendly losses. A war characterized by retaliatory and pre-emptive strikes is exactly what is currently happening between Israel and radical Palestinians and it will obviously never lead to a cease-fire or peace.

The problem of terrorism cannot be solved by simply killing or capturing terrorists, since it is impossible to hunt all of them down. A military victory over terrorism in the traditional sense cannot be achieved. It has to be defeated in the mind. And this objective cannot be reached by soldiers or policemen alone. Assuming that this is the case, the question arises why so much injustice and cruelty must occur when in the end a compromise will have to be reached anyway? The answer is simple and shocking: A certain threshold of pain has to be reached before hostile parties will show the required willingness to compromise and reach a peace agreement. The situation usually escalates because both parties will be convinced to the very end that they can win a clear victory. This conviction will even be confirmed by the support provided by other countries. From the ethical point of view, this support from other countries has a war-protracting effect and increases the suffering, destruction and loss.

The exercise of power and the use of force can be as morally wrong as the decision to abstain from the use of force. Anyone who has the ability to take action in order to counter a foreseeable danger and does not act will automatically be responsible for this inaction. With regard to states that have the appropriate means to counter-violence and terrorism this implies that they have an obligation and responsibility to use these means even for the welfare of other people. Consequently, the strengthening of international law, for instance, will not reduce but increase the number of interventions. President Bush's threat to launch a pre-emptive attack against the so-called 'rogue states' must be seen in this regard.

Nor is a complete renunciation of force a credible alternative since that deliberately disregards the chance to prevent injustices from occurring. Defence and protection from terrorism must also be seen as a social responsibility and a religious obligation. The capability to fight terrorism must not be sacrificed for an abstract principle – as noble as it may be from an ethical perspective. Such ethical scruples are seen by terrorists as a weaknesses, things to be exploited uncompromisingly. To effectively protect a state, it will be necessary for governments to take the fight against terrorism to the very edge of the legal and ethical border.

When is prevention justified, especially when it accepts death and injury of people as unavoidable? The answer depends primarily on the objectives pursued and on the consequences that any refusal to pursue these objectives would have. Only absolutely vital objectives justify injury or death of people, provided there are no other ways and means to achieve the same objective. Not only friendly but also enemy damages and losses must be in a rationally and ethically justified proportion to the envisioned objectives. From the ethical point of view, the use of force always creates a conflict situation since damage is inflicted on some people in order to avert damage from other people. A conflict situation occurs when one ethical requirement can only be met if another ethical requirement is violated. The question is: can the ethical requirements be weighed against each other in order to find a solution? The answer is 'no' since these requirements are different but equally binding and cannot be compared, which precludes any rational optimization.

There is no one absolutely correct strategy for fighting terrorism. But there is the possibility of minimizing to a great extent the amount and kind of force used, thus minimally infringing on ethical principles. The armed forces must have military equipment at their disposal that allows them to accomplish their tasks with superiority and, at the same time, avoid, or at least limit, unintentional damage to others. This calls for precision weapons and weapons with non-lethal effects. Politicians have to realize that military equipment has an ethical dimension beyond budgetary constraints. They have a moral and political duty to make the appropriate equipment available as soon as it is technologically feasible.

I will now conclude this paper and summarize its findings in the form of seven principles for a strategy **against** terrorism and **for** a just peace. Of course there are more principles concerning a strategy against terrorism, but I will concentrate only on those that are directly concerned with terrorism and a just peace.

5. PRINCIPLES FOR A STRATEGY AGAINST TERRORISM AND FOR A JUST PEACE

1. **The aim in fighting terrorism must be a just and permanent peace.**
   It is not enough merely to strive for a just war against terrorism. The overriding aim must be a just and lasting peace. The deployment of armed forces should only be seen as a transitional phase. After this, other pre-planned stabilization and consolidation phases must follow, employing civilian sources and means, and lead to a just and permanent peace. There must not only be a concrete, realizable plan, but an allocation of the necessary resources to accomplish it. If these conditions are not met, the use of military force is politically wrong and ethically irresponsible.

2. **The use of military force to fight terrorism must be the absolute last means taken.**
   It is only justifiable if a serious wrongdoing can only be ended or preventatively repulsed in this way. In using military

240 ALPHART VON HORN

force there must be no other alternatives promising success.
The UN should have agreed on a mandate for the use of
military force.

3. The use of military force must be clearly defined.
The quality and quantity of the use of force must not block
the way for a future reconciliation of the opposing parties.
The regulations of international laws of war and human
rights must therefore receive special emphasis. The military
objectives must be set so that they will, with great probability, lead to military successes and be of such vital consequence that the expected losses and damage on all sides can
be justified.

4. The use of military force against terrorism must be simultaneously conducted in an offensive and preventive manner.
The key point is to prevent terrorism from succeeding.
Therefore planned terror activities must be identified and
prevented well before their realization. The most important
pre-requisite for this is comprehensive, international
co-operation, particularly in the areas of exchange of information, assessment of the situation, intelligence, tracking
and destruction of terrorist forces. Recognized terrorists must
not be allowed to escape. They must be hunted internationally. The highest degree of effectiveness must be attained by
technology, organization and training. Quick elimination of
the terrorist leaders must have priority over the pursuit of
followers and supporters.

5. Preventive wars must remain the exception.
Presently, the UN charter has not embraced the new quality of the global threat from terrorism. A new article must
therefore be introduced which legitimizes and regulates a
similar multilateral preventive UN reaction as in the case of
a war of aggression. It is therefore important to work out a

stringent list of criteria by which the number and types of future preventive wars can be limited.

6. **The fight against terrorism is only successful in co-operation with the affected population and the national security and law-and-order organisations.**
Islamic terrorism can thus only be overcome in conjunction with and not in opposition to the Muslim states. The country affected by terror should not be excused from its national responsibilities because the terror is and remains above all a national problem of the affected state and must be solved in that country. The responsibility therefore lies not only with the intervening states but also with the affected population and its leaders and politicians. They have the 'ownership of responsibility.'

After a military intervention the national sovereignty and responsibility must therefore be returned as quickly as possible to the security and law-and-order organisations of that state. Of course, these must be checked and reorganised by UN personnel and suitable training as well as material support given. Even these measures must be planned before an intervention and the necessary resources must be available in fact.

7. **Terrorism must be outlawed world-wide.**
Terrorism is an ethical and religious evil. States that tolerate and/or support terrorist organizations on their territory must be persistently forced by the UN by means of international sanctions and if necessary by military intervention, to give up terrorism. It is crucial that this be no mere threat but backed by real sanctions and military interventions. If this cannot be guaranteed politically, militarily and economically then no threats should be made.

Contributors

Carl CEULEMANS is an assistant professor in the Department of Philosophy at the Royal Military Academy, Brussels. He obtained a PhD in political science at the Vrije Universiteit Brussel. His fields of research are military ethics and social and political philosophy.

He was co-author of *Moral Constraints on War. Principles and Cases* (2002), and has published in a number of journals (e.g., *Res Publica, Belgian Journal of Political Science, Journal of Military Ethics, Militaire Spectator, Vrede en Veiligheid. Tijdschrift voor internationale vraagstukken, and Ethiek & Maatschappij*). He was also guest co-editor of a special issue of the journal *Professional Ethics: A Multidisciplinary Journal* on the subject of military obedience.

Nick FOTION is professor of philosophy at Emory University, Atlanta. He has published several articles about military ethics. Some recent publications include *John Searle* (2002), *Moral Constraints on War* (2002), *Transforming and Expanding the Kasher/Yadlin Theory on Ethics of Fighting Wars Against Terrorism* in *Journal of Military Ethics* (2005) and *From Speech Acts to Speech Activity in John Searle*, in B. Smith (Ed.) *John Searle* (2003).

David PRATT is a commander in the Chaplain Corps of the U.S. Navy and a combat veteran. Educated at Berkeley California, he has previously published articles on war and moral theology. His dissertation at the Catholic University of Leuven (Belgium) is on moral action and deliberation in Martha Nussbaum.

Wim SMIT studied moral theology at the Catholic University of Leuven (Belgium) and is now a Catholic Chaplain of the Belgian Royal Military Academy in Brussels, and a member of the *Center for Theology and Military Ethics*. He is completing a PhD in theology on the topic of *Terrorism, Counterterrorism and the Violations of*

Human and Civil Rights. He has published articles on military ethics and inter-religious education, and recently, *The New 'World Ethos' as a Challenge for Religious Education*, in *Lline. Lifelong Learning in Europe* (2004).

Claude SELIS holds masters degrees in philosophy and in oriental history. He was a Catholic Chaplain at the Belgian Royal Higher Institute of Defence and the Royal Military Academy from 1996 to 2005. He is a founding member and the Director of the *Center for Theology and Military Ethics*. His specialisation is on violence, war, and peace in the Bible.

Fred VAN IERSEL holds the *Chair for Religion and Ethics in the context of the Armed Forces*. In 1999 he established the *Office for Military Ethics of the Dutch Ministry of Defence*. Since December 2002 he is part-time Chief of Catholic Prison Chaplaincy in the Netherlands. He is a professor at the faculty of theology at the University of Tilburg (The Netherlands). Some of his English articles are *Military Obedience: A Source of Moral Dilemmas?*, in *Professional Ethics* (2002); and *Civil-Military Cooperation: the Ethical Challenges*, in W. de Wolff (Ed.), *The Role of the Military and the Role of Humanitarian Aid Organisations in Emergencies* (2002).

Johan VERSTRAETEN is professor in moral theology at the Catholic University of Leuven (Belgium). He specialises in business ethics, the social teaching of the Catholic Church, and the just war tradition, on which he wrote his dissertation, and recently *From Just War to Ethics of Conflict Resolution. A Critique of Just-War Thinking in Light of the War in Iraq*, in *Ethical Perspectives* 11 (2-3) (2004), 99-110.

Alphart VON HORN is an engineer and retired major general of the German army. He is the former Chief of Staff of the *NATO Headquarters Stabilization Forces* (SFOR) in Sarajevo (Bosnia-Herzegovina). Von Horn is often invited as an authority to international congresses and seminars. His viewpoints are built upon his numerous personal military experiences.

PRINTED ON PERMANENT PAPER • IMPRIME SUR PAPIER PERMANENT • GEDRUKT OP DUURZAAM PAPIER - ISO 9706

N.V. PEETERS S.A., WAROTSTRAAT 50, B-3020 HERENT